ESSAYS IN TWENTIETH CENTURY AMERICAN DIPLOMATIC HISTORY DEDICATED TO PROFESSOR DANIEL M. SMITH

Edited by

Clifford L. Egan
University of Houston

and

Alexander W. Knott
University of Northern Colorado

UNIVERSITY
PRESS OF
AMERICA

Library of Congress Catalog Card Number: **81-40030**

Professor Daniel M. Smith

iii

Contents

Preface

Daniel Malloy Smith, Professor of History at the University of Colorado, died on 28 July 1976 in Boulder, Colorado, at the age of 54. In recognition of his achievements as a teacher, writer, and historian, ten of his graduate students have dedicated this volume of essays in twentieth century American diplomatic history to his memory.

Born in Sanford, North Carolina, on 12 July 1922, he served in the United States Navy in World War II as a Photographer's Mate First Class aboard the U.S.S. Cabot in the South Pacific. Following his tour of duty, he entered the University of California at Berkeley and received his B.A. degree in 1949, won election to Phi Beta Kappa, received his M.A. in 1950, and, studying under Professor Armin Rappaport, earned his Ph.D. in American history in 1954. After four years as an instructor at Stanford University, Smith joined the Department of History at the University of Colorado in Boulder where he rose to the rank of professor and served as chairman of the department from 1969 to 1975.

An outstanding lecturer and distinguished scholar, he attracted large numbers of students. Numerous graduate students studied under him also, and he directed more than twenty doctoral dissertations. A professional historian, with an "absolute devotion to the business of being an historian" as his friend Gerald Wheeler has stated, Dan Smith specialized in the diplomacy of the Wilsonian period, winning for himself the reputation of a "realist" interpreter of the period. His was a world view in every sense of the term, for he analyzed how nations behaved regardless of their social and economic systems. Totally dedicated to history, he held a profound belief in its relevance to contemporary problems.

His best known work, and also his own favorite, was the interpretive monograph, The Great Departure: The United States and World War I, 1914-1920 (New York, 1965), though he produced six other volumes of history, including Robert Lansing and American Neutrality 1914-1917 (Berkeley and Los Angeles, 1958) and the widely used text, The American Diplomatic Experience (Boston, 1972). He is

survived by his wife, Aladeen, his daughter, Stephanie, and two sons, Daniel Bennett and Gregory Malloy, who share his name as well as his devotion to history.

The editors wish to thank Mrs. Aladeen Smith for her skillful editorial assistance and for her general support of the project; she actually merits· the title of co-editor. They would also like to thank the University of Houston for generous clerical and financial help, without which this project could not have been completed. We are grateful also to Professor Boyd H. Hill, Jr., currently chairman of the Department of History at the University of Colorado at Boulder, for allowing us to print his eulogy, "The Legacy of Daniel Smith," given on 31 July 1976 at Professor Smith's memorial service.

The Legacy of Daniel Smith

When I came to the University of Colorado in the summer of 1964, one of the first members of the Department of History I met was Dan Smith. He was handsome, intelligent, and an excellent raconteur. I already knew of Dan by reputation as a first-class scholar of American diplomatic history, and I quickly learned from my colleagues that he was considered an outstanding lecturer as well. He was the star of the historians in both research and teaching, and for these reasons alone he will long be remembered. He directed a score of doctoral dissertations and any number of master's theses. He did for his graduate students what the Harvard law professor did in The Paper Chase: he took their minds of mush and molded them into systematic tools of analysis. Hundreds of under-graduates who enthusiastically signed up for his courses left with the impression that they had received excellent instruction and penetrating observations about United States history. I know because many of them told me of the satisfaction and stimulation they had received from Dan's lectures and discussions. He carried on the great tradition of inquiry developed by historians of the nineteenth century and handed on to those of the twentieth, and he did it with style.

At my first meeting with Dan, I was impressed with his zeal for his job. His enthusiasm was contagious. He had all the natural gifts that are necessary for being a compelling teacher and a convincing scholar, and he had honed the skills needed to communicate his historical insights to others. He was a shrewd observer of the human condition, and he possessed the ambition and capacity for leadership among his colleagues. When he became chairman of the History Deparment, he exercised his executive authority in such a way that his colleagues' stature and efficiency were enhanced, for he gave as much attention to administration as to his teaching and research, and he did these very different tasks equally well. This in itself is an extraordinary accomplishment, especially when we remember that his first term of office coincided with the tumultuous era of student strikes and riots.

What is Dan Smith's legacy to those of us who were privileged to know him? Impressionable students were set on a course of self-discipline and hard work in the pursuit of understanding about the historical past. Colleagues were affected by his stern model of performance in teaching and research. Friends were amused and entertained by his affable charm and his genuine warmth. Dan was hard-driving: he was hard on himself, and he was hard on others, but his demands were for a purpose. He did not have to articulate his philosophy; he exemplified it. He believed in the meaning of <u>arete</u>, the Greek ideal of excellence. He expected it, and he was never content unless he achieved it himself or saw it demonstrated in the activity of others, whether in the classroom, at a departmental meeting, or on the football field.

Such people are not always easy to be around, but they leave more behind them when they are no longer there in person. During the latter part of Dan's career, it became fashionable in academic circles to lower standards in order to appear more "humane" and "understanding." Publication was supposed to be at odds with good teaching, and empathy often passed for accomplishment. Dan never succumbed to this new philosophy of education. He did not believe that students were helped by substituting personality for intellect, nor that historians can advance the profession by giving up on the hard tasks of research and publication. And ultimately he was proven correct. He lived to see a turning away from permissiveness and the questioning of the intellectual enterprise. His ideals prevailed, and we should all be grateful that he never relaxed them. He should be proud that he has left behind a family of loving achievers, a set of cantankerous but mournful colleagues, and hundreds of graduates who were all exposed to his realistic, uncompromising philosophy.

Dan's life was rich and exciting, and his early experiences no doubt helped to determine his choice of profession as a diplomatic historian. Four years with the navy in the Pacific Theater between 1942 and 1946 gave him personal experience with one of the historian's most perplexing problems--warfare. After his tour of duty in World War Two, he went through Berkeley like a rocket and quickly embarked upon a teaching career at Stanford. After moving to Colorado in 1957, he confounded his colleagues

by producing seven volumes of history which were uniformly well written and well reviewed. He received a teaching award in 1966 while turning out articles at a prolific rate. He acted as editorial consultant for more than a dozen publishers while performing the difficult role of director in the training of graduate students. In retrospect, the corpus of works produced by Dan Smith would satisfy the most rigorous and self-demanding of scholars.

All of us have some sort of yearning for immortality, and none more than the historian. Dan's works, his students, his family, and his life as remembered by his friends are his legacy--intellectual and moral achievements that can never be erased.

In the seventh century two Irish monks once sat down and tried to classify all of the sins of the age in a work called De duodecim abusivis saeculi, "Twelve Abuses of the Age." They castigated the young man without obedience, the rich man who giveth not alms, the master without virtue, and the unjust king. But the first sin of all was committed by the scholar without works. Dan did not commit this sin: he was a scholar rich in works, and I refer to all of his accomplishments, not just to his publications.

Dan's character and personality were those of a hard-working, hard-driving man, and his colleagues can most easily recall this side of their friend, but they should also remember a softer side of his character, a gentler side, his smile, the gleam of amusement and humor in his eye, and the obvious joy he took in his garden and flowers. I personally was roused from apathy or gloom by his hearty laugh, which promoted optimism and good cheer, and this is what I remember best. The walls of the second story of Hellems Hall reverberate with the joyous sounds of Dan's laughter, and that is another enduring part of his generous gift to us.

When I reflected upon Dan Smith's legacy, I wondered what Dan himself might have said on such an occasion, and while such a thought is presumptuous, I could not help but

consider that he might have approved of the four-fold cure of Epicurus as a fitting farewell:

> In God there is nothing to fear
> In Death there is nothing to feel
> What is good is easily won
> What is ill is easily borne.

31 July 1976   Boyd H. Hill, Jr.

THE HOUSE MISSIONS:
UNOFFICIAL DIPLOMACY IN THE NEUTRALITY PERIOD
Billie Barnes Jensen

I

While most American presidents have had a serious concern with their place in history, Woodrow Wilson, a onetime practicing historian, had a particularly well-developed sense of the past.[1] Before he took office, and in the early months of his term, it is clear that he hoped to leave for future historians the image of a progressive reformer. Not long after taking office, however, Wilson found that foreign affairs were demanding an increasingly large amount of his time and attention, with the result that a second self-image began to develop for the President. Certainly he was encouraged in this by Colonel Edward M. House, his unofficial adviser, who stressed to the President the possibilities for world statesmanship arising from the war in Europe. In only one of many examples, House wrote to Wilson lauding him for "the path you are blazing as a standard for future generations, with permanent peace as its goal and a new ethical code as its guiding star . . . ."[2] On another occasion House wrote: "The history of this war must necessarily be largely the history of today, and no President has ever been given so splendid a chance to serve humanity as a whole."[3] Playing such a part was hard to resist, and Wilson began to see himself in the role of peacemaker. As the leader of the most important neutral nation, Wilson contemplated the possibility of turning a tragic war into an opportunity for permanent peace. It was in the pursuit of this peacemaker image that Wilson encouraged the unofficial diplomatic plans of Colonel House-- plans which resulted in the three House missions to Europe between 1914 and 1916.

Unofficial diplomacy has long had its uses, of course. The choice of a private citizen to carry out negotiations, or even to serve as a discreet connection between major powers, is recognized as a potentially effective diplomatic tool. On the other hand, the practice has pitfalls ranging from the tendency of another power to treat an unofficial representative with something less than respect, to the

1

jealousy and hostility that may be aroused in those legally charged with carrying out the nation's foreign policy. The House missions are representative of some of the best and the worst in unofficial diplomacy.

All of House's diplomacy was based on his friendship with Woodrow Wilson, and, indeed, House's power was totally dependent on his relationship with the President. He had no official position until the second Wilson administration, and although public office was his for the asking, he declined most offers pleading frail health. This selflessness, along with House's supportive, complimentary, and conciliatory attitude, helped entrench him both in Wilson's affection and in his political favor. Alexander and Juliette George maintain that House furthered his foreign policy projects by playing on the President's ambition, his desire "to achieve everlasting distinction," and his need for affection. House was also willing to appeal to the President's vanity, lavishing praise on him as the world's wisest leader while at the same time criticizing Wilson in the privacy of his diary.[4] In another work that investigates the relationship between House and Wilson, William Bullitt and Sigmund Freud described House as Wilson's "little brother" or "love object."[5] While the thoughtful observer may be unwilling to accept the Bullitt-Freud psychological analysis, nonetheless it is quite clear that there was a special relationship between Wilson and House. Wilson, in his florid nineteenth century style, addressed House in very affectionate, and perhaps misunderstood, phrases. House's replies were no less warm. Many images have been left us--in the House-Wilson letters, in House's diary, in the memoirs of close associates--attesting to the closeness of the two men. For anyone reading deeply in the literature of the Wilson period, the images persist: Wilson's eyes misting over as House leaves on a European peace mission; House providing restful humor and a brief relief from the President's political cares over dinner; House, self-effacing, ever in the background, praising Wilson's greatness. These and other glimpses into the private lives of the two friends certainly help to explain the willingness of the President to by-pass traditional channels and use House as an instrument of unofficial diplomacy. As Wilson's physician, Admiral Cary Grayson, noted in a generally hostile description, House "occupied a position unlike any other in the history of our country."[6]

2

At the time Colonel House and Woodrow Wilson first met in November, 1911, Wilson was one of several contenders for the Democratic nomination for the Presidency, and House was an obscure Texan best known for his behind-the-scenes political manipulations in the Lone Star state.[7] Each man must have recognized in the other a source of political advantage: Wilson was looking for support in his presidential bid, and House was searching for a way to extend his political interests to the national level. From House's account, the first meeting was propitious and as he noted in a letter to his brother-in-law, "never before have I found both the man and the opportunity."[8]

The friendship thus begun matched two interesting personalities. While House came from a home of wealth on the southwestern frontier, Wilson came from a very religious family of moderate means, and he grew up in Reconstruction days in the southeast. House's comfortable wealth, combined with a physical frailty resulting from a boyhood accident, had turned him away from typical patterns of ambition. He was interested in politics, but he would have been unable to withstand the rigors of campaigning, and his intolerance of warm climates made it impossible for him to hold office in his native state or in Washington, D.C. Wilson, by contrast, was clearly ambitious for the world's offices and honors, even though he sometimes clothed that ambition in idealistic rhetoric. In Wilson, House found a man who could achieve power and let him share it; in House, Wilson found a useful practical politician who seemed to want nothing for himself. In addition to this, there was an intangible attraction between the two men from their first meeting. In House's words, "We knew each other for congenial souls at the very beginning."[9] When Wilson recalled the first meeting over three years later, he was reported to have said, "We had known each other always, and merely came in touch then, for our purposes and thoughts were as one."[10] Such intangible matters must be considered in studying the relationship between Wilson and House, since the role House played in Wilson's nomination and election, while helpful, was still not important enough to explain House's later influence with the President.

House's part in Wilson's nomination has been traditionally viewed as threefold. He was supposed to have played an important role in obtaining the support of William Jennings Bryan for Wilson at the nominating convention in Baltimore; he is credited with being a key figure in gaining the support of the Texas delegation for Wilson; and finally, he is often commended for giving important advice to Wilson and the Democratic National Committee.[11] Recent scholarship tends to weaken the claims of House supporters that he played a central role in the nomination, however, and House did not even attend the Baltimore convention, leaving shortly before the meeting for one of his frequent trips to Europe.[12] In one of the letters he wrote to Wilson just prior to his departure, House noted that while his "deep interest" in Wilson's success was calling him to the convention, he was physically unable to attend. He noted: "I have done everything that I could do up to now to advise and anticipate every contingency."[13] This rather self-serving statement appears almost ludicrous in the face of events which followed.

By going to Europe, House missed one of the most exciting nominating conventions in American history--one which called for all the political wisdom the Wilsonians on the scene could muster. Generally speaking, the Wilson nomination owed much to a combination of luck, skill, and hard work which Arthur Link has called "one of the miracles of modern politics."[14] Few of the people connected with Wilson's candidacy were modest about the part they played in the proceedings, adding to the difficulty of assessing the contributions of each. By absenting himself from the convention, however, Colonel House lessened the credit he could logically claim. House's role in the subsequent election was a minor one, certainly not sufficient to purchase for him the high position he soon gained with the President.

Although House's personal influence with Wilson just after the election was not easily measurable, it became obvious, to insiders at least, that the influence was there;[15] and House was soon sought out as a man in a position to help office-seekers--most of them loyal Democrats who had been out of office for sixteen years. In all the clamor, House was the one man who stood out as apparently

4

Colonel Edward M. House, Edward M. House Papers,
Yale University.

selfless, refusing a cabinet position and not using his influence to build a political organization for himself. Fortunately for his future career as an unofficial representative of Wilson, House was of some influence in naming men to posts where they would be important in planning and implementing foreign policy. Several of these men would later be of great use to him.

II

Colonel House called his 1914 mission to Europe the "Great Adventure," a title that reflects very well the spirit in which the trip was undertaken. House was in the habit of visiting Europe in the summer, and during his trip in 1913 he had begun to make contacts which were to be valuable to him later when he undertook missions for Wilson. During the 1913 trip, for example, House met Sir Edward Grey,[16] the British Foreign Secretary, an acquaintance that was further cultivated when Grey's secretary, Sir William Tyrrell, spent some time during the ensuing winter in the United States. It was during discussions with Tyrrell that House began emphasizing the two major themes connected with the "Great Adventure": disarmament and the less defensible idea of channeling the energies of the major powers into a beneficial exploitation of the "waste places of the earth."[17] In the hope of using these ideas to improve the world situation, House told Tyrrell that he would like to go to Europe to "bring about an understanding between France, Germany, England, and the United States, regarding a reduction of armaments, both military and naval."[18]

Although Tyrrell's visit had triggered House's ambitions for a trip to England and Germany in 1914, the ideas of a grand scheme for disarmament and the utilization of the "waste places of the earth" as a diversion for the major powers had long been brewing with the Colonel. In his novel, Philip Dru, the Colonel had suggested that the major powers divide the earth into spheres of influence for the purposes of benevolent exploitation. It is interesting that Walter Hines Page, American ambassador in England, had been toying with a similar idea. On 28 August 1913, he wrote to House that some way should be found to allow the European nations to escape from their costly militarism:

6

"If we could find some friendly use for these navies and armies and kings and things--in the service of humanity-- they'd follow us." He suggested that perhaps something could be done for "the good of the tropical peoples," and that "cleaning up of backward lands" could be accomplished without annexing "a foot of land."[19] This letter to House, along with a memorandum written at about the same time and a letter written in August to Wilson, caused Burton J. Hendrick, Page's biographer, to write that along with Tyrrell's visit, "Page's letters of this period had apparently implanted in Colonel House's mind an ambition for definite action. . . . Page's ideas on the treatment of backward nations had strongly impressed both the President and Colonel House."[20] Hendrick gives Page perhaps more credit than is due when one considers that House had been considering just such an idea at least as early as 1912 in Philip Dru. A few months after that, in January, 1913, he discussed a plan with Edward S. Martin that would have provided for "Germany to exploit South America in a legitimate way; that is, by development of its resources and by sending her surplus population there."[21] Later, in the spring, House furthered his rather vague plan by cultivating a relationship with the German ambassador to the United States, Count J. H. von Bernstorff. A meeting between House and Bernstorff was arranged through a mutual friend and, according to House's account, he suggested to the German representative that "it would be a great thing if there was a sympathetic understanding between England, Germany, Japan, and the United States." He also told the Count that these nations might wield an influence for good, and that "they could ensure peace and the proper development of the waste places, besides main- taining an open door and equal opportunity to every one everywhere."[22] House hinted in his diary that the same subject was discussed with Grey on his 1913 trip, for he told Grey of this meeting with Bernstorff.[23]

House's meeting with Tyrrell is interesting because it set a pattern for British treatment of House's plans in the future: Tyrrell was encouraging; he wished to keep lines of communication open; but he was noncommittal regarding what the British might do, specifically; and he turned House's attention to the Germans. Here, as later, it was clear that the British wished to make the Germans assume

7

the role of obstructionists, and they would be delighted to use House to push matters they had long desired, such as a reduction in German naval building. Both the British and the Germans knew House's potential influence on the President; both sides wished to keep the United States friendly; and neither wished to be blamed for obstructing high-sounding principles or peaceful intentions. Tyrrell was successful in convincing House that, should he visit Europe, his first stop should be in Germany.[24]

Encouraged by his talks with Tyrrell, House approached the President on 12 December and received Wilson's approval to proceed. House's preparations for the trip--gathering information and paving the way with diplomats--occupied much of his time from December, 1913, to May, 1914. It is interesting to note that after the war broke out House complained that he had gone to Europe too late, and thus his plan had no chance of success. Yet he could only blame himself, for he had the opportunity to go to Europe months before he did.

Finally, late in April, House asked the President whether he was certain the time was ripe for his departure, to which Wilson replied, "The object you have in mind is too important to neglect."[25] House asked the President to write a letter and "put in it something which would give me an excuse to show it to the Kaiser." The object of the letter was to show the relationship between House and the President, but House suggested that it need not contain any information on the mission he was undertaking.[26] Wilson complied four days later with a letter that said, "It is hard to say goodbye, but knowing what I do it is delightful to think of what awaits you on the other side, and it is particularly heartening to me to know that I have such a good friend and spokesman."[27] When House left for Germany on 16 May, that which awaited him "on the other side" was a Europe on the brink of war--not a promising climate for his "Great Adventure."

Once in Germany, House was swept into a series of activities centered on meeting high officials. American Ambassador James Gerard arranged for House to have conversations with Admiral Alfred von Tirpitz, the Minister of Marine; Foreign Secretary Gottlieb von Jagow; Arthur

Zimmermann, the Undersecretary of State for Foreign Affairs; and even the Kaiser himself. Although House had been warned that it would be futile to talk to von Tirpitz because the Admiral's ideas were very different from those of the Wilson administration,[28] House made the effort anyway. He spent an hour with the Admiral at a party given by Ambassador Gerard, and he found that his disarmament ideas were unwelcome. Von Tirpitz, House reported, argued forcefully for the "highest possible order of military and naval organization."[29] The Admiral insisted that Germany's armaments were not offensive, and that the German government believed peace could best be maintained by putting fear into the hearts of Germany's enemies. He also made it clear that he did not trust the English. In the face of von Tirpitz's attitude, House did a little muscle-flexing of his own, pointing out the character and courage of President Wilson. He noted: "I wanted official Germany to know that if any international complications arose between our two countries, they would have to deal with a man of iron courage and inflexible will."[30]

The highlight of House's Berlin jaunt came in his meeting with the Kaiser. Charles Seymour reports that although it was quite unusual, House held out for, and was granted, a private interview with the German ruler. House found the Kaiser to be less hostile toward the British than his Minister of Marine, but he was no less committed to the German navy. Near the end of their conversation, House told the Kaiser that he and the President felt that perhaps an American might be able to instigate a project for smoothing out difficulties in Europe, and House said that he had undertaken such work. The Kaiser asked that he might be kept informed of this project through Undersecretary Zimmermann.[31]

Soon after the interview with the Kaiser, House left Germany for Paris. He had accomplished little. He had found a situation in which militarism was running "stark mad,"[32] and although he had been received politely, there was little cause for optimism as he turned toward France and Great Britain. Nevertheless, after reaching Paris, House sent a report to the President noting that he had been "as successful as anticipated," and had "ample material to open negotiations at London." He was, he said,

"altogether . . . very happy over what has been accomplished." He was even planning to set up a meeting between Sir Edward Grey and the Kaiser.[33]

House remained in Paris from 2 June through 9 June, but he made no attempt to broach his proposals with any government officials. House had his sights set on England, and he wrote ahead to Ambassador Page to "prepare the way" for negotiations. He hoped to see the British, return to Germany, and, with his mission completed, leave for the United States late in July.[34]

House arrived in England to the sweet music of praise. Ambassador Page, House confided to his diary, "was kind enough to say that he considered my work in Germany the most important done in this generation."[35] Soon afterwards, House received a letter from President Wilson bestowing yet more compliments: "You have, I hope and believe, begun a great thing and I rejoice with all my heart. You are doing it, too, in just the right way with your characteristic tact and quietness. . . ."[36]

The British leaders were friendly and helpful to House in his talks with them. At a meeting on 17 June, House reported, Grey was "visibly impressed" by his account of the German trip, but when specific matters were discussed, such as the possibility of a meeting between Grey and the Kaiser, there was a less enthusiastic response.[37] The 17 June meeting was followed by a series of talks with members of the government in which House continued to discuss the prime points of his mission, disarmament and the "waste places" idea. Throughout, the English remained more inclined to talk than to commitment. Through late June and early July, Grey was ostensibly working on a statement he would transmit to the Kaiser by means of a letter from House, but he was slow to act. Ambassador Page, in a letter to Wilson, gave reasons why he felt the British were approaching the House proposals so warily: "They're trying to find something to say to Germany, which is hard because they don't fundamentally trust the Germans. Grey is deeply in earnest, but he can't get rid of the fear that the Germans may misuse his approaches and turn them against him."[38]

Once Grey had overcome what Page described as his "fears," House turned to drafting the letter to the Kaiser. On 7 July he wrote to a friend that the "Great Adventure" had advanced rapidly enough to permit such a communication. He was hoping for a prompt answer that would "permit another step forward."[39] Significantly, while House was proceeding optimistically on his way, he had taken little notice of the assassination of the Archduke Francis Ferdinand in Bosnia on 28 June; but Ambassador Gerard was more concerned about the general European situation. On 7 July, he wrote to House to report his visit with the Kaiser at Kiel. Gerard had met with the German ruler and von Tirpitz before the news of the event in Bosnia arrived; but after word of the assassination came, the Kaiser cancelled Gerard's scheduled stay on the royal yacht, and on returning to his post, the ambassador reported that "Berlin is quiet as the grave . . . ."[40]

Undaunted by the worsening European situation, House sent his letter to the German Emperor. Transmitted through Zimmermann, the message was dated 8 July. In it, House reviewed his Berlin visit and then described his activities after leaving Germany. In England, the Kaiser learned, House had consulted Grey and the Prime Minister as well as the other important members of the government, and he had found them sympathetic, although they were forced to move cautiously to avoid offending France and Russia. Having laid the background, House wrote that while he felt much had been accomplished, there was much more to be done since the world was in a condition of "unusual foment." House appealed to the Kaiser's prejudices by pointing out that if more were to be done, it must be accomplished by a "sane and reasonable understanding among the statesmen of the Western Peoples, to the end that our civilization may continue uninterrupted." House then asked for a reply from the Kaiser to permit "another step forward."[41] House did not submit this letter to Wilson before sending it to Germany. Writing to the President on 9 July, House enclosed a copy of the message and noted that it had been shown to Page for consideration. He added that he hoped Wilson approved.

Once House had written to the Kaiser, matters of diplomacy were replaced by more relaxing activities. As

Page reported to the President: "House is happy, having sent his letter to the Kaiser, and he is now enjoying himself." Page said that Grey was pleased with the House activities but reported that the shadow of European events was beginning to fall over the island, and that Grey was disturbed by the "Servian unrest" and the mobilization in Russia and in Germany.[42] By the time House left England on 21 July, there were only a few days left before the conflagration burst upon Europe. Thus, Wilson did not even receive a full verbal report on House's activities before events had overtaken them. When House and the President met, they would discuss House's summer trip in terms of what might have been.

What had House accomplished by his sojourn in Europe? Arthur Link has written that the House mission "might conceivably have saved the peace of the world, to the eternal credit of New Freedom diplomacy, if it had come a year before instead of upon the eve of Armageddon."[43] Ray Stannard Baker felt that it served to illustrate the "real disparities" between House and Wilson in matters of foreign policy. It seemed to him to illustrate Wilson's attitude of "faith without complete understanding, of trust without actual commitment."[44] It should be said in summary that House's stay in Europe had accomplished no definitive results in the matter of his two-pronged plan to try to bring peace to Europe. He was unable to interest either Great Britain or Germany in disarmament, and he was unable to channel their energies into renovating the "waste places of the earth." Further, House was strangely unaware of the extent of his failure. On leaving Europe he was optimistic about the possibility of negotiations, and yet the shot had been fired at Sarajevo. On the morning before House's departure from England, Grey sent him word the British were gravely concerned about the "Austro-Serbian situation."[45] On 31 July, however, after House had returned to America, and as European armies were marching, the Colonel was optimistic enough to write Wilson: "I have a feeling that if a general war is finally averted, it will be because of the better feeling that has been brought about between England and Germany."[46]

House's trip did have some importance in European politics. The friendliness with which he was received by

British statesmen had its effect on the Colonel. Perhaps more important, the trip emphasized his pro-British tendencies. After viewing both Germany and England in that crucial summer, he was never able to place the blame for the war on the British, for he had noted himself that while Germany had been concerned with military glory, the British were concerned with Ascot and garden parties. From this point forward, House was never really neutral.

Late in July, House landed in Boston, but surprisingly he made no immediate effort to report to the President in person. Having no desire to face the summer heat in Washington, House went directly to Pride's Crossing, Massachusetts, from whence he viewed the disintegrating situation in Europe and wrote letters to Wilson. In one of these he made it quite clear that he was still ready to represent Wilson abroad:

> What I particularly want to say to you is that if either now or at any time soon you feel that you may be able to use me to your advantage in the troubles, I shall be, as always, entirely at your command. Both Germany and England know that I hold your confidence, and I would perhaps understand better how to proceed than one new to the situation as I am in close touch with both Governments. For the moment, I do not see what can be done, but if war comes, it will be swift and terrible and there may be a time soon when your services will be gladly accepted. It is then I would hope to be useful to you.[47]

While House was looking forward to future negotiations, there was still some unfinished business with regard to the mission just completed. He had yet to receive, when he arrived back in the United States, a reply to his letter to the Kaiser. The answer, dated 1 August, came from Zimmermann, conveying the thanks of the German ruler. Zimmermann then added that the Kaiser's "strong and sincere efforts to conserve peace have entirely failed." He blamed Russia for the condition of European affairs, and added, "There is no chance now to discuss the possibility of an understanding, so much desired, which would lay the foundation for permanent peace and security."[48] This

letter would later provide the basis for House to engage in some further negotiations, but in August, 1914, it was viewed merely as the end of the unsuccessful mission of the summer.

III

House began thinking of a second mission to Europe soon after returning from the first. From the summer of 1914, through the end of the year, he made himself available for advice on matters of foreign policy, and he cultivated the acquaintance of those who might be useful to him should he undertake another mission abroad. In addition, the British ambassador in Washington, Cecil Spring-Rice, and the American ambassador in Great Britain, Walter Hines Page, were proving to be of limited usefulness to their governments, and House was among those willing to point out their limitations to Wilson. Further, the Colonel was quick to note that Secretary of State William Jennings Bryan was not respected by European nations, and House carried on a subtle campaign to discredit the Secretary with the President. All of these things may have served to illustrate to Wilson the desirability of continuing House's type of unofficial negotiation.

The early fall of 1914 saw House strengthening his connections. He wrote in September that he was laying plans to make himself "persona grata" with all the nations involved in the war, stating: "I have been assiduously working to this end ever since the war broke loose." By so doing, he felt, he would be "trying to think out problems in advance" rather than leaving them to chance.[49]

In mid-December, Wilson spoke to House about the possibility of his going abroad to "initiate peace conversations." By House's account, Wilson placed the matter exclusively in his hands. "He desires me to take charge of it and to go whenever I think it advisable. . . . He felt that I was the one to undertake it. . . ." House assured the President that he was willing to go at any time.[50]

From this point, there were a series of discussions and letters aimed at securing a warm welcome in England and Germany when the Colonel should go abroad. Both of these

countries were, because of House's maneuverings, forced to walk a diplomatic tightrope. They could not flatly refuse to consider peace parleys, for very unfortunate propaganda might result. On the other hand, they could not appear to welcome talks openly since public opinion at home and opinion among their allies would thus be aroused.

As 1915 began, the two major belligerents were still toying with the idea of House's mission; they wished to retain the friendship of the United States, yet they were distinctly unhappy about the prospect of risking peace negotiations to do so. On 2 January, Grey wrote to Spring-Rice on the proposed mission, and a few days later the British ambassador passed the message contained in the letter on to House. It was a pessimistic communication, discouraging in tone, but House took heart from one passage in which Grey said that if there was a hope of satisfactory settlement, he would consult his allies.[51]

House went to Washington on 12 January to confer with the President. Regarding the decision on his mission, House reported in his diary that he and the President "had exactly twelve minutes' conversation before dinner, and during those twelve minutes it was decided that I should go to Europe January 30." House believed that everything that could be done through the regular ambassadors had been done, and that the time had arrived to "deal with the principals."[52]

Before his departure, House conferred with the British, French, and Russian ambassadors in Washington at a meeting which was far from satisfactory. He then had a discussion with Bryan that was painful for both of them. It was during this conversation that the Secretary of State learned that House was to have the mission Bryan desired for himself. House noted that Bryan was "distinctly disappointed" that he had not been chosen, but the Colonel explained that the mission was to be unofficial and that Bryan's presence in Europe would attract far too much attention. Bryan was gracious enough to say that if he could not go to Europe, he was glad that it was House who had been chosen instead.[53] House finally sailed for Europe on 30 January 1915, on the Lusitania. In the months since

his last mission, he had worked hard to pave the way for negotiations, but he had achieved little in the way of success. Great Britain had extended a rather unenthusiastic invitation, but Germany had not yet sent one at all.

When House's first mission had failed to achieve peace, he had turned to the twin ideas of disarmament and his "waste places" theory in the hope of finding some basis for negotiations. On his 1915 trip, he developed two new ideas to help guide his mission: "freedom of the seas," and his "second convention" idea.[54] By "freedom of the seas," House meant an international agreement by which only implements directly used in war would be considered contraband, and free trade should be allowed in all other items during wartime. Further, a blockade had to be effective to be declared. By the "second convention" idea, House meant that a second conference should be called at the same time as or immediately following the peace conference, and this second convention would be used to establish some sort of permanent peace. Both of these ideas had been in House's repertoire before the trip, but during his mission he brought them out, refurbished them, and suggested them to the governments he contacted when the possibilities of initiating peace negotiations seemed dim.

Since he had no official invitation to visit Germany, House began his 1915 mission in England. Almost immediately after House's arrival in London on 6 February, he sought and received an appointment with Sir Edward Grey. In this conference, and those that followed, Grey expressed his friendship and willingness to cooperate, but the Colonel found it quite difficult to pin Grey down to any specific commitment on the subject of peace negotiations. The official attitude the British presented to House was that they were willing to participate in parleys at any time that Germany and her allies were sincerely ready to negotiate. After nearly every conversation, House noted that the British had cast doubts on the sincerity of the Germans.[55]

While the British were delaying any commitment on negotiations, House found them to be particularly interested in the question of American participation in a postwar peace conference. This coincided with House's "second convention" idea, which may be seen in a letter from House

16

to Wilson reporting a talk in which Grey had urged that the United States take part in the postwar conference. As the Colonel wrote: "I evaded this by suggesting that a separate convention should be participated in by all neutrals as well as the belligerents, which should lay down the principles upon which civilized warfare should in the future be conducted." House explained that this convention would adopt rules for "governing the game."[56]

Meanwhile, House made a concession to the British that Arthur Link regards as especially significant. At a meeting held on 10 February, House told Grey that he had "no intention of pushing the question of peace," admitting that before talks began the Allies should be allowed to try their spring offensives in the hope that Germany would be in a less advantageous position thereafter.[57] Link states that "this was, altogether, a momentous declaration, one that changed the character of House's mission at the very outset." Thus, Grey no longer had to fear immediate American pressure. This "assured the Foreign Secretary that the Washington government would use its influence to achieve only a settlement acceptable to the Allies."[58]

Another way in which House seemed to be favoring the British was in delaying his scheduled trip to Germany. Wilson was being pressured by his ambassador in Germany, James Gerard, who wired the State Department on 11 February that "if a reasonable peace proposition were offered Germany very many men of influence would be inclined to use their efforts to induce Germany to accept the proposition." He also feared that "if peace does not come immediately, a new and protracted phase of the war will commence."[59] In the weeks which followed, Gerard continued to urge action.

House found himself in a difficult situation. The same letter which invited House to visit Germany--written by Zimmermann on 4 February--also made it clear that the Germans were not going to accept the evacuation and indemnification of Belgium as a part of the peace settlement.[60] Since House believed the German ambassador in Washington, Johann von Bernstorff, had intimated that such a settlement was possible, he was disillusioned about the possibilities that awaited him in Berlin. House's

doubts, fed by British pressure, and Wilson's impatience, fed by the dispatches of Ambassador Gerard, caused the President to come as close to rebuking House as he ever did in the neutrality period. He wrote: "It will, of course, occur to you that you cannot go too far in allowing the English Government to determine when it is best for you to go to Germany because they will naturally desire to await some time when they have the strategic advantage. . . ." He added that House ran the risk of appearing to be the spokesman of the British rather than the President.[61]

On receiving this cable, House sent a long explanation to the President, pointing out the difficulty over Belgium, and cautioning that to go to Germany at once would be to risk losing the "sympathetic interest" shown by Britain. He noted that "if there was any reason to believe that Germany was ready to make such terms as the Allies are ready to accept, then it would be well to go immediately, but all our information is to the contrary. . . ."[62] A vote of confidence was soon forthcoming from the President who wrote that House's cables helped him to understand the situation. "I am of course content to be guided by your judgment as to each step," he wrote.[63]

Slightly over a month after House arrived in England, he left for the Continent. On 5 March, he wrote to Wilson, "Berlin is now calling for me," but, unfortunately, he had little reason to be optimistic. The Germans, to be sure, had invited House to come to their country, but they had given him very little reason to hope that they were willing to accept any basis for negotiation that would be acceptable to the British and their allies. With an immediate establishment of peace negotiations unlikely, House turned to his ideas of "freedom of the seas" and the "second convention."

En route to Berlin, House stopped in Paris. While Grey had warned him that the French were not interested in beginning peace negotiations, House believed that he should consult with Théophile Delcassé, the Foreign Minister. Although Delcassé received House in a cordial manner, the Colonel was forced to report to Wilson that the French were in "no mood for peace talks."[64] On 18 March

18

1915, House left Paris for Berlin. When he arrived in the German capital, he found that the Germans were in no mood for peace talks either. The Germans, House reported to Wilson, were so inflamed by war propaganda that they expected "extravagant results."[65] House feared that discussions were futile. "It is plain at the moment that some serious reverse will have to be encountered by one or the other of the belligerents before any government will dare propose parleys." The best move, he believed, would be to "wait until the fissure appears."[66]

House did find some reason for optimism while in Germany, since he encountered a few "fair minded" Germans who had a "clear vision of the situation" in their country and who were favorably disposed toward peace.[67] The Colonel also found that the members of the Foreign Office were encouraging about future negotiations--the idea of the "second convention" was acceptable to them. On 23 March, Foreign Secretary von Jagow approved the concept in principle, although he was not willing to discuss any details connected with it,[68] and the next day Zimmermann expressed enthusiasm for the idea.[69] House wrote to Wilson on the same day that all the ministers he had seen had agreed that Germany was quite willing to back the United States in her desire for a "second convention."[70]

House also found the Germans receptive to his ideas about "freedom of the seas." As he explained to Wilson, "I have sown this thought of the Freedom of the Seas very widely here, and already I can see the result." He added, "I think I can show England that, in the long run and looking at the matter broadly, it is as much to her interest as it is to the other nations of the earth." Not surprisingly, House was able to report to the President that the Chancellor and Zimmermann thought the naval idea was the best possible beginning for peace negotiations.[71] With the thought that something might be accomplished with England on this basis, House left Germany saying that he was fairly satisfied with the situation. Wilson replied that the "suggestion you are to carry to London seems to me very pleasing and may be the opening we are looking for. . . ."[72]

It could hardly be said that House had accomplished much by his trip to Germany. He had learned that the Germans were by no means interested in any peace parleys that included the evacuation of conquered territory, although they could be interested in a plan which would restrict the British navy. House could have learned either of these things without visiting Berlin.

Before he returned to England, House met with the American ambassadors to Italy and Spain.[73] He also went again to Paris where he had conferences with Delcassé and French President Raymond Poincaré. These talks were not successful from the standpoint of promoting peace, for as House wrote in his diary, "I would have made a mistake if I had attempted to talk peace at this time." The French, he felt, considered the Americans to be pro-German and to be pushing peace measures to aid Germany.[74] Nevertheless, House noted that the conferences with the two went smoothly enough.[75]

House had hoped that upon his return to England he might get negotiations started on the basis of his "freedom of the seas" notion, but before the Colonel had a chance to confer with British officials, he received a letter from Grey rejecting the idea.[76] When House met with Grey upon his return to London, however, he found some hope in Sir Edward's utterances. Grey pointed out that such a plan as House's would require that the British public be "educated," and House said that he would endeavor to do that.[77] House also used this glimmer of hope as the basis for continued correspondence with Zimmermann.[78]

House was still in England when the Lusitania was sunk on 7 May, and his pro-English feelings were intensified by that event. His first dispatches to Wilson were filled with talk of American intervention,[79] but by 13 May he had softened his position somewhat.[80] Although House had never been truly neutral in his attitude toward the European belligerents, he had never before expressed such strong sentiments to the President as he did over the Lusitania sinking. Thereafter, there could be no doubt that House believed the cause of right was on the side of England and her allies. Nevertheless, the Colonel was still trying to find some basis for opening talks, and he dis-

cussed with Grey the possibility of relieving the tense maritime situation by having the British end their food blockade of Germany in exchange for Germany's giving up submarine warfare and the use of asphyxiating gases. As might be expected, the idea was not taken seriously.

With the collapse of these negotiations, House began to think of returning to the United States. On 25 May, he wrote to Wilson that there was nothing new in England and that the Europeans seemed to be settling down for a long war. "I want very much," he wrote, "to see you and to go over the situation in person."[81] On 1 June, House cabled that he was thinking of returning on the fifth and noted that he hoped this met with the President's approval.[82] Wilson replied: "You have been so invaluable to me over there and can be of such great service to me here in these times of perplexity that I am at a loss to advise but I am perfectly willing that you should act on your own judgment. . . ."[83] Meanwhile, House had confided to his diary that war with Germany was inevitable, and therefore he decided to return to the United States.[84]

House had been in Europe four months, and yet as far as peace negotiations were concerned, he had accomplished nothing. The military stalemate in Europe created an extremely difficult situation for anyone seeking to end the war. From a personal point of view, House had managed to strengthen his ties with the nations at war, especially Great Britain. Perhaps most important of all, House was in England at the time of the Lusitania disaster. This event, which would have had a strong effect on him in any case, was made doubly impressive by his British surroundings at the time. Thereafter, he was not only strongly pro-British, but he also was convinced that it was inevitable that the United States enter the war on the Entente's side. It was in this frame of mind that House returned to the United States, there to involve himself in the Lusitania considerations and the crisis over Bryan's resignation as Secretary of State.

IV

By October, 1915, House was again considering a trip to Europe. Having thought about the world situation

21

through the summer and fall, he outlined for the President a procedure which would "either end the war in a way to abolish militarism or that would bring us in with the Allies to help them do it."[85] House's plan for accomplishing this end was to ask the Allies if it would be agreeable to them for the United States to demand that hostilities cease. The American demand should be made on the grounds that the neutrals of the world were suffering along with the belligerents, and had as much right to demand parleys. "If the Allies understood our purpose, we could be as severe in our language concerning them as we were with the Central Powers." The Allies could then accept the demand of the United States and if the Central Powers followed suit, a "master-stroke" of diplomacy would be accomplished. If they did not, "we could then push our insistence to a point where diplomatic relations would first be broken off, and later the whole force of our Government, and perhaps the force of every neutral--might be brought against them." According to House, when the President heard this idea, which was later to develop into the House-Grey Memorandum, he was "startled" by the plan, but "he seemed to acquiesce by silence."[86] By 14 October, House noted that the President was "cordially acquiescing" in his "intervention" plan. It was now, he wrote, "only a question as to when and how it should be done." The matter, House said, had been left in his hands.[87]

House took the first step by writing to Sir Edward Grey. He asked whether Grey felt the time was propitious for the United States to intervene between the belligerents, proposing parleys on the basis of "the elimination of militarism and navalism." House continued, explaining that the weight of the United States would be thrown on the side that accepted the proposal. The Central Powers, he felt, might not wish to agree to the terms, which would then make it necessary for the United States to join the Allies.[88] President Wilson, upon reading the letter before it was sent, inserted the word "probably" before the promise of joining the Allies.[89] On the day he composed the message to Grey, House wrote in his diary that it was one of the most important letters he had ever written.[90] Thus began the negotiations leading to the House-Grey Memorandum.

House also mentioned the possibility of renewing his activity on behalf of peace to German Ambassador Johann von Bernstorff. The peace, House explained, would be based on Germany's giving up militarism and England's giving up navalism. Bernstorff's reaction, according to House, was gratifying: "He was intensely interested and suggested that it would be a good time for me to go to Europe and make such a proposal direct."[91] Other assurances from the Germans came in December when Ambassador Gerard reported to House that the Chancellor was sounding out the members of the Reichstag, presumably to be able to follow public opinion in the matter. Gerard reported that many members of the body, not only the socialists, were in favor of peace.[92]

On 15 December, House was in Washington to discuss the proposed mission with the President. The Colonel noted in his diary that he suggested to Wilson that the mission might be deferred until later, but that the President "thought I should go immediately."[93] Since House and Wilson decided that the mission would not include Berlin unless an invitation from the German government was forthcoming, House, in conversations with Bernstorff, dropped the hint that his itinerary depended on the Germans. "He [Bernstorff] declared that I would be welcome in Germany if any one would be upon such a mission."[94] The Colonel intimated to Wilson, however, that he had a distrust both of German diplomatic methods and of Bernstorff's invitation. "I insisted that his Government communicate with me at London through Gerard so as to confirm Bernstorff's assertion that I would be welcome. . . . I do not believe it would be wise to go to Berlin without direct assurance other than from Bernstorff."[95]

House sailed for Europe on 28 December 1915. When he arrived on this third mission, House was prepared to give assurances to the British that the United States would enter a postwar conference for the purpose of guaranteeing the peace, and assurances that if American peace offers were rejected in Germany, the United States would probably enter the war on the side of the Allies. House was in no sense trying to arrange a situation by which the United States might ultimately be aligned, by any chance, with the Central Powers. The question at stake, as far as he was

concerned, was whether the United States would be brought into the war by another of the submarine "outrages" that had caused such crises in 1915, or whether the country would enter the war on the basis of the moral and political issues involved. This latter consideration, which House approved, would have involved intervention to force the writing of a just peace but not, he assumed, to bring about an unconditional victory for the Allies. This view shows House's concern with the balance of power in Europe and the danger that it might be upset by the outcome of the war.

House received a warm welcome in Great Britain and immediately entered into a series of talks with British leaders, explaining his mission and renewing his discussions on the "freedom of the seas." He told Sir Edward Grey that he felt public opinion in the United States had progressed to a point where the country might be able to enter an agreement for world peace. House's statement was supported by Wilson in a message on 9 January, in which he noted that he "would be glad if you would convey my assurance that I shall be willing and glad when the opportunity comes to cooperate in a policy seeking to bring about and maintain permanent peace among civilized nations."[96] House was quite aware that the assurance he had thus received from the President was precedent-shattering. As he wrote, "It marks a definite departure in the policy of our Government and for this, as well as for other reasons, is of historic value."[97]

While House's friendly discussions with the English were taking place, conversations between the United States and Germany on the Lusitania matter took a turn for the better. Wilson cabled House that the optimistic outlook in the negotiations with the German ambassador might alter the American attitude toward Great Britain. As soon as the problems with Germany were adjusted, he warned, "the demand here especially from the Senate will be imperative that we force England to make at least equal concessions to our unanswerable claims of rights."[98] Since British officials had repeatedly explained to House that any substantial surrender to the demands of the United States on shipping questions might well result in a change of government, House was especially disturbed by Wilson's cable. He

feared any change in government would damage his negotiations and force him to re-establish trust. Fortunately for House, if not for the cause of world peace, he soon received word from State Department Counsellor Frank Polk that a settlement with Germany was being delayed.[99]

Meanwhile, satisfied that he would be well-received in Germany, House made plans for his departure to the Continent. He had a final conference with Grey on the night of 19 January. This followed a rather discouraging luncheon House had had with Page, who was quite pessimistic about the trip to Germany, and who told House that the whole undertaking was a mistake.[100] In view of Page's opinion, House asked Grey about the impending trip to Germany and received complete approval for it.[101]

Travelling by way of France and Switzerland, House arrived in Berlin on the morning of 28 January, and was met by members of the staff of the American embassy. Following a busy day spent with newspapermen and others desiring interviews, House was the guest of Ambassador Gerard at dinner.[102] Since House stayed only four days in Berlin, his contacts were not extensive, but he did talk with Chancellor Theobald von Bethmann Holweg and with von Jagow of the Foreign Office. The Chancellor intimated that evacuation of the conquered territory might be considered by Germany in return for an indemnity, but House advised that the Allies would never consider such a proposition. Generally, House was not impressed by the Chancellor, and he felt he had gained nothing from their conversation on this occasion. He found von Jagow to be somewhat more reasonable, although he noted in his diary: "I went to bed with a feeling that not much had been accomplished by my discussions with the Chancellor and Von Jagow."[103]

On 30 January, House left Germany, retracing his steps to England. Since he felt he could not write freely from Germany, it was not until 3 February that he sent his observations on Berlin politics to the President. He was, he reported, well received in Germany, and because the Chancellor was in the ascendancy over the military group, the atmosphere was more congenial than it had been during his 1915 trip when Admiral von Tirpitz and General Erich

von Falkenhayn were in favor. Unfortunately, House felt the civil arm of the government would not be in control long--especially, he noted, unless the United States decided to take "measures" against the Allies. This would be impossible to do, House stressed, in a manner that would satisfy Germany.[104]

Once back in France House proceeded with discussions centered on his intervention plan. On 3 February, he was able to report "interesting and satisfactory" talks with both Premier Aristide Briand and Jules Cambon of the Foreign Office. He outlined, for the benefit of the French, "the entire situation as it seems to me."[105] Not surprisingly, he found the French to be more sympathetic with the United States' shipping problems than the English had been.

In a dispatch from France, House tried to impress upon Wilson the seriousness of the European situation:

I cannot begin to tell you by letter how critical the situation is everywhere, not only as between themselves, but with us as well. In my opinion, hell will break loose in Europe this spring and summer as never before; and I see no way to stop it for the moment. I am as sure as I ever am of anything that by the end of the summer you can intervene.[106]

Interventionism formed the core of House's talks with the French. Of this he wrote to Wilson, "I dare not cable . . . further than to say that it was the most important conference I have had in Europe and that it was along the line of my conversation with Lloyd George before leaving London."[107] In other words, intervention should be accomplished by the President at the end of the summer offensives.

On leaving France, House summarized the accomplishments of his visit for the President. He had tried, he said, to create a favorable atmosphere for his negotiations, and, prompted by the slowness of the British, he had decided to talk frankly with the French. The result was "surprisingly satisfactory."[108]

When House returned to England, he and Grey went over the diplomatic situation in great detail and "finally agreed that it would be best for you [Wilson] to call a conference for the discussion of peace terms." This would be preferable to intervention on the submarine issue. The Allies were to agree to the conference, and then, if Germany declined, the United States would throw her weight behind a movement to bring Germany to terms. His discussions with Grey so encouraged the Colonel that he wrote to Wilson: "If you can hold the situation at Washington clear of all complications, sending no notes, protests, etc., etc., to any of the belligerents, it looks as if something momentous may happen." House's report of this conference was full of confidence. He would, he wrote, bring the substance of his talks with Grey before other officials, and "if they consent it should mark the beginning of the end of the war." He predicted that after his return to Washington, Wilson would be able to initiate "the great movement we have in mind."[109]

By 11 February, House was able to assure the President that when he left England it would be with absolute understanding that Wilson was to propose a conference and act as mediator "when the time is propitious."[110] The Colonel's optimism was rooted in a conference of that day in which the mechanics of the intervention plan were worked out. House agreed to cable Grey at regular intervals, offering the intervention of the President. Grey would ignore these messages until the time arrived for mediation, then he would show the message to his allies. House cautioned those present at the conference--Grey, Arthur Balfour and Herbert Asquith-- that they would run a risk if they waited until Germany had a decisive victory, since American help would then be useless.[111] In summary, House believed that the conference was "very satisfactory, but not entirely conclusive."[112]

On 14 February, a general meeting was held between House and the most important figures of the British government. After some discussion of specific terms that might be considered at a peace conference, the group turned to the issue of when the United States should demand that a conference be held. As might be expected, the British were unwilling to designate a specific time.

They were only willing to agree that intervention would be most effective when the Allies could make a "deep dent" in German lines.[113]

On 15 February, Grey agreed to write a memorandum of the understanding which had been worked out between House and the British leaders so the Colonel might have a copy to take to the President.[114] House was pleased at what had been accomplished, as he wrote to Wilson:

> After many conferences with Sir Edward Grey and his colleagues, I am satisfied with the result. They cordially accept the suggestion that you preside over the convention when it is held, provided our general understanding is carried out. No action however is to be taken until they signify their readiness. There is a difference of opinion only as to time.[115]

As it turned out, of course, this difference of opinion proved to be of primary importance.

It was with a feeling of accomplishment that Edward House set out for the United States on 25 February 1916, on board the Rotterdam. After his two earlier missions had failed to bring about the peace negotiations he sought, House at last had reason to believe that he had accomplished something of lasting importance. With the memorandum he had initialed with Grey, House now believed that he had provided the machinery by which the United States would be enabled either to end the war or to enter it on the side of the Allies. House returned to the United States carrying the memorandum that could have taken the United States into the war a year earlier than it finally did and on what House considered to be higher moral grounds than finally turned out to be the case.

V

It is difficult to evaluate the House missions. On the surface, they were clearly failures. No peace negotiations resulted from House's efforts; the war began and it continued as if he had done nothing. In a deeper sense, too, House was, at least in part, a failure. He disrupted regular channels of diplomacy and planted seeds of distrust

28

on the part of the President against some of the regularly constituted diplomats in the United States and abroad. He sometimes gave the President false hope, and he frequently sent misleading dispatches back from Europe. In many ways, House illustrates the disadvantages of sending a man on a diplomatic mission whose philosophies are generally unknown, and who has not been tested by the usual process of elective politics or Senate confirmation. Indeed, House's political philosophy sometimes smacked of authoritarianism, an element of his thinking which was displayed in such widely separated examples as his utopian novel, Philip Dru, which was written in 1911-1912, and in his unfortunate praise for Mussolini in the 1930's. More often, though, the Colonel's faults lay not with authoritarianism, but with a sort of naive idealism. In this he was like Wilson, but in House the tendency was less pronounced than it was in the President.

As an unofficial representative of the United States, and as an individual who spent as little time in Washington as possible, House was sometimes not as well informed as a regular representative of the government would have been. This resulted in a type of tunnel vision when House was pursuing his objectives overseas. True, House was a keen observer, and certainly he was provided with any information he requested, but he was not fully and continuously informed about the total political, diplomatic, and military situation, and when he was on a mission he tended to see only his immediate objective.

Another of the problems with House's negotiations was a certain lack of realism with regard to the intentions of the European leaders. This was a problem growing out of his own diplomatic methods; for when House encountered resistance to the specific matter he had gone abroad to propose, he turned to discussions of concepts anyone could consider with relative safety. Disarmament and freedom of the seas, for example, are matters which most nations can endorse in principle as long as they are not pushed on details. Thus, House let himself believe the diplomats facing him in Europe were of a mind with him, when, in reality, they were simply humoring him for the sake of retaining the good favor of a major neutral power. House, who could be every inch a practical politician, could also display an impractical side. Certainly, as Arthur Link has

29

observed, House sometimes heard what he wished to hear.[116] Similarly, Keith Nelson has asserted that there were times when House behaved "as if nations would inevitably honor the pledges they had given."[117] Wishing to believe that he was accomplishing a great deal, and wishing to be remembered along with Wilson as a great peacemaker, House saw his European missions in something less than a realistic way, and he misled the President as well as himself. This was especially true in the case of the House-Grey Memorandum.[118]

House's missions may well have contributed to the formation of a dangerous image of Wilson abroad. Arthur Link believes that the most enduring image of Wilson among his English critics was "of a well-intentioned idealist so naive as to be almost completely visionary, a kind of Don Quixote tilting at European windmills."[119] Indeed, the House negotiations contributed to such an image among the European leaders. The ideas House brought to Europe were visionary, and to men engaged in a brutal war they must have seemed an unaffordable luxury. In the end, such ideas proved expensive to the United States in such matters as the President's distress over the failure of the House-Grey Memorandum, or, on a larger scale, the later disillusionments of the peace conference.

Another of the pitfalls of unofficial diplomacy, arousing the hostility of regularly appointed officials, is evident in the House missions. Perhaps the best example of this comes with Wilson's first Secretary of State, William Jennings Bryan. Bryan and House had been acquainted for some time, and the Secretary was gracious about House's efforts in 1914 and 1915. Bryan resented the close relationship of House and the President, however, and he wished to be Wilson's representative in Europe himself. One of Bryan's biographers wrote that failing to get a mission overseas gave Bryan "perhaps the most drastic disappointment of his career."[120] Although this is something of an exaggeration for a man who had thrice lost the Presidency, it was nevertheless a great blow to Bryan when House was chosen. After all, Bryan considered himself to be the primary advocate of peace in the Wilson administration. Later, when Bryan met with Wilson to inform the President he was resigning, the Secretary said, "Colonel House has been Secretary of State, not I, and I have never had your full

confidence."[121]   Bryan would probably have been even more resentful of House if he knew that the Colonel had made it clear to Wilson that the Secretary of State was not respected overseas. On 1 August 1914, for example, House wrote: "Please let me suggest that you do not let Mr. Bryan make any overtures to any of the powers involved." House went on to explain that the Europeans regarded Bryan as "purely visionary," so that overtures made through him would lessen Wilson's personal influence.[122]

House's relationships with the two American ambassadors most intimately connected with his work were generally quite good. James Gerard in Germany was always cooperative, and although he was occasionally a bit impatient about House's delays when Gerard thought peace was in sight, there is seldom any criticism of House found in the ambassador's writing. Indeed, a book he wrote about his experiences in Germany, Face to Face with Kaiserism, was dedicated to House. Walter Hines Page in England was strongly supportive of House during his first two missions, but by the third he had lost enthusiasm for House's course. Page's reaction at the time of the third mission is a curious combination of practical wisdom and unbridled prejudice. He was wise enough to see the flaws in House's scheme, discussing the plan as "purely academic and nonsensical stuff,"[123] and even writing to Wilson that House was "living in an atmosphere of illusion."[124] On the other hand, Page's anger was based not on concern for a practical American stance, but on his strong attachment to the British cause. He fervently desired that the United States enter the war on the side of the Allies, and he did not wish to be part of any plan that risked bringing the war to a close before the Germans were defeated. His despair over House's mission led him to consider, at least in private, the possibility of resigning.[125]

Page might have lost patience with House sooner than he did if he had realized that the reports the Colonel sent to the President were not always favorable to Page. Indeed, one historian argues that House gradually assumed the duties of Page and his counterpart in Washington, Spring-Rice, as well.[126] It is possible that House's negative reports about Bryan, Spring-Rice, Page, and others arose from a great concern that the United States have the best possible representation in a difficult time. It

is also possible that, consciously or not, House recognized Bryan, Page, and Spring-Rice as competitors. After all, these were the men who might have been expected to carry out the missions House secured for himself. Whatever his purpose, House's presence probably contributed to Bryan's distress with the Wilson administration and gradually lessened the usefulness of Page and Spring-Rice.[127] In the long run, the weakening of the ambassadors at such a critical time probably did the nation a disservice; however, Bryan's replacement by Robert Lansing was no tragedy.

While the number of House's specific accomplishments is small, he was nevertheless successful in achieving some objectives. In Philip Dru, House had clearly placed himself among the ranks of those who favored a retreat from a policy of isolationism. When the outbreak of war in Europe focused the attention of House firmly on foreign policy, he directed even more effort to the task of concentrating the attention of President Wilson on the important developments in diplomacy. The President, who had devoted most of his attention to domestic politics, was ultimately forced by world events to play a major role in foreign affairs; and it was House who early realized the President's reluctance in this new area of statesmanship. It was House who bent his efforts toward making the President realize the importance of the role the United States was destined to play in the conflict. House was frequently impatient with the President, especially in the early months of the war, and he complained in his diary that the President was unwilling to face his international responsibilities. Undiscouraged, House used his influence throughout the neutrality period to take the United States into the stream of international events. He was well aware, for example, that our traditional policy would preclude any participation in peace negotiations. Approaching the problem circumspectly at first, House developed his "second convention" idea--an idea which eventually helped establish in Wilsonian policy some of the basis for the League of Nations. There were, of course, many men who were sponsoring ideas of a permanent settlement that would embrace an end to militarism and navalism, but none of them stood as close to the President as Edward House.

An important aspect of House's desire to make the country take its place among the nations of the world was

his belief, after the spring of 1915, that a desirable settlement could come only if the United States participated in the conflict. House saw that there were two ways in which this participation might occur and, of the two, the most desirable was for American participation to be placed on a moral basis. He believed that if the United States entered the war, the President should announce that the chief reason was to guarantee a just peace. This would create a great moral advantage for the United States when the peace conference finally met. Wilson could then use this advantage to build a really permanent peace. On the other hand, House believed that if United States intervention ultimately came about because of some outrage, some act of "frightfulness" on the part of the Germans, then Wilson's influence would only equal that of the Allied leaders. Perhaps the greatest difficulties that arose at the peace conference were based on the fact that Wilson was trying to wield a great moral power that he lacked because the United States entry into the war was not actually based on moral principles.

House was convinced that America should enter the war on the side of the Allies. His own sentiments were with the Allies from the beginning of the war and, after the sinking of the Lusitania, he made no attempt to keep his sentiments from the President. Nevertheless, he was quite proper in his dealings with the Central Powers, and it is a credit to his abilities as a diplomat that Ambassador Bernstorff wrote after the war that he had considered House to be neutral throughout the period.[128]

Colonel House succeeded in one main purpose during the neutrality period. He saw that the United States was committed to participation in a conference to secure a permanent peace, and his arguments, along with those of others who shared his views, helped formulate Wilson's decision to enter the war on the side of the Allies.

House's approach to foreign policy was, in the beginning, a curious mixture of realism and idealism. On his first mission to Europe, his idealistic plans for peace were impractical in view of the realities of European politics. As the war in Europe progressed, House's outlook became increasingly realistic; his second mission to Europe showed that he still relied on idealistic phrases but, by the

third mission, his offer of peace negotiations was combined with a probable guarantee of assistance to the Allies. He recognized that the interests of the United States were tied to those of the Allied powers and he acted accordingly. He feared a Europe dominated by a victorious Germany and thus realized the necessity of maintaining strong relations with France and England. House shrewdly recognized that a decisive victory by either side in the war might render impossible a European balance of power following the conflict, and his concept of an organization to maintain a permanent peace was an attempt to maintain this equilibrium. Nevertheless, he misjudged the ability of President Wilson to lead the country into such a consortium of nations.

Although he was inept and naive at times, Edward M. House was, as an unofficial diplomat, an important force in the American assumption of international responsibilities.

[1]Much of the material in this essay is based on letters and other papers located in the Manuscript Division of the Library of Congress and the Yale University Library. The author wishes to thank the librarians of both institutions for permission to use the collections cited here.

[2]Edward M. House to Woodrow Wilson, 22 August 1914, Woodrow Wilson Papers, Library of Congress, Washington, D.C. (hereafter cited as Wilson Papers).

[3]House to Wilson, 30 November 1914, ibid.

[4]Alexander L. George and Juliette L. George, Woodrow Wilson and Colonel House: A Personality Study (New York, 1956), pp. 162-63.

[5]Sigmund Freud and William C. Bullitt, Thomas Woodrow Wilson: A Psychological Study (Boston, 1967), pp. 68-69, 145-46, 213-14.

[6]Cary T. Grayson, "The Colonel's Folly and the President's Distress," American Heritage 15 (October 1964): 7.

[7]For a description of this part of House's career, see Rupert N. Richardson, Colonel House: The Texas Years (Abilene, 1964).

[8]House to Dr. S. M. Mezes, 25 November 1911, quoted in Charles Seymour, ed., The Intimate Papers of Colonel House (Boston, 1926-1928), 1:46.

[9]Arthur D. Howden Smith, Mr. House of Texas (New York, 1940), p. 42.

[10]Verification for this statement comes from the President's daughter, Eleanor Wilson McAdoo, The Woodrow Wilsons (New York, 1937), p. 146, and from House's Diary, the entry of 25 January 1915, Edward M. House Papers, Yale University Library, New Haven, Conn. (hereafter cited as House Papers). Unless otherwise noted, the House Diary entries cited hereafter are from the copy in the Yale University Library.

[11]The view stressing the importance of House in the 1912 campaign may be found in Seymour, Intimate Papers, 1:66-67, and in Smith, Mr. House of Texas, pp. 45, 53.

[12]Two of Wilson's biographers have played down House's role. See Ray Stannard Baker, Woodrow Wilson, Life and Letters (Garden City, N.Y., 1935-1939), 3:194-95; Arthur S. Link, "The Wilson Movement in Texas, 1910-1912," Southwestern Historical Quarterly 48 (October 1944): 169-85; Arthur S. Link, Wilson: The Road to the White House (Princeton, 1947).

[13]House to Wilson, 20 June 1912, quoted in Seymour, Intimate Papers 1:64-65.

[14]Arthur S. Link, "The Enigma of Woodrow Wilson," American Mercury 65 (September 1947): 306.

[15]For example, William Gibbs McAdoo, who became Wilson's Secretary of the Treasury (and later son-in-law), wrote that House's apartment, especially during the formation of the cabinet, was "one of the most important spots on the political map of the United States." William Gibbs McAdoo, Crowded Years (Boston and New York, 1931), p. 181.

[16]For Grey's description of his acquaintance and negotiations with House, see Viscount Grey of Fallodon, Twenty-Five Years 1892-1916 (New York, 1925), 2:123-37.

[17]Both are ideas which House had discussed in his utopian novel, Philip Dru: Administrator (New York, 1912). For a discussion of the foreign policy ideas in this novel see Billie Barnes Jensen, "Philip Dru: Blueprint of a Presidential Adviser," American Studies 12 (Spring 1971): 49-58.

[18]House Diary, entry of 2 December 1913. This diary entry is quoted in part in Seymour, Intimate Papers 1:242-44.

[19]Page to House, 28 August 1913, quoted in Burton J. Hendrick, The Life and Letters of Walter H. Page (Garden City, N.Y., 1922), 1:270-71.

[20]Ibid., pp. 278-80.

[21]House Diary, entry of 22 January 1913, quoted in Seymour, Intimate Papers 1:239. In Philip Dru, South America was to fall within the sphere of the United States for exploitation. It is interesting to contemplate the furor which might have been generated if the public had known that one of Wilson's advisers was harboring a plan that would have invited Germany to exploit South America and nullify the Monroe Doctrine.

[22]House Diary, entry of 9 May 1913, quoted in ibid., p. 240.

[23]House Diary, entry of 3 July 1913. House seems to have approached the Austro-Hungarian ambassador, Constantin Dumba, with the plan too. See Seymour, Intimate Papers 1:242, and Constantin Dumba, Memoirs of a Diplomat (Boston, 1932), p. 215.

[24]He even gave House specific advice on how to approach the Kaiser. House Diary, entry of 2 December 1913.

[25]Ibid., entry of 28 April 1914.

[26]Ibid., entry of 11 May 1914.

[27]Wilson to House, 15 May 1914, Wilson Papers.

[28]House to Wilson, 28 May 1914, ibid.

[29]House Diary, entry of 27 May 1914. There are some slight discrepancies between the account of this passage in Seymour, Intimate Papers 1:549-51, and the copy of the House Diary at Yale. Part of the material that appears in Seymour is from an undated passage in the diary which precedes the entry of 27 May.

[30]House Diary, entry of 27 May 1914.

[31]Ibid., entry of 1 June 1914. This entry is worded differently in the copy of the House Diary at Yale and in the account in Seymour, Intimate Papers 1:252-57. The account in Seymour is made up of the June first entry plus a memorandum at the beginning of the diary, and some passages are phrased differently.

[32]House to Wilson, 29 May 1914, Wilson Papers. This passage originally read, "The situation is extraordinary. It is militarism run stark mad." House changed "militarism" to "jingoism" on the copy he sent to Wilson, but not on the copy he retained. See Arthur S. Link, Wilson: The New Freedom (Princeton, 1956), p. 315.

[33]House to Wilson, 3 June 1914, Wilson Papers.

[34]Hendrick, Walter H. Page 1:297.

[35]House Diary, entry of 12 June 1914, quoted in Seymour, Intimate Papers 1:259.

[36]Wilson to House, 16 June 1914, Wilson Papers.

[37]House Diary, entry of 17 June 1914.

[38]Walter H. Page to Wilson, 5 July 1914, Wilson Papers.

[39]House to Hugh Wallace, 7 July 1914, ibid.

[40]James Gerard to House, 7 July 1914, quoted in Seymour, Intimate Papers 1:270.

[41]House to the Kaiser, 8 July 1914, Wilson Papers.

[42]Page to House, 12 July 1914, ibid.

[43]Link, Wilson: The New Freedom, p. 318.

[44]Baker, Woodrow Wilson, 5:50.

[45]House Diary, entry of 20 July 1915, quoted in part in Seymour, Intimate Papers 1:276.

[46]House to Wilson, 31 July 1914, Wilson Papers.

[47]Ibid.

[48]Zimmermann to House, 1 August 1914, quoted in Seymour, Intimate Papers 1:279-80.

[49]House Diary, entry of 5 September 1914, quoted in part in Seymour, Intimate Papers 1:332.

[50]House Diary, entry of 16 December 1914.

[51]Grey to Spring-Rice, 2 January 1915, quoted in George M. Trevelyan, Grey of Fallodon (Boston, 1937), pp. 357-58.

[52]House Diary, entry of 12 January 1915.

[53]Ibid., entry of 13 January 1915.

[54]Seymour stated that the phrase "freedom of the seas" originated with House, although the general principle was well known before. Intimate Papers 1:408.

[55]See, for example, House Diary, entries of 10 and 11 February 1915, and House to Hugh Wallace, 12 February 1915, Wilson Papers.

[56]House to Wilson, 9 February 1915, quoted in part in Seymour, Intimate Papers 1:362-63. House did not explain what he meant by "civilized warfare."

[57]House Diary, entry of 11 February 1915, quoted in Arthur S. Link, Wilson: The Struggle for Neutrality (Princeton, 1960), p. 219.

[58]Ibid.

[59]Gerard to Bryan, 11 February 1915, U.S. Department of State, Foreign Relations of the United States, 1915, Supplement (Washington, 1928), pp. 9-10.

[60]Zimmermann to House, 4 February 1915. A copy of this letter was enclosed with House to Wilson, 18 February 1915, Wilson Papers.

[61]Wilson to House, 20 February 1915, ibid.

[62]House to Wilson, 23 February 1915, quoted in Seymour, Intimate Papers 1:380-83.

[63]Wilson to House, 26 February 1915, Wilson Papers.

[64]House to Wilson, 15 March 1915, ibid.

[65]House to Wilson, 19 March 1915, ibid.

[66]House to Wilson, 20 March 1915. The published version in Seymour, Intimate Papers 1:400-402, varies from the copy in the Wilson Papers.

[67]House to Wilson, 22 March 1915. The copy in Seymour, Intimate Papers 1:402-403 is dated 21 March; that in the Wilson Papers is dated 22 March, with a postscript dated 26 March.

[68]House Diary, entry of 23 March 1915.

[69]Ibid., entry of 24 March 1915.

[70]House to Wilson, 24 March 1915, Wilson Papers.

[71]House to Wilson, 27 March 1915, quoted in Seymour, Intimate Papers 1:410-11.

[72]Wilson to House, 1 April 1915, Wilson Papers.

[73]In Nice and Biarritz. He also stopped in Switzerland.

[74]House Diary, entry of 16 April 1915, quoted in Seymour, Intimate Papers 1:424.

[75]House Diary, entry of 17 April 1915, quoted in ibid., p. 416.

[76]Grey to House, 24 April 1915. A copy was enclosed with House to Wilson, 7 May 1915, Wilson Papers.

[77]House to Wilson, 30 April 1915, quoted in Seymour, Intimate Papers 1:426.

[78]House to Zimmermann, 1 May 1915, quoted in ibid., pp. 430-31.

[79]House to Wilson, 9 May 1915, quoted in ibid., pp. 433-34; House to Wilson, 11 May 1915, Wilson Papers.

[80]House to Wilson, 13 May 1915, Wilson Papers.

[81]House to Wilson, 25 May 1915, quoted in Seymour, Intimate Papers 1:456-57.

[82]House to Wilson, 1 June 1915, Wilson Papers.

[83]Wilson to House, 1 June 1915, Ray Stannard Baker Collection, ibid.

[84]House Diary, entry of 30 May 1915, quoted in Seymour, Intimate Papers 1:453-54.

[85]House Diary, entry of 8 October 1915. This section is quoted in Seymour, Intimate Papers 2:84-85, in an undated passage.

[86]Seymour, Intimate Papers 2:84-85.

[87]House Diary, entry of 14 October 1915.

[88]House to Grey, 17 October 1915. A copy of this letter was enclosed with House to Wilson, 17 October 1915, and was returned to House with Wilson's letter of 18 October 1915, House Papers.

[89]House Diary, entry of 19 October 1915; Wilson to House, 18 October 1915, House Papers.

[90]House Diary, entry of 17 October 1915.

[91]House to Wilson, 19 November 1915, Wilson Papers.

[92]Gerard to House, 7 December 1915, quoted in Seymour, Intimate Papers 2:104.

[93]House Diary, entry of 15 December 1915. House noted that Secretary of State Robert Lansing believed that a delay of the visit would be desirable.

[94]House to Wilson, 16 December 1915, Wilson Papers.

[95]House to Wilson, 22 December 1915, quoted in part in Seymour, Intimate Papers 2:107-108.

[96]Wilson to House, 9 January 1916, Wilson Papers. This and many of the following items in the Wilson correspondence for the period of the third House mission were transcribed from code by Ray Stannard Baker.

[97]House Diary, entry of 10 January 1916.

[98]Wilson to House, 11 January 1916, Wilson Papers. Baker dates his transcript 12 January.

[99]Polk to House, 21 January 1916, House Papers.

[100]House Diary, entry of 19 January 1916.

[101] Ibid. This section is quoted in Seymour, Intimate Papers 2:136.

[102]House Diary, entry of 26 January 1915, quoted in Seymour, Intimate Papers 2:137-38.

[103]House Diary, entry of 28 January 1916, quoted in ibid., pp. 140-43.

[104]House to Wilson, 3 February 1916, quoted in part in ibid., pp. 146-47.

[105]House to Wilson, 3 February 1916, Wilson Papers. During this trip to the Continent, House wrote several letters of the same date, but he numbered them so that the proper order may be ascertained. This, for example, was "no. 11."

[106]Ibid.

[107]Ibid.

[108]House to Wilson, 9 February 1916, quoted in Seymour, Intimate Papers 2:163-65.

[109]House to Wilson, 10 February 1916, Wilson Papers.

[110]House to Wilson, 11 February 1916, ibid.

[111]House Diary, entry of 11 February 1916.

[112]House to Wilson, 11 February 1916, Wilson Papers.

[113]House Diary, entry of 14 February 1916, quoted in Seymour, Intimate Papers 2:179-82.

[114]House Diary, entry of 15 February 1916, quoted in ibid., pp. 182-83.

[115]House to Wilson, 16 February 1916, Wilson Papers. For interesting recent accounts of reactions among British leaders to House's proposal, see John Milton Cooper, Jr., "The British Response to the House-Grey Memorandum: New Evidence and New Questions," Journal of American History 59 (March 1973): 958-71, and Michael G. Fry, Lloyd George and Foreign Policy (Montreal and London, 1977), 1:216-40.

[116]Arthur S. Link, Wilson: Confusions and Crises, 1915-1916 (Princeton, 1964), p. 141.

[117]Keith L. Nelson, "What Colonel House Overlooked in the Armistice," Mid-America 51 (April 1969): 75.

[118]See Link, Wilson: Confusions and Crises for an excellent discussion of the aftermath of the House-Grey Memorandum.

[119]Arthur S. Link, The Higher Realism of Woodrow Wilson and Other Essays (Nashville, 1971), p. 118.

[120]J. C. Long, Bryan, the Great Commoner (New York, 1928), p. 325.

[121]So Wilson told House, House Diary, entry of 24 June 1915, quoted in Link, Wilson: The Struggle for Neutrality, p. 422.

[122]House to Wilson, 1 August 1914, Wilson Papers.

[123]John Milton Cooper, Jr., Walter Hines Page: The Southerner as American, 1855-1918 (Chapel Hill, 1977), p. 326.

[124]Page to Wilson, 5 January 1916, Wilson Papers. The letter is misdated 1915, but it is filed with the appropriate year in the Wilson Papers.

[125]Cooper, Walter Hines Page, p. 327.

[126]Mary Kihl, "A Failure of Ambassadorial Diplomacy," Journal of American History 57 (December 1970): 636-53.

[127] Ibid., p. 653. No campaign against Gerard was necessary since Wilson had a low regard for him and was unhappy about having to appoint him. House Diary, entries of 17 January and 13 February 1913.

[128]Johann H. Bernstorff, Memoirs of Count Bernstorff (New York, 1936), pp. 133-34.

THE JAPANESE REACTION TO THE KELLOGG-BRIAND PACT, 1928-1929: THE VIEW FROM THE UNITED STATES

Stephen John Kneeshaw

On the night of 18 September 1931, a small explosion damaged the Japanese-controlled South Manchurian Railway near Mukden.[1] This seemingly minor episode inaugurated a series of crises which culminated later in the decade in World War II. The Manchurian crisis, planned and implemented by Japan's Kwantung Army, uncovered as sham the promise, progress, and stability of the 1920's, exploding not only a small bomb, but more importantly illusions that the Treaty of Versailles and the League of Nations, the Washington Conference agreements, and the Kellogg-Briand Pact could preserve the peace in a time of crisis. Japan's Manchurian maneuvers reflected the strategic and economic significance of the territory to the island empire, the perceived threat of Communist Russia in the north, and the intensification of social and economic turmoil from the Depression. In other words, this was hardly a minor episode for the Japanese.

Following the incident, the Western powers struggled unsuccessfully to restore the peace of the Far East. This peace-shattering situation, especially the inability to end the tensions, "reflected the tragic unwillingness of all concerned to pay the necessary price for peace."[2] The affair also revealed the impotence of the peace-keeping machinery established during the 1920's, especially the Kellogg-Briand Pact, the newest of the instruments devised to guarantee a peaceful world. The failure might have been foreseen had world leaders recognized that Japan was notably unreceptive to the agreement to renounce war as national policy. Japanese reaction to the treaty was not studied carefully by diplomats of that age; nor has it been studied adequately by historians since that time.[3]

Japanese-American relations had been deteriorating steadily since the time of American involvement in the peace negotiations following the Russo-Japanese War of 1904-1905. President Theodore Roosevelt's intervention at the Portsmouth sessions, and the resultant displeasure among the Japanese citizenry about the treaty of 1905, triggered the new age of mistrust and animosity. In the decade and

a half following the Treaty of Portsmouth a series of events further marred Japanese-American relations: the school segregation and immigration crises along the west coast, the California debate over alien landholding (meaning Japanese landholding), the troubles with the Twenty-One Demands made on China during World War I, and the diplomatic impasse over a racial clause at the Paris Peace Conference compounded the discord.[4] The capstone was the Immigration Act of 1924 with its Japanese exclusion clause shutting off all immigration into the United States from Japan. Japan did not question the right of the United States to regulate the flow of immigrants into the country; however, the Japanese were certain that this proposal was aimed directly at them, and that "insult" stung their national pride. The race-inspired restrictions of 1924 had the tragic consequence of widening the growing estrangement between the United States and Japan.[5] There seemed to be no break in the tension until the end of the 1920's when the opportunity came for Japan to join with the United States and other nations in the Kellogg-Briand Pact.

Given the unredressed grievances of the Japanese, it would not have surprised the world powers if Japan had refused to initial the treaty that carried the name of the American Secretary of State, Frank B. Kellogg. After all, in the Japanese mind the United States had done nothing to ease the diplomatic tension so evident in Japanese-American relations. Repeatedly since the Roosevelt era the ideals of peace and amity set forth in the Kellogg treaty had been negated by the realities of racially motivated diplomatic and political maneuvers. The Japanese leadership temporarily put those memories behind, however, and agreed to become one of the original signatories of the outlawry agreement, prompting enthusiastic commentary. For example, Professor James T. Shotwell of Columbia University, whose promotion of a Franco-American accord in early 1927 had initiated the movement toward the Kellogg-Briand Pact, wrote that Japanese acceptance of a pledge to eliminate war as an instrument of national policy "ought definitely to mark the passing of the old regime in the area of the Pacific, the regime which looked rather to the weight of armaments than to the discovery of mutual interests, which has encouraged distrust rather than confidence in friendly and peaceful intercourse." Shotwell felt confident that the Japanese government would abide by its pledges to the other signa-

tories in keeping with its postwar diplomatic attitude of showing "the most scrupulous regard for its honor and the fulfillment of its commitments."[6]

Shotwell was also sensitive enough to the tensions in Japanese-American relations and knowledgeable enough of history to understand that there might be future difficulties with Japan's agreeing to the renunciation of war in her international dealings. In addition, the Columbia University scholar identified three other problem areas that irritated the Japanese leadership as formal consideration was given to the Kellogg treaty: overpopulation of the home islands; Japanese-American troubles over immigration; and Japan's economic role in Manchuria and possible conflict with China.[7] Shotwell's reading of the Japanese reaction to the Kellogg-Briand Pact was only partly correct. Other issues were to intercede as the Japanese people and government debated the value of the Kellogg treaty and questioned whether Japan should ratify the multilateral agreement for the renunciation of war.

For several months after the April, 1927, proposal by French Foreign Minister Aristide Briand that the United States and France agree "to outlaw war" in their relations with one another, consideration of the idea was limited to informal political and public dialogue because President Calvin Coolidge refused to recognize the proposal.[8] Finally, late in December, after almost nine months of increasing public pressure, Secretary of State Kellogg proposed to France that the idea of renouncing war be multilateralized. He suggested that invitations be extended to several nations to join with the United States and France in this international effort to arrest the use of war as an instrument of national policy.[9] Already editorial discussions about outlawing war had appeared in a number of Japanese papers with "the outstanding fact in this discussion . . . the practically unanimous approval of the general principle which had been set forth by M. Briand."[10] It appeared that Japan would eagerly accept an invitation to align herself with those nations that supported the renunciation of war.

In the first week of the new year, mixed signals began emanating from Tokyo. The New York Times reported on 5 January that rumors were circulating that Japan approved

44

the Kellogg proposal "in principle," believing that any general agreement for the renunciation of war would be "a great step toward world peace."[11] Within forty-eight hours, however, the Times reported that the Japanese were "puzzled" by Kellogg's proposal. Most officials and press observers credited Kellogg with "a sincere effort to extend the area of organized peace," but there was some doubt about its practicality and uncertainty as to how the multilateral compact could work. Premier Giichi Tanaka gave official voice to the skepticism when he told newsmen that Japan had "its own special circumstances" to consider and that the government would not define the national attitude "in the meantime," or until a formal proposal had been made to Japan by the United States.[12]

Within days of the Premier's announcement, the Japanese press began debating the "special circumstances" Tanaka had mentioned. In editorial commentary reflecting the official Japanese attitude, Osaka Mainichi argued that the immigration issue stood as "an obstacle" to Japanese agreement to any American proposal, "not because Japan ever desires to exploit the possibility of war as a means to an end, but because the [immigration] question is so important to us that we would not feel justified in undertaking any far-reaching engagement without having it settled."[13] Otherwise, press comments manifested sarcasm and cynicism, as Tokyo Jiji contrasted the high-minded idealism of renunciation with the hard-headed reality of "aggressive" design by the United States: it was "more than baffling" that the United States should be debating simultaneously the merits of proposals to renounce war and to increase the size of her navy.[14]

By March greater balance had been restored to the public commentary in Japan. The press conceded that Kellogg had attempted to provide rational solutions to the problems of world war: Kellogg's "logic is impressive" was one comment. Yet failure seemed inevitable despite his sincerity because "his proposals are impractical."[15] By April, the skepticism had solidified. According to a New York Times dispatch, "The present attitude of Japanese public opinion toward all peace plans is a friendly but distinctly skeptical interest."[16]

45

Drawing on the growing line of criticism in the United States that the Kellogg proposals were weak or even worthless because of the lack of enforcement machinery, government officials in Tokyo began to voice their uncertainty about "peace by slogan," arguing that "if the war outlawry compact stood alone not much would be hoped from it." There was some corresponding hope from Japan that if the anti-war treaty were joined to arbitration and conciliation agreements, it could become "a powerful instrument for safeguarding peace."[17] More beneficial still would have been American acceptance of membership in the League of Nations.[18] There seemed to be general agreement that the "simplest way to insure peace" would be for the United States to join the League, and some viewed that as a natural consequence of American acceptance of the outlawry ideal.[19] Thus, the Tokyo <u>Nichi Nichi</u> editorialized that the proposed agreement should be valued "because it is a link connecting America and the League."[20]

These hopes for American involvement with the League were dismissed out of hand by American spokesmen. Secretary of State Kellogg, for example, argued that the Kellogg treaty "no more entangles us in the political affairs of foreign countries than any other treaties which we have made."[21] Yet the hope remained strong in Japan that the United States would be drawn inevitably into the League by her own diplomatic dealings on renunciation with the powers. That hope countered some of the skepticism and criticism of the treaty idea in Japan.

The various points of disagreement continued to be discussed publicly and in the press through the spring of 1928. Immigration problems were the most openly debated of the several issues, although some mention was made of "the possibility of trouble between Japan and China or Russia and Japan over Manchuria."[22] Nevertheless, with a formal draft treaty before the powers for consideration, the time had arrived for at least a preliminary decision on acceptance or rejection of the Kellogg proposals. On 23 June, the Secretary of State submitted a full draft treaty to fourteen governments containing his own "construction" of the treaty with reference to certain "considerations" that had been raised in diplomatic correspondence with the powers.[23] In effect, Kellogg reiterated the points he had made in a qualifying statement circulated on 23 April

excluding from the treaty all questions involving self-defense and obligations under the League Covenant, the Locarno agreements, and the French treaties of alliance throughout Europe.[24] With the powers making note of the qualifications, acceptances of the proposal flooded into Washington in mid-July, with the Japanese statement of willingness to join in the accords coming on 20 July.[25] The formal treaty was signed in Paris on 27 August.

At the signing ceremonies, only Briand was singled out to speak. He proudly hailed the "unforgettable hour" in history, witnessing that "today's event marks a new date in the history of mankind." Speaking from Tokyo after the signing was confirmed, Premier Tanaka echoed Briand's sentiments that the treaty signaled "the dawn of a new day." "Japan hails that dawn," he continued, "and she rejoices in the prospect of an age of continuous peace. The treaty will ever mark an epoch in history. It always will stand as the portal to an era wherein it is officially proclaimed that war is unworthy of civilized man."[26]

There appeared to be no problems with regard to Japanese approval of the Kellogg Pact because it was assumed that the major issues had been resolved. In fact, that was not the case, and in the months following the Paris ceremonies a whole new set of difficulties emerged to threaten Japanese adherence to the Kellogg-Briand Pact. The first criticism concerned the wording of Article I of the anti-war agreement: "The High Contracting Parties solemnly declare in the names of their respective peoples that they condemn recourse to war for the solution of international controversies, and renounce it as an instrument of national policy in their relations with one another."[27] For months critics of the agreement had questioned the phrases relating to the renunciation of war, arguing especially that words alone would not stop war, but rather that implementing machinery needed to be included to guarantee enforcement. American defenders of the treaty were prepared to answer Japanese criticisms on that particular point, but the Japanese chose to single out as the basis for their objections a phrase that seemed to most observers to be totally innocuous: "The High Contracting Parties solemnly declare in the names of their respective peoples. . . ."[28]

In early June, 1928, during consideration of proposed draft agreements, the Japanese chargé in Washington cautioned Assistant Secretary of State Robert Olds that the Japanese leadership was concerned about the phrase "in the names of their respective peoples," fearing that the Emperor's power to make treaties would be undercut by the wording.[29] To the American mind the worries seemed unfounded, and the phrase in question remained as part of the first article. In late September, however, the New York Times reported that Tokyo sources had uncovered some continuing concern among Japanese political leaders that the treaty would infringe on the Emperor's prerogatives.[30]

Opposition members from the Minseito party brought their criticism to the Privy Council which had to give approval to the treaty.[31] In a move that political observers regarded as designed to embarrass the governing Seiyukai party, the opposition claimed that the phrase "in the names of their respective peoples" was derogatory to the Emperor's power to make treaties and incompatible with the Japanese constitution. The Tanaka government rebutted the charge, pointing out that "the documents were drawn in the name of the Emperor and that ratification by the Emperor on the advice of the Privy Council is provided in full constitutional form." It was also argued that "the words complained of form a rhetorical expression theoretically uttered by the Emperor in common with other heads of states as meaning, for the sake of, or in the interests of, their respective nations."[32]

The government's position that the article's phrasing did not conflict with the rights of the Emperor was endorsed by most influential Japanese who regarded the Minseito naysaying solely as a political maneuver. Support for the critical charge had come principally from what the New York Times defined as "a body of super-patriotic fanatics" (Kenkokukai) who opposed Tanaka personally and politically.[33] Although it was destined to surface again on the Tokyo scene after the first of the new year, concern about the phrase diminished.

With one objection overcome, for the time at least, another problem soon appeared. In October, American Chargé Edwin L. Neville advised Secretary Kellogg that

"the members of the Privy Council are also exercised over the possibility that China's adherence to the Treaty to Outlaw War may be construed as implying Japan's recognition of the Nationalist Government as the Government of China."[34]

This new obstacle was founded on an American precedent. Article III of the Kellogg-Briand Pact allowed that "this Treaty shall . . . remain open as long as may be necessary for the adherence by all the other Powers of the world." Once the invitation had been accepted, Article I provided that contracting parties would have renounced war as an instrument of national policy "in their relations with one another." In the United States, a number of people interpreted this as allowing for the Soviet Union to gain recognition from the United States, voiding the policy of nonrecognition that had prevailed since 1917.[35]

In fact, a recent State Department ruling regarding Chinese-American ties seemed to make the Russian connection inevitable. On 25 July 1928, the American minister in China signed a bilateral trade agreement with representatives of the Nationalist government. The United States previously had not recognized the legitimacy of the Nanking-based regime and the commercial pact contained no express clause of recognition.[36] Two months later, however, the State Department announced that its legal experts had determined that the signing of the trade accords had constituted full de jure recognition of the Nationalist government. Further, it was conceded that the recognition dated from the July signing of the treaty and, therefore, no other declarations of recognition would be required.[37] Assuming that recognition could be extended unintentionally by the mutual agreement to a treaty, it appeared that official Russian-American and Sino-Japanese relations would flow naturally from full consent by the four states to the Kellogg-Briand Pact.

Political and legal experts in the United States began speaking to this issue of Russian recognition. Republican Senator William E. Borah of Idaho, longtime champion of Russian recognition and ardent supporter of the Kellogg treaty, regarded the dual steps of Russian adherence to and American ratification of the treaty as constituting recognition.[38] John Bassett Moore, an eminent lawyer and

a former treaty expert for the State Department, also judged that recognition had occurred "when a government is permitted by the original parties to a treaty to adhere to it, no matter whether this permission is given by one of the powers directly or indirectly, this does, in fact, recognize the adhering government, and not only that, but as a government representing the people over whom it professes to rule."[39] But the State Department was not prepared to concede that recognition of the Soviet Union was an inevitable consequence of the Kellogg treaty's being signed and ratified.

While the recognition debate raged outside the State Department, departmental experts were drawing up a lengthy memorandum on "Recognition by Means of Treaty." This statement of 15 November advised that recognition might or might not occur through the instrument of a bilateral treaty "as convenience or necessity might dictate." But the same was not to be presumed for a multilateral pact.[40] Obviously the State Department did not intend for the adherence of the Soviet Union to the Kellogg treaty to constitute recognition by the United States.

Four days later Kellogg communicated the gist of the memorandum to the American embassy in Tokyo:

> This Government considers that the signing by the United States of a bilateral treaty, such as was signed by United States and Nationalist Government, implies recognition. It does not consider that adherence by an unrecognized Government to a multilateral treaty of which the United States is a signatory or to which it is a party entails recognition. . . . Adherence of other Government is its unilateral act. Recognition is primarily a matter of intention. Intention on part of the United States to recognize such Government can not be imputed to the United States by an act of the other Government.

The Japanese government could draw its own conclusions on the matter. As the Secretary of State noted, "It is of course for the Japanese Government to decide what action on its part would constitute recognition

of Chinese Nationalist Government and whether ratification by Japan of treaty renouncing war to which China has adhered would constitute recognition of Nationalist Government."[41] The American decision apparently convinced Japan that recognition of China would not occur by consenting to the Kellogg treaty because this objection did not surface again.

Through December and into January, 1929, the anti-war agreement seemed to be gaining greater acceptance among the Japanese leadership and people.[42] It was reported early in January that even American rejection, if that should occur, would not condemn the treaty to defeat in Japan. But there was some fear that the United States might attach reservations to its consent. In such a case, it was believed that Tanaka's enemies in the Diet would agitate for Japanese interpretations, including guaranteed freedom of action in Asian territories.[43] A "Japanese Monroe Doctrine," comparable to the American doctrine in the Western Hemisphere and to Austen Chamberlain's reserving of British freedom of action in "certain regions of the world," would have assured Japan freedom of action in case of hostilities in Manchuria.[44]

Tanaka, who opposed any Japanese reservations, was strengthened in his stand when the American Senate approved the Kellogg treaty overwhelmingly, attaching only an explanatory report from the Foreign Relations Committee stipulating that the statement "in no respect changes or qualifies our present position or relation to any pact or treaty existing between other nations or governments."[45] Still, attempting to ward off reservations, Tanaka advised the Diet that his government would continue to pursue an equitable solution to the immigration problem with the United States and "to take appropriate steps" in Manchuria should any disturbances jeopardize Japan's "vital interests" in the area. In the meantime, he contended that no justification existed for Japan to reject "an instrument for world peace," the importance of which "can hardly be underestimated."[46]

Before further action could be taken, the opposition moved to take the political lead again as Deputy Yukio Ozaki proposed a resolution calling for a change in the wording of the treaty to remove the controversial phrase

"in the names of their respective peoples" before submitting the pact to the Emperor.[47] The government took the position that "in the names of their respective peoples" meant "on behalf of their respective nations"--consistent with the constitution and imperial prerogatives--and to show that Washington agreed with this definition. According to political analysts, "this 'discovery' took the wind out of Deputy Ozaki's sails." The governmental denial that any conflict existed with the constitution was accompanied by a stern reminder that the Diet had no role to play in treaty making.[48]

The several signatory states continued to submit their notices of consent to Washington as the treaty stipulated. After the 29 March approval by France, only Japanese consent was needed to make agreement unanimous among the fifteen original signatories, as was required before the Kellogg-Briand Pact could go into effect. The Privy Council's delay in approving the pact was interpreted as evidence that wording remained a controversial matter in Tokyo.[49] Furthermore, there seemed to be evidence that the Cabinet and the Foreign Office had divided in the debate, the Foreign Office supporting Tanaka, with some members of the Cabinet wanting an explicit reservation. "Old-fashioned Councillors" continued to view the wording as significant. According to a Hugh Byas byline in the New York Times, "the harmless phrase has become as provocative as a hostile flag and a sense of proportion has temporarily disappeared," and "reason has been obscured by the clouds of patriotic emotion."[50]

Tensions mounted as Tanaka promised early ratification and the opposition predicted the imminent fall of the government.[51] At this point, Tanaka requested the resignation of Etsujiro Uyehara, Parliamentary Under-secretary for Foreign Affairs, who had openly criticized the Privy Council for playing politics with the Kellogg treaty. "A scapegoat had become necessary," the New York Times communicated from Tokyo, "and M. Uyehara, by attracting the lightning to himself, may have saved the government and the treaty."[52] Having appeased the opposition with a political sacrifice of sorts, and after letting the turmoil and tension cool for some six weeks, Tanaka sent the pact to the Emperor for submission to the Privy Council.[53] Late in June the Privy Council accorded the treaty its approval "by

a sweeping majority," although it chose to attach an inter-pretation--but not a formal reservation--on the troublesome phrase in the first article.[54] On the following day, after months of controversy and debate, the Emperor signed the Kellogg-Briand Pact, completing the process of approval by the fifteen signatory states.[55]

Writing in June, 1929 about "the progress of the world," Albert Shaw of the Review of Reviews speculated that the constitutional debate in Japan over the phrase "in the names of their respective people" was simply a screen to hide more substantive concerns, especially the need to maintain total freedom for possible action in Manchuria to guarantee strategic and economic security.[56] The same charge might be leveled in regard to each of the several issues in dispute.

Most important, Japan's reluctance to offer final endorsement to the Kellogg-Briand Pact should be read as a smoke screen to veil genuine concern and displeasure about the unwillingness of the United States to treat Japanese and Americans equally. The immigration problems of the Roosevelt era and the 1920's continued to poison the diplomatic atmosphere between the United States and Japan. After the exclusion of the Japanese in 1924, the race issue ceased to be important in the United States; but this was not the case in Japan where the population observed the onset of exclusion as a national day of mourning, remembering the insult to Japanese pride each year on 1 July.[57]

Certainly the Japanese exhibited some concern over the recognition question with China and with the dilemma over Manchuria; but the race issue was the strongest and the deepest issue for the Japanese. Despite some commentary to the contrary, there was little chance of war between the United States and Japan during the 1920's.[58] But as former diplomat Kikujiro Ishii noted, in Japanese-American relations there was "one serious problem": it was not the naval issue, it was not China, it was not Japan's position in the Pacific, it was not the Open Door. The problem was the race question.[59] For the Japanese, exclusion was a matter of national pride and honor; and in Japanese-American relations it was the primary cause of misunder-standing, distrust, resentment, and frustration.

Putting aside the Manchurian and immigration troubles for the time at least, and certain that Kellogg's "considerations" would allow for any necessary military action as "self-defense," the Tanaka government elected to be a party with the other world states to the Kellogg treaty. After all, without enforcement machinery the Kellogg-Briand Pact could do little damage to Japan, but acceptance of the treaty might bring benefits stemming from partnership with her international colleagues. In fact, there was little genuine enthusiasm for the anti-war agreement in Japan, for Japanese leaders knew that the treaty was impotent. This helps to explain the willingness of Japan to violate the treaty blatantly in Manchuria in 1931 and afterwards.

President Herbert Hoover proclaimed the implementation of the Kellogg-Briand Pact on 24 July 1929, one month after the Japanese approval had been received in Washington. Even before the proclamation, however, the anti-war agreement was under siege as China and Russia confronted each other militarily in Manchuria. This first test of the pact proved it worthless, and the treaty could hardly be said to have gained strength during the decade that followed.

In 1931 the Manchurian incident brought the United States and Japan to diplomatic loggerheads again. Japan was committed to protecting her rights and interests in China, which, according to the Japanese, could be done only with military force. This action challenged the policy objectives of the United States and threatened to disrupt the entire structure of the postwar world. The United States had pledged to support the peace machinery and the security system founded upon the Washington Conference treaties (especially the Nine-Power Pact) and the Kellogg-Briand Pact, and she hoped to block any action to alter the existing order by military force.[60] The Manchurian affair raised "clear and disturbing" issues that the United States could not ignore.[61] The policies of President Hoover and Secretary of State Henry Stimson would not allow for strong American action, however; the times were too hard at home and too uncertain overseas. The weak American policy of nonrecognition, backed by public opinion but not by military force, allowed the Japanese armies, in the words of Secretary Stimson, to "gallop across the grass."[62] Japan continued her aggressive movement across Asia and the

Pacific unchecked until the morning raid of 7 December 1941 on Pearl Harbor. At that moment, the United States abandoned pacifism and nonrecognition for activism and war.

Hoover and Stimson invoked the Kellogg-Briand Pact in their condemnations of Japanese actions in Manchuria, but they refused to support their demands with any military sanctions. Public opinion alone was not sufficiently strong to arrest the movements of Japan or to enforce the Kellogg-Briand Pact. Very simply, the pact was found wanting. It was worthless, powerless, and devoid of enforcement machinery. The words of praise extended to the treaty by Kellogg, Briand, Tanaka, and others had been delusory because the treaty itself was worthless since no one seemed willing to fill the enforcement gap.

Reflecting on the Manchurian episodes of 1929, Assistant Secretary of State William Castle lamented that events were making the Kellogg-Briand Pact "look like 30 cents."[63] Later events revealed that Castle had mistakenly inflated its value.

[1]See Robert H. Ferrell, "The Mukden Incident: September 18-19, 1931," Journal of Modern History 27 (March 1955): 66-72; Robert H. Ferrell, American Diplomacy in the Great Depression: Hoover-Stimson Foreign Policy, 1929-1933 (New Haven, 1957), pp. 120-37; and Sadako N. Ogata, Defiance in Manchuria: The Making of Japanese Foreign Policy, 1931-1932 (Berkeley, 1964).

[2]L. Ethan Ellis, Republican Foreign Policy, 1921-1933 (New Brunswick, N.J., 1968), p. 363.

[3]If the Japanese reaction is mentioned at all, it appears in the general discussion of negotiation and approval of the pact, but without any specific or detailed analysis of the Japanese attitude. When historians focus upon Japan, the emphasis tends to be minimal. For example, Akira Iriye gives only two sentences to the Japanese reaction. Iriye, After Imperialism: The Search for a New Order in the Far East, 1921-1931 (Cambridge, 1965), p. 238. Iriye has lamented the lack of good works pertaining to Japanese-American relations in the 1920's, except for those concerning naval issues. Iriye, "1921-1931," in Ernest R. May and James C. Thomson, eds., American-East Asian Relations: A Survey (Cambridge, 1972), p. 233.

[4]On Japanese-American relations in the early twentieth century, see Thomas A. Bailey, Theodore Roosevelt and the Japanese-American Crises (Stanford, 1934); Roger Daniels, The Politics of Prejudice: The Anti-Japanese Movement in California and the Struggle for Japanese Exclusion (Berkeley, 1962); Raymond A. Esthus, Theodore Roosevelt and the Struggle for Japanese Exclusion (Berkeley, 1962); Raymond A. Esthus, Theodore Roosevelt and Japan (Seattle, 1966); Akira Iriye, Pacific Estrangement: Japanese and American Expansion, 1897-1911 (Cambridge, 1972); Charles E. Neu, An Uncertain Friendship: Theodore Roosevelt and Japan, 1906-1909 (Cambridge, 1967); Burton F. Beers, Vain Endeavor: Robert Lansing's Attempt to End the American-Japanese Rivalry (Durham, N.C., 1962); and Roy W. Curry, Woodrow Wilson and Far Eastern Policy, 1913-1921 (New York, 1957).

[5]Robert A. Divine and Gerald E. Wheeler both have termed the exclusion clause an "insult" which, in Divine's words, became "a permanent source of friction" between the two countries. Divine, American Immigration Policy, 1924-1952 (New Haven, 1957), p. 23; Wheeler, Prelude to

Pearl Harbor: The United States Navy and the Far East, 1921-1931 (Columbia, Mo., 1963), p. 34.

[6]James T. Shotwell, War as an Instrument of National Policy and Its Renunciation in the Pact of Paris (New York, 1929), pp. 240-41.

[7]Ibid., pp. 240-53.

[8]Briand to the Associated Press, 6 April 1927, U.S. Department of State, Foreign Relations of the United States (hereafter cited as FRUS), 1927 (Washington, 1942), 2:612. The best study of the origins of the Kellogg-Briand Pact remains Robert H. Ferrell, Peace in Their Time: The Origins of the Kellogg-Briand Pact (New Haven, 1952).

[9]Kellogg to Paul Claudel, 28 December 1927, FRUS, 1927 2:627.

[10]Shotwell, War as an Instrument of National Policy, p. 248.

[11]New York Times, 5 January 1928.

[12]Ibid., 7 January 1928.

[13]Ibid., 10 January 1928.

[14]Ibid., 15 January 1928.

[15]Ibid., 4 March 1928.

[16]Ibid., 1 April 1928.

[17]Ibid., 3 April 1928. On the growing criticism in the United States, see Stephen John Kneeshaw, "The Kellogg-Briand Pact: The American Reaction" (Ph.D. diss., University of Colorado, 1971).

[18]New York Times, 15 April 1928. On the question of American entanglement with the League, see Kneeshaw, "The Kellogg-Briand Pact," pp. 88-112.

[19]New York Times, 4 April 1928.

[20]Ibid., 15 April 1928.

[21]John Bakeless, "The Kellogg Treaty: A Survey of Comment and Opinion from the World's Press," Living Age 335 (November 1928): 220.

[22]David Bryn-Jones, Frank B. Kellogg: A Biography (New York, 1937), Appendix I: 297. Kellogg's public assurances were repeated in a variety of letters in his private correspondence. Kellogg was aware that "a significant movement against the treaty" had developed among influential editors in the United States who were concerned about the question of entanglement. But he endeavored to convince them--usually with success--that "it took the greatest pains not to make any guarantees on behalf of the United States." Kellogg to William E. Borah, 26 July 1928; Kellogg to Mrs. Whitelaw Reid, 19 July 1928;

Kellogg to Robert McCormick, 21 July 1928; Kellogg to Walter Lippmann, 21 July 1928; Kellogg to William Randolph Hearst, 11 December 1928, Frank B. Kellogg Papers, Minnesota Historical Society, St. Paul.

[23]New York Times, 24 April 1928.

[24]Kellogg to Myron T. Herrick, 23 June 1928, FRUS, 1928 (Washington, 1942), 1:90-95.

[25]Kellogg to Herrick, 23 April 1928, ibid., pp. 34-39. After World War I, France engaged in a variety of diplomatic activities to guarantee her sécurité against Germany. A large French army and the protections afforded by the League and the Locarno treaties provided the first parts of the French security system; she added an elaborate network of alliances to include Belgium, Poland, Czechoslovakia, Rumania, and Yugoslavia. Her plan was to surround Germany and prevent any aggressive German moves against France. In the apt description of Robert H. Ferrell, France suffered from "pactomania." Ferrell, Frank B. Kellogg (New York, 1963), p. 110.

[26]Tanaka to Edwin L. Neville, 20 July 1928, FRUS, 1928 1:123-24.

[27]New York Times, 28 August 1928.

[28]For the full text of the treaty, see FRUS, 1928 1:153-56.

[29]Memorandum by Olds of conversation with Japanese Chargé Awada, 12 June 1928, ibid., p. 85.

[30]New York Times, 22 September 1928.

[31]Two major political parties dominated in Japan in the 1920's: Seiyukai, headed by Tanaka Giichi, pursued a foreign policy emphasizing reliance on the military; Minseito, under career diplomat Shidehara Kijuro, favored a more cautious foreign policy, believing that diplomacy (rather than force) offered the best method of protecting the empire. See James William Morley, ed., Japan's Foreign Policy, 1868-1941: A Research Guide (New York, 1974), pp. 43-44.

[32]New York Times, 22 September 1928.

[33]Ibid.

[34]Neville to Kellogg, 8 October 1928, 711.9412 Anti-War/70, U.S. State Department records, RG 59, National Archives, Washington, D.C. (hereafter cited as D/S File #).

[35]See Stephen John Kneeshaw, "The Kellogg-Briand Pact and American Recognition of the Soviet Union," Mid-America 56 (January 1974): 16-31.

[36] For a full text of the trade agreement, see *FRUS, 1928* 2:475-77.

[37] *New York Times*, 28 September 1928.

[38] Ibid., 13 September 1928. Meanwhile, the Secretary of State was advising Borah's Senate colleagues that recognition would not be an inevitable consequence of accepting the treaty. Kellogg to Reed Smoot of Utah, 16 September 1928, Kellogg Papers. Borah's position changed a short time later and he conceded that recognition had not occurred. *New York Times*, 20 November 1928; Claudius O. Johnson, *Borah of Idaho* (New York, 1936), p. 361.

[39] "Kellogg Pact--Recognition of Russia," undated memorandum, Box 158, John Bassett Moore Papers, Manuscript Division, Library of Congress, Washington, D. C. Also see John Bassett Moore, *The Collected Papers of John Bassett Moore* (New Haven, 1944), 6:349, 478.

[40] "Recognition by Means of Treaty," 15 November 1928, D/S File #711.9412 Anti-War/74.

[41] Kellogg to American embassy, Tokyo, 19 November 1928, D/S File #711.9412 Anti-War/75.

[42] Addressing an early December meeting of the Japan Society in New York, Katsuji Debuchi, Japanese ambassador to the United States, termed the Kellogg treaty "a great bulwark of peace for the future." *New York Times*, 4 December 1928.

[43] Ibid., 8 January 1929.

[44] For the Chamberlain statement, see Chamberlain to Alanson B. Houghton, 19 May 1928, *FRUS, 1928* 1:68.

[45] U.S., Congress, *Congressional Record*, 70th Cong., 2d sess., 15 January 1929, 70:1730. Senatorial consent was voted 85-1.

[46] *New York Times*, 22 January 1929.

[47] Ibid., 24 February 1929.

[48] Ibid., 5 April 1929.

[49] Ibid.

[50] Ibid., 14 April 1929.

[51] Ibid., 26 April 1929.

[52] Ibid., 20 April 1929.

[53] Ibid., 11 June 1929.

[54] Ibid., 27 June 1929. Count Uchida, who had signed the treaty in Paris for Japan, resigned in protest, contending that the attaching of an interpretation by the Privy Council was "a slur on his conduct as imperial plenipotentiary."

[55] Ibid., 29 June 1929.

[56]Albert Shaw, "Japan and the Kellogg Pact," Review of Reviews 79 (June 1929): 34.

[57]Divine, American Immigration Policy, p. 23; Wheeler, Prelude to Pearl Harbor, p. 33.

[58]Wheeler, Prelude to Pearl Harbor, pp. 31, 35-36.

[59]Iriye, "1921-1931," pp. 240-41.

[60]Mushakoji Kinhide, "The Structure of Japanese-American Relations in the 1930s," trans. by Shumpei Okamoto, in Dorothy Borg and Shumpei Okamoto, eds., Pearl Harbor as History: Japanese-American Relations, 1931-1941 (New York, 1973), pp. 595-606.

[61]Norman A. Graebner, "Hoover, Roosevelt, and the Japanese," ibid., p. 25.

[62]Ferrell, American Diplomacy in the Great Depression, p. 137.

[63]Ellis, Republican Foreign Policy, p. 327; Ferrell, American Diplomacy in the Great Depression, p. 57.

61

SIR RONALD LINDSAY AND THE BRITISH
VIEW FROM WASHINGTON, 1930-1939

Benjamin D. Rhodes

In November, 1929, soon after his appointment as British ambassador to the United States, Sir Ronald Lindsay wrote an American friend: "The Embassy at Washington has been my ambition ever since I went there more than twenty years ago, and you may guess what a pleasure it is to me now to realize it."[1] An experienced career diplomat who twice married Americans, Lindsay served in Washington until his retirement in August, 1939. Unhappily for Lindsay, however, his decade as ambassador coincided with a series of Anglo-American disagreements, primarily over economic issues. During the administration of Herbert Hoover, the structure of reparations and war debts began to crumble and trade stagnated in the face of intense economic nationalism on both sides of the Atlantic. In the Far East, the two nations failed to form a common front for containing Japanese expansion. The record of the New Deal was equally inauspicious. President Franklin D. Roosevelt was widely blamed for the spectacular failure of the London Economic Conference of 1933, and the following year Britain ended the debate over war debts by defaulting. Even the 1938 Anglo-American Trade Agreement was reached only after exasperating negotiations. Not until the approach of war in 1939 were there signs of improvement as King George VI made a highly successful visit to Washington and President Roosevelt sought to modify the neutrality laws to permit the sale of munitions to Britain and France.[2]

To what extent was Lindsay responsible for the dismal state of Anglo-American relations? Certainly the six-foot-four-inch Lindsay, with his relaxed geniality and wealth of anecdote, made an excellent impression upon the American diplomatic establishment. In the State Department, he was generally viewed as a man with whom it was a pleasure to do business. But to some extent Lindsay, whose personal approach to diplomacy was rather stiff and old-fashioned, was somewhat of a liability to Anglo-American relations. He enjoyed close relations neither with President Hoover nor with Secretaries of State Henry L. Stimson or Cordell Hull, although his relationship with Roosevelt, a fellow aristocrat, was cordial and businesslike. Moreover, Lindsay found it

difficult to tolerate what he considered to be the provincialism and ineptitude of American congressmen, and he was frequently frustrated by the "archaic" constitutional division of authority between the congressional and executive branches of government.[3] Nevertheless, the main source of Anglo-American friction lay not in personality clashes, but in the economic problems remaining from World War I and aggravated by the Depression. Despite the disputes of the thirties, there was never any possibility of an open breach between the two governments, for behind the quarrels there remained a consciousness that the two nations shared similar democratic values and interests. No one was more aware of this central fact than Lindsay. Describing himself as a "practical diplomatist," Lindsay conscientiously strove to deflect America from isolationism because he believed the two nations shared a common interest in achieving a European balance of power characterized by "reasonableness and peace." In his cultivation of American friendship, Lindsay relied upon a high degree of personal charm, combining a businesslike approach with the more traditional diplomatic techniques of courtship. "America," he observed rather patronizingly to Anthony Eden, "is still extraordinarily youthful and sensitive. She resembles a young lady just launched into society and [is] highly susceptible to a little deference from an older man."[4]

Lindsay's appointment as ambassador to the United States was the high point of his career. Born in Scotland on 3 May 1877, he was the fifth son of the Earl of Crawford. Educated at Winchester, he did not attend a university but instead entered the diplomatic service in 1899. Demonstrating ability in Russian and Persian, Lindsay advanced in rank from attaché at St. Petersburg and Teheran to Second Secretary at Washington (1905-1907) where he served under ambassadors Sir Mortimer Durand and James Bryce. During the First World War, he was Under Secretary of the Egyptian Ministry of Finance after which he returned to Washington as First Secretary. Lindsay's first ambassadorial appointment was at Constantinople in 1925; he was transferred to Berlin as ambassador in 1926. Two years later he returned to London as Permanent Undersecretary of State for Foreign Affairs where his work "proved of great value, especially as an approved and well-trained understudy." His first wife, Martha Cameron, the daughter of Senator J. Donald

Cameron of Pennsylvania, died in 1918. In 1924, Lindsay married the cousin of his first wife, Elizabeth Sherman Hoyt of New York.[5] An experienced and wealthy landscape architect, Lady Lindsay was described by her husband as "positively incoherent with delight" at the prospect of returning to the United States. On 18 March 1930, the Lindsays arrived at New York on board the Aquitania accompanied by two servants, a private secretary, and a Scottish terrier named "Sandy" (who performed a "roly-poly" at Lady Lindsay's first press conference). The following day they traveled to Washington and established temporary quarters at the Mayflower Hotel pending the completion of the new British embassy on Massachusetts Avenue.[7]

The paralysis caused by the Depression was already evident at the time of Lindsay's arrival, and he was quick to recognize the political vulnerability of President Hoover. Conceding that it was normal for a president to lose some public support during his first year in office, Lindsay detected such a collapse in Hoover's prestige that "one hears men comparing his loss of popularity with that which Mr. Taft incurred in 1909-1910 -- an ominous comparison indeed."[8] Nevertheless, Lindsay never questioned Hoover's basic intelligence and administrative ability, noting that the President possessed a "remarkable genius for organization and an immense grasp of detail." Hoover's primary short-coming, reported Lindsay, was a striking lack of political experience and ability. In Lindsay's judgment, Hoover was a man of "no skill in politics," and he found Hoover, when confronted by the "complete and perfect unreason [of] pure American politicians," to be "dumbfounded and struck with impotence."[9] Hoover's political effectiveness was not enhanced by his "ungainly mannerisms and inability to ingratiate himself," nor by his personal distaste toward such necessary but unpleasant tasks as enforcing party discipline. "What he has to learn," contended Lindsay, "is to hit back and to show his teeth both to his open enemies and to his disloyal friends."[10]

One hopeful example of presidential leadership noted by Lindsay was Hoover's attempt to improve American relations with Latin America through the publication of the J. Reuben Clark Memorandum repudiating the Roosevelt Corollary to the Monroe Doctrine. Theodore Roosevelt's

Corollary of 1905 had angered Latin Americans by justifying American intervention in the Caribbean on the basis of the Monroe Doctrine. But the Clark Memorandum, published with Hoover's blessing, found that there was nothing in the Monroe Doctrine to support a policeman's role in Latin America for the United States. "A rose by any other name would smell as sweet," commented Lindsay, "but South and Central Americans have not for a long time liked the smell of this particular variety."[11]

Yet Lindsay observed numerous examples of Hoover's lack of political acumen during his initial year as ambassador. An early embarrassment to the President was the "severe snub" inflicted by the Senate when it rejected the nomination of John J. Parker to the Supreme Court.[12] A few months later Hoover disappointed Lindsay by signing the Hawley-Smoot Tariff Act by which "he let slip a splendid opportunity for proving that his relationship with enlightened opinion was not purely platonic." It was Lindsay's feeling that the extremely inactive role taken by Hoover during the tariff debate would be interpreted in Congress and throughout the country as evidence that he lacked "the fibre necessary for leadership."[13] Nor was Lindsay impressed by Hoover's rather passive role in the 1930 congressional elections in which the Democrats gained almost a tie in both houses of Congress. The President confined his efforts to making several "long and rather dull speeches," but failed to "appeal to the imagination of the people as a politician." Lindsay did not view the Republican setback as necessarily fatal to Hoover's re-election chances in 1932, however, recognizing that tradition favored the party out of power during mid-term elections, and that a revival of the economy might resurrect Republican fortunes.

Lindsay was quick to identify Governor Franklin D. Roosevelt of New York as a logical successor to Hoover. His personal honesty and anti-Tammany record, combined with his landslide re-election to the Governorship made Roosevelt, he reported, the leading candidate for the Democratic nomination. But Lindsay consistently misjudged the willingness of the American people to accept a physically handicapped leader. Roosevelt's paralysis, Lindsay predicted, "is likely to prove a serious disability,

though I never saw a man who, from the hips upwards, was more completely alive than he."[14]

Lindsay's disillusionment with President Hoover's leadership deepened during 1931. Basically Lindsay lacked confidence that Hoover's program of modest spending upon public works and loans to farmers would reverse the deflationary cycle and restore public confidence. Moreover, Lindsay found it difficult to comprehend Hoover's unrelenting opposition to direct federal relief. Hoover, he believed, was "ignoring practical difficulties" by insisting that the cost of relief must be met by the states and private charity. How, he asked, were poor southern states to contend with the burden of unemployment and natural catastrophes? To Lindsay it was "becoming more and more evident that nothing but a return of prosperity is likely to bring about his re-election."[15]

Then on 20 June 1931, Hoover dramatically proposed a one-year moratorium on war debts and reparations. Initially Lindsay viewed the moratorium, which would postpone approximately $160 million in British war debt payments, as a turning point in the fortunes of the Hoover administration. But within a few months, Lindsay's original pessimism returned as Britain was forced off the gold standard and American bank failures and unemployment continued their runaway course.[16] Also dismaying to Lindsay was Hoover's increasing emphasis upon the argument that the origins of the Depression lay not in America but Europe. Such a theme was foreshadowed by Hoover when he received Lindsay and author H. G. Wells in October, 1931. Apparently irritated by one of Wells's comments--although Lindsay could "remember no remark by Wells that could reasonably have been regarded as provocative"--the President launched into a lengthy and ill-humored lecture stressing the virtues of America's past policy of isolation. In view of America's unhappy involvement with European affairs during and after World War I, Hoover said, the nation's only desire was to "get out" and "to leave Europe to extricate herself from her difficulties as best she may."[17] Equally disappointing to Lindsay was Hoover's 1931 State of the Union address in which he placed the responsibility for the continued Depression largely upon European economic dislocations and the Democrats in Congress. It was evident, he concluded, "that even the

few who still hoped for inspiration and leadership from Mr. Hoover are disappointed."[18]

Lindsay's feeling of despair was further accentuated by the undisciplined performance of Congress when it assembled in December, 1931. One major disappointment was the overwhelming congressional hostility to Hoover's statesmanlike request that the World War Foreign Debt Commission be recreated to make temporary adjustments in the outdated war debt agreements. Furthermore, Lindsay was appalled by the prolonged argument in the Senate over the selection of a president pro tempore, a debate in which a filibuster was directed against Senator George Moses of New Hampshire in part because he had once referred to congressional progressives as "sons of the wild jackass." Venting his frustration in caustic dispatches to the Foreign Office, Lindsay contended that "Congress has given an exhibition of irresponsibility, buffoonery and ineptitude that could hardly be paralleled in the Haitian legislature." Having "proved unequal to its responsibilities and the needs of the country," Congress offered a prospect that could only be appreciated by "such critics of democracy and representative government as Messrs. Mussolini and Stalin." Rather superciliously, Lindsay ascribed the failures of Congress to incompetence and political opportunism on the part of congressmen who were "quite incapable of understanding the complexities of the present situation or realizing the national issues at stake, still less of originating or applying constructive relief measures."[19] By the end of the year, Lindsay had succumbed to what he described as "an atmosphere of unrelieved gloom, in which the dark and menacing clouds are illuminated only by flashes of panic apprehension."[20]

Yet a brief ray of hope seemed to appear in early 1932 when Congress approved the creation of Hoover's Reconstruction Finance Corporation. It was a "bold and constructive" development, reported Lindsay, an indication that Congress had finally "appreciated the seriousness of the situation" and had "temporarily abandoned its exploitation for party purposes."[21] But Lindsay's hopefulness was tempered by the severe weakness of the municipal bond market. In New York, he quipped, the situation was said to be so serious that Mayor James Walker, a notorious

playboy, was thinking of running for Vice-President.[22] Nor was Lindsay impressed by the President's message to Congress upon the subject of improving law enforcement. He found it to be "not a very inspiring document" and indicative of "Mr. Hoover's hesitancy and evasiveness and his reluctance to face disagreeable facts." It was symbolic of Hoover's chronic "ill-luck" that no sooner had he conceded the need for an improvement in law enforcement than the nation was shocked by the brutal kidnapping of the Charles A. Lindbergh baby.[23] By March, 1932, Lindsay's hopes for an economic improvement were once again disintegrating. Amid continued bank failures, increased unemployment, and industrial stagnation, he detected "no signs of business recovery." The nation's economy, he feared, was "incapable of rallying from a condition of physical coma and moral despair."[24] A month later he remarked that he had been expecting "bread riots" for the past three months and warned that such outbreaks were to be considered likely during the presidential campaign.[25]

It was now politics rather than the faltering economy which absorbed Lindsay's attention. A few months previously he had noticed a "fairly perceptible rise in Mr. Hoover's stock," although he felt it was primarily attributable to "the unconvincingness" of the prospective Democratic opponents.[26] As the economic collapse intensi- fied, however, Lindsay wrote with alarm of "the national bankruptcy in single-minded, constructive leadership" and predicted that the re-election of President Hoover was "very unlikely."[27] Of the Democratic candidates, he considered Franklin D. Roosevelt to be "far and away" the leading prospect. But he still believed Roosevelt's paralysis an insurmountable political obstacle, notwithstanding the "superb courage with which he has faced and overcome his infirmities." The most likely result was a deadlock between Roosevelt and former New York Governor Alfred E. Smith, with the convention eventually turning to a dark horse such as former Secretary of War Newton D. Baker or possibly the financier Owen D. Young.[28] Roosevelt's defeats in the Massachusetts and California primaries further confirmed Lindsay's view that it would be necessary for the Democrats to choose a compromise candidate. "Certainly," he predicted, "Mr. Franklin Roosevelt's impetus has now been stopped."[29]

When the Republicans met at Chicago, they adopted a conservative platform and nominated Hoover for a second term. ("Don't change toboggans in the middle of the slide" could have been his slogan, Lindsay remarked.) Lindsay had expected the Republican convention to be "dull, and this expectation was not disappointed." He was tremendously pleased, however, by the absence from the platform of any pledge to collect the war debts, thereby implying that Hoover, if re-elected, might enjoy a free hand.[30] In a jocular mood, Lindsay told Secretary of State Henry L. Stimson that he was "very grateful for the platform in our plank at Chicago on the subject of the debts." But Stimson was not amused and replied that Lindsay would not make fun of the platform if he appreciated the political danger which had been avoided.[31]

As for the Democrats, Lindsay was "mercifully disappointed" when the forecasted deadlock failed to develop and Governor Roosevelt received the nomination.[32] He did, however, feel some minor concern over the Democratic pledge (attributable to the influence of publisher William Randolph Hearst) to oppose the cancellation of war debts. Yet he recognized that in America political platforms were frequently forgotten after an election, and he took solace from the fact that Roosevelt had made no mention of the debts in his acceptance speech.[33] In Lindsay's view, the Democratic candidate was an ambitious and politically sensitive aristocrat: "a gentleman in every sense of the word." Roosevelt's intellectual endowment, Lindsay believed, was "not conspicuously great," but because he had "no intellectual pride" Roosevelt was not reluctant to seek the advice of experts when confronted with an unfamiliar problem. Despite Republican charges that "a vote for Roosevelt is a vote for Moscow," Roosevelt's "so-called radicalism" was non-existent and Lindsay could "see nothing to justify fears of a dangerously advanced policy." But Roosevelt's running mate, Speaker of the House John Nance Garner of Texas, appeared to Lindsay as dangerously unfit, "a man after Mr. Hearst's heart, with a closed mind and the xenophobia of a Boxer." Because Garner's "stock-in-trade" was composed of "demagogy, the cruder forms of patriotism, and the petty tricks of politics," it behooved all to "pray for the life of Mr. Franklin Roosevelt" should he win the election, and a Democratic victory was all but certain. Roosevelt, although no longer possessing "the charm and

69

good looks which characterized him twelve years ago," was by far the better candidate, outshining the "awkward, undramatic Hoover."[34] On election day Lindsay's judgment was vindicated when Roosevelt won a decisive victory, giving him an opportunity to guide policy on national rather than sectional lines. Lindsay still feared, however, that Roosevelt "was hardly a great enough man to accomplish this."[35]

The first year of the New Deal substantially rejuvenated Lindsay's enthusiasm for American politics. President Roosevelt's performance as a politician elicited from Lindsay such superlatives as "masterful," "courageous," "realistic," and "highly stimulating."[36] Especially striking in Lindsay's estimation was Roosevelt's finesse in dealing with the press and his skill in public speaking. To Lindsay the new President's inaugural address was "inspiring both in its language and its delivery," although he conceded that the national banking crisis had contributed to the high drama of the occasion.[37] Roosevelt's first "fireside chat" Lindsay described as "an astute and highly effective innovation," and his speeches in general were characterized by "a fine speaking voice and a clear and confident delivery."[38]

Roosevelt's attractiveness to Lindsay was based on more than just charm and rhetorical ability; indeed, Lindsay was an enthusiastic admirer of the New Deal reforms. Except for some pragmatic reservations concerning the National Recovery Administration and Roosevelt's liking for monetary experimentation, Lindsay welcomed the new Democratic improvisations in such areas as public works, agricultural price supports and production controls, and federal relief to the destitute. Above all, Lindsay admired the New Deal because it seemed to herald the demise of the system of "ruthless, rugged individualism" and the small business oligarchy which controlled it. Whereas Republican business leadership had been characterized by "rapacity, blind egoism, and moral insensitiveness," the New Deal sought to eliminate exploitation and social irresponsibility while retaining such traditional concepts of individualism as initiative and free competition. The ultimate result, Lindsay believed, would be neither state capitalism nor state socialism, but a "controlled economy on the Russian plan, organized on lines of American efficiency."[39]

Moreover, Lindsay applauded Roosevelt's success in restoring public confidence in the federal government and presidential leadership. In contrast to "the fearful, furtive fumbling of the Great White Feather,"[40] as Lindsay rather unkindly referred to Hoover, Roosevelt had demonstrated "a power of leadership and of inspiring confidence and devotion to a degree which is almost miraculous."[41]

Yet Lindsay's admiration for Roosevelt the politician did not always extend to Roosevelt's abilities as a statesman. From Lindsay's viewpoint, Roosevelt was not a good judge of men, relying on advisers of "second-rate ability" who would willingly "go along" with his views.[42] Lindsay was especially distrustful of the youthful professorial members of the "brain trust," noting that their ideas were frequently impractical and contending that "the professorial mind in administration is notoriously dangerous."[43] Rexford G. Tugwell seemed to Lindsay as both the most radical and most intelligent of the President's advisers, although he appeared to possess "a distinct anti-British bias" and an arrogant "chip on the shoulder" attitude. Another former professor, Assistant Secretary of State Raymond Moley, despite "a somewhat shifty appearance," was a man of honesty but of "definitely second-rate ability."[44] Nor was Lindsay impressed with the leadership qualities of Secretary of State Cordell Hull. In the spring of 1933, when Prime Minister J. Ramsay MacDonald and his economic advisers journeyed to Washington to discuss debts and the forthcoming economic conference, Hull was content to "sit in with you gentlemen" and confined himself to "an occasional disquisition in general and theoretical terms" on the desirability of removing obstacles to international trade.[45] As a man of the "utmost integrity, dignity and charm," Hull would patiently reply at great length to any question asked by diplomatic callers, "but when they return to their houses," noted Lindsay, "they usually have difficulty in remembering anything he has said which deserves to be reported."[46]

In Lindsay's view, Roosevelt's most conspicuous weakness was his amateurish grasp of economics. During his first meeting with Roosevelt at Warm Springs, Georgia (29 January 1933), the President-elect's remarks on the war debts, international trade, and stabilization of currencies ("I do not think he knows much about it") left Lindsay with

71

the distinct impression "that on all economic subjects he is rather weak."[47] Roosevelt's vacillating policy toward the debts during the spring of 1933 did little to allay Lindsay's apprehensions. Finding an overall settlement impossible, the President briefly flirted with asking Congress for a new moratorium before finally suggesting to MacDonald that Britain make a partial payment. Nevertheless, Lindsay continued to seek a moratorium even, in a conversation with Moley, alluding to the "we forgive our debtors" phrase of the Lord's Prayer.[48] As the 15 June 1933 deadline approached, Lindsay twice met with Roosevelt to explore possible solutions. On the whole, he found Roosevelt to be "extraordinarily fresh and vigorous," although there were still "plenty of contradictions" in his economic views.[49] When Lindsay suggested a token payment of only $5 million, Roosevelt objected on psychological grounds, pointing out that in America a token was regarded as a small worthless coin. Lindsay readily agreed with Roosevelt that $10 million would be a more "distinguished" figure, and in the end the Cabinet decided to pay the larger figure as "an acknowledgement of the debt pending a final settlement."[50] To Lindsay, the President and the State Department had displayed both "patience and good temper" throughout the whole "anxious business." But, he conceded to Sir John Simon, "I don't know how my nerves can stand a third such crisis."[51]

That Roosevelt was "constantly out of his depth" and "in these complex economic matters an almost complete amateur and an opportunist"[52] was again demonstrated to Lindsay by the spectacular failure of the London Economic Conference. The purpose of the conference, which Roosevelt had inherited from the Hoover administration, was to coordinate international measures against the Depression. In the spring of 1933, Roosevelt welcomed the conference with enthusiasm. But, preoccupied with pressing domestic matters, he delayed in selecting the American delegation and did not thoroughly consider the implications of international measures such as currency stabilization upon his domestic recovery program. Roosevelt then compounded the confusion by dispatching his "amateurish and muddled" message of 3 July 1933, in which he rejected currency stabilization and largely repudiated his original position. But Lindsay did not subscribe to the explanation that Roosevelt's conduct was proof of mental instability; rather

the President's nationalistic outburst was attributable to the requirements of American politics and to his own dilettantism in international economics. Notwithstanding his performance in foreign affairs, Lindsay insisted that Roosevelt should be credited with restoring America's confidence and with igniting an economic recovery that promised to produce material benefits for the entire world.[53]

Anglo-American economic disputes continued to dominate Lindsay's attention throughout the fall and winter of 1933-1934. Negotiations on the revision of the war debt settlement stalemated in October. As an expedient, it was decided to repeat the token payment procedure, although Lindsay and Sir Frederick Leith-Ross, who represented the British Treasury, shrewdly offered only $7.5 million and Roosevelt, ignoring his reputation as a "Yankee trader," readily accepted.[54] The President's trading instincts were fully in evidence, however, during the "pig versus whiskey" controversy that arose simultaneously with the repeal of the Eighteenth Amendment. At issue was the extent of concessions which Britain would make on the importation of American pork products in return for the right to export whiskey and other alcoholic beverages to the United States. The President wanted to drive a hard bargain, telling the press that the British position was unacceptable and that "there will be no more Scotch whiskey for you this winter."[55] Lindsay did not permit the dispute to disturb his sense of humor. When Roosevelt held his annual diplomatic reception, the same day on which repeal became effective, Lindsay remarked to Pierrepont Moffat, chief of the State Department's Division of Western European Affairs, "You are now looking at a parade of the best-dressed men in town and have you stopped to think that the one thought each and every one has in mind is, 'How much whiskey can I sell in this country?'" Not to be outdone, the President told his press conference that he had learned that Assistant Secretary of State R. Walton Moore had sent Sir Ronald Lindsay a "very, very good Virginia ham" and had received in return a bottle of Scotch. Early in 1934, the problem was settled when the administration decided to abandon its liquor quota system ("an administrative riot," Herbert Feis called it) in order to forestall massive bootlegging.[56]

Lindsay's exasperation over Roosevelt's handling of economic matters was compounded when the President signed the Johnson Act of April, 1934. In xenophobic terms, the bill forbade loans to any nation in default upon its war debt (Lindsay began to refer sardonically to the act's author, Senator Hiram Johnson of California, as the "Iron Canceller."[57]). Subsequently, Attorney General Homer Cummings ruled that token payments would no longer enable the debtors to avoid the stigma of default; payment of the full amounts due on 15 June 1934 would be required to avoid the loan ban of the Johnson Act.[58] On 17 May Lindsay met with Roosevelt and Undersecretary of State William Phillips to explore possible solutions. Throughout the conversation, Roosevelt, displaying his "usual breezy optimism and amazing candour," avoided appearing as a debt collector and adopted instead the attitude of a friendly counselor whose only desire was to be helpful. "His ideas," Lindsay noted, "were frequently haphazard and even self-contradictory and his ignorance of economics was often evident." Roosevelt suggested that the British divert attention from the distasteful word default by sending a prestigious mission to Washington for a new round of negotiations, but Lindsay, expressing his "absolute horror," rejected the idea as impractical. Moreover, the President demonstrated an interest in receiving payments in kind, yet Lindsay felt that Roosevelt did not grasp the distinction between payments made by the delivery of goods, based upon the German reparations experience, and payments based upon the exchange of goods, which Britain had long advocated. The President startled Lindsay by stating that he would like to draft the diplomatic note in which Britain would justify its inevitable default. Cloaked in his role as friendly adviser, Roosevelt "actually recommended" to the now bemused Lindsay that the British note stress the necessity of reducing the tax burden of the average British citizen so as to remove "social injustice."[59] In a private letter to Sir Frederick Leith-Ross, Lindsay reported that Roosevelt had "talked some of the most ridiculous financial nonsense I have ever heard." That a head of state could "be so woefully ignorant of the most elementary economic facts" was not only strange but laughable. "I did not," Lindsay concluded, "telegraph more than the general sense of his remarks because it is unwise to inject prejudice by the display of absurdity."[60]

As the debts faded from public attention, Lindsay was able to concentrate again upon internal American politics. Following Roosevelt's superb performance as a politician, Lindsay felt that Republican chances in the 1934 congressional campaign were poor. Thus, when Ogden Mills addressed himself to the theme of "rugged individualism 1934 convertible model" (convertible in the sense that the listener could have his tariff up or down) and warned of the "Big Bad Dictator" and of threats to freedom posed by a planned economy and an entrenched bureaucracy, Lindsay felt the former Secretary of the Treasury had become "hard of political hearing."[61] Although there was "plenty of mud-slinging" by the Republicans, Lindsay felt the optimism of Postmaster General James A. Farley "as he superintends the ladling out of the relief money" to be fully justified.[62] The unprecedented gains recorded by the Democrats left Roosevelt "bestriding the scene like a Colossus."[63]

Yet Lindsay soon discerned a potential threat to Roosevelt's leadership in "the plague and affliction" of Senator Huey Long. To Lindsay, the populistic Louisiana Democrat, strutting on the Senate floor in a pink shirt, resembled "the bluebottle fly (Musca vomitoria)." Both shared "the same frantic, relentless activity, the same intolerable, strident note, the same maddening elusiveness, the same origin in corruption, the same affront to the decencies and the same menace to health." The prospect of Long's elevation to the White House filled Lindsay with dread, although assassination soon removed the "kingfish" from Lindsay's list of worries.[64] Immediately, however, another obstacle to Roosevelt appeared when the Supreme Court began to declare major New Deal social reforms unconstitutional. A reactionary court might well produce serious class antagonism, Lindsay believed, since the majority of Americans favored the "disciplinary regulation of big business" as well as the fixing of hours and wages, unemployment insurance, and old-age pensions. Early in 1935, he observed that the Constitution might be revised so as to weaken the Court.[65] Despite Long and the Supreme Court, Lindsay knew that Roosevelt was unbeatable. His prospective opponents in 1936 were but "sacrificial oxen," including Senator Arthur Vandenberg of Michigan and "a Republican Governor from someplace or other" (a super-cilious reference to Governor Alfred Landon of Kansas). More than a year before the election, he observed that "one

might safely bet 5 to 3 on Mr. Roosevelt."[66]

To Lindsay's surprise the "colourless" Landon, although lacking either a national reputation or organization, easily proceeded to capture the Republican nomination. With the assistance of a good cabinet, such a "dependable wheelhorse" might make an "excellent president," Lindsay thought, but he was highly skeptical of Landon's prospects against Roosevelt.[67] The President's subsequent impressive victory and the unimpressive showing of Union Party nominee William Lemke (a "freak candidate") came as a relief to Lindsay. A potent factor in Roosevelt's success, Lindsay believed, was his "beautiful delivery and fine phrasing" over the radio, which helped to nullify the Republican bias of the press.[68]

Although Lindsay's political instincts concerning the presidential election proved highly accurate, he failed to anticipate the 1937 battle over the Supreme Court. Having attended Roosevelt's inauguration on 20 January 1937, Lindsay reported that Roosevelt intended to consolidate previous gains and "adopt conciliatory methods where possible, both toward the Supreme Court and business."[69] Thus, the President's "bombshell" in which he proposed the addition of as many as six new justices to the Court, shocked Lindsay. He sympathized with Roosevelt's main purpose of "reconstructing the decrepit edifice of the Constitution," noting that "it is not easy for one . . . to admire an instrument which makes it impossible to prohibit child labour by national statute." But Roosevelt's contention that the plan would increase judicial efficiency seemed disingenuous and oblique. Still, at the outset, he felt that Roosevelt was likely to get his way "more or less."[70]

By March, 1937, Lindsay recognized that substantial public and congressional opposition had developed. For once, he noted, Roosevelt's "remarkable political acumen" seemed to have deserted him. But he felt the charge that Roosevelt was taking a short cut to a virtual dictatorship exaggerated and "altogether nonsensical."[71] As the crisis intensified during the early summer, Lindsay's apprehension mounted. Not only had Roosevelt split his party "from top to bottom," but his unwise proposal had accentuated the prevalent drift toward isolation through neutrality

legislation.[72] Lindsay felt "very uneasy" about the loss of personal and political influence suffered by Roosevelt, pointing out that it was certainly not in the interest of Britain to have the President's prestige suffer a "severe prejudice."[73] When Roosevelt was forced to concede defeat, Lindsay could see only negative results: the President had sacrificed the election landslide, opened irreparable wounds in the Democratic party, and seriously impaired chances for further reform legislation.[74] The 1937 business recession further eroded the President's influence. Lindsay took this development in stride, however, contending with remarkable accuracy that the situation was similar to "the slump of 1924," and that a resumption of the economic advance could be expected by the spring or summer of 1938.[75]

Having served as ambassador for over seven years, Lindsay, now sixty years old, began to contemplate retirement. When Foreign Secretary Anthony Eden offered Lindsay a one-year extension of his appointment from 11 March 1938 to 11 March 1939, Lindsay promptly accepted, but not without private and official hesitation. The private considerations he cared not to discuss "because when they lie like lead on one's own mind, they usually seem as light as feathers to everyone else." As for the official reasons, Lindsay conceded candidly: "I do not discharge my duties with all the zest which an Ambassador ought to have at his command," and he signified a desire to retire on pension in the spring of 1939 or earlier if that should be desired by the Foreign Office. In London, Lindsay's attitude was highly appreciated. As Sir Robert Vansittart noted, "Sir R. Lindsay sees life in the right light, and sits looser as he grows older. He will still be under 62 when he retires, and we could have done with a lot more of him. But it is a refreshing example to find anyone with so little of the limpet in him. One comes across that very seldom."[76] Yet circumstances forced a change in Lindsay's plans: he was asked to stay on in Washington beyond the spring of 1939 so as to supervise the royal visit in June. Officials in the Foreign Office felt that Lindsay's long experience would be valuable in resolving the many "difficult and tricky questions" which were bound to occur, and that "if we were to take him away just before it might well seem very odd to the Americans."[77] Moreover, King George himself requested Lindsay stay on for the royal tour.[78] Therefore, Lindsay, who felt that "nothing but good" could come from

the trip, agreed to accept an extension of his commission until 30 June 1939.[79]

Anxiety over the rise of European fascism dominated Lindsay's thinking during his final two years in Washington. When the Czechoslovakian question assumed crisis proportions in the fall of 1938, Lindsay argued for a firm British stand against Nazi demands. He would not oppose "a wise accommodation," but he felt that there would be "a certain letdown of American friendliness" in the event of a British capitulation to Adolf Hitler. Although Americans generally hoped to avoid participation in another European war, Lindsay felt that American involvement was "likely." Disgust over Nazi brutality more than anything would lead to American intervention. Unlike World War I, though, American neutrality would last far less than two and a half years.[80]

When he considered the question of "how the United States can be favourably predisposed towards us for the contingency of a major crisis arising in Europe," Lindsay's mind turned to the subject of an Anglo-American trade agreement, an idea being zealously promoted by Secretary of State Hull. From Lindsay's viewpoint, such an agreement was highly desirable, but more for political than economic reasons. With war likely, America's friendship was imperative, he reasoned, and should Britain sacrifice an agreement because of minor economic disputes comprehensible only to experts, it would be guilty of a "first-class political crime."[81]

The negotiation proved especially arduous for Lindsay. He and Hull had never enjoyed close personal relations, and the trade negotiations did not enhance either man's estimate of the other. Hull frequently bored Lindsay with lengthy monologues extolling the virtues of his trade policy. Hull's remarks, in the ambassador's view, tended to be "long, discursive and often very obscure."[82] Lindsay found it difficult to read Hull's rather repetitious speeches "without allowing one's mind to wander to other topics."[83] For his part, Hull considered Lindsay to be "difficult to deal with." Lindsay's chief shortcoming, Hull explained in his memoirs, was that he confined his contacts to an elite group of Republican socialites, thereby making it difficult for him to appreciate Hull's point of view.[84] In view of Lindsay's general admiration of the New Deal, the lack of rapport

Sir Ronald Lindsay arriving at the White House
12 April 1939, National Archives.

between the two was probably due more to matters of style and personality than to issues of substance.

More than a year later the talks reached a critical phase, bringing Lindsay "personally to that state of bitterness and exasperation which usually results from dealing with [the] United States Government." Hull, he complained bitterly, was unreasonable in his demands and insisted upon putting Britain "through the mangle of American politics."[85] Suddenly all the obstacles to an agreement were swept away when Roosevelt and Hull relaxed the American terms. To Hull, the agreement was the capstone of his desire to remove the causes of war by expanding trade; to Lindsay, the chief significance of the agreement was that it had strengthened Anglo-American political ties.

While the European crisis preoccupied Lindsay, he remained a keen student of American politics. The conservative trend evident in the 1938 election (the Republicans gained 81 seats in the House of Representatives and six in the Senate) did not particularly upset the British ambassador, for he felt the result was not an isolationist reaction but had been decided largely upon such domestic issues as the recession and widespread labor violence.[86] By the winter of 1938-1939, he believed that the American people were acquiring a war mentality because of the new emphasis upon rearmament and the hysterical public reaction to Orson Welles's sensational radio portrayal of "The War of the Worlds."[87] Meanwhile, the 1940 presidential campaign intruded into every aspect of American life. Administration pledges not to request higher taxes or to expand federal power projects were issued with a view toward the "appeasement" of the business community; in short, the President's policy was to "take business for a petting party."[88] Lindsay blamed political partisanship for the defeat of Roosevelt's attempt to liberalize the neutrality act to benefit Britain and France. Had Roosevelt been willing to renounce all third term ambitions, Lindsay believed, he might well have succeeded. Instead Roosevelt was thwarted by a determined isolationist minority, and by summer Congress was drifting indecisively in "a lamentable display of incompetence, partisanship, and log-rolling."[89]

On the eve of his retirement, Lindsay considered it quite likely that Roosevelt would run again in 1940,

especially if war seemed imminent. In Lindsay's view, the Democratic alternatives to Roosevelt were generally unappealing: Vice-President Garner and Secretary of State Hull were too old, Harry Hopkins was too controversial, William Douglas had "disappeared into the Supreme Court," while the nomination of such progressives as Robert La Follette and Fiorello La Guardia would split the Democratic party. "So," he concluded, "Mr. Roosevelt himself appears once more as the logical candidate to succeed himself in 1940."[90]

Lindsay's leave-taking, already once delayed, proved elusive as the arrival of his successor, Lord Lothian, was postponed until August. Suffering in Washington's heat and humidity, Lindsay considered his fate to be "most unfair." As Lindsay complained to the Foreign Office, "I think that more consideration is due to me than to him [Lord Lothian] and that I am not getting it."[91] On 26 August, Lindsay was finally able to sail on the Aquitania, arriving in Britain on the very eve of World War II. Ten days later, in a more relaxed and amiable mood, he concluded his diplomatic service with a brief note of appreciation to Lord Halifax. As a young man Lindsay recalled that he had often heard it said, "From Hell, Hull, and Halifax, Good Lord protect us! Now it happens that in recent times I have had such constant and such pleasant relations with two of these terrors that I almost approach the third without trepidation, and I wish to thank you most sincerely for the part you have thus taken in speeding me on my way."[92] In a gracious reply, Halifax expressed to Lindsay the thanks of the entire Foreign Office "for your part in bringing American opinion to where it now stands, though, no doubt, you have been assisted a bit by Hitler."[93]

The compliment was well deserved as Lindsay had played a major role in improving relations. He could take personal credit for having tactfully handled Britain's default of its war debt in 1934 and for having conducted the difficult negotiations which led to the Anglo-American Trade Agreement of 1938. Lindsay's final diplomatic accomplishment was the arranging of the highly successful royal visit to the United States (7-11 June 1939) which served as a subtle appeal to American emotions. Lindsay, however, would have disclaimed personal credit for the renewed vigor

of the Anglo-American understanding since he believed that personalities were relatively unimportant in determining the course of international relations. No amount of logic or diplomatic persuasion could induce Americans to abandon isolationism unless they first became convinced that the national interest was at stake. His advice to the Foreign Office was to avoid a direct "political approach" to the United States; instead, the most fruitful strategy for winning American goodwill was to combine the use of psychology with timely economic concessions.[94] His role in formulating British policy toward Europe was minimal, but Lindsay's recommendations regarding policy toward the United States were listened to with respect, especially once the approach of war forcibly impressed the British with the need for closer ties with America.

As an observer of American affairs, Lindsay was hardly infallible. Frequently his observations were cautious and conventional and many displayed the influence of such prominent journalists as Walter Lippmann, Frank Simonds, and Arthur Krock. Convinced of the superiority of the British cabinet system, Lindsay frequently exaggerated the deficiencies of Congress and the American constitutional structure. On the other hand, he demonstrated unusual ability in analyzing the major political trends of the thirties. His political forecasting was surprisingly accurate (his only major error was in predicting that Franklin D. Roosevelt would be unable to overcome his opponents and the two-thirds rule at the 1932 Democratic convention). He foresaw the downfall of the Hoover administration and business leadership; however, unlike many contemporaries he did not see the New Deal as a radical reform movement but as merely a moderate brand of liberalism. Notwithstanding his uninhibited criticisms, Lindsay was impressed by many aspects of American life in the thirties. He applauded the social welfare reforms of the New Deal, and he was pleased by the ease of establishing friendships with Americans. Moreover, he found that from official Washington he and other diplomats received "all, and possibly more than all, the courtesy and consideration which we could possibly receive from any other post in the world." Had Lindsay's unvarnished personal expressions inadvertently become public knowledge, his effectiveness surely would have been damaged: in the eyes of nationalistic Americans, he might have become the modern day equivalent of Mrs. Frances

Trollope. But this "first class representative" (as Sir Robert Vansittart called him) retired without mishap to his home in Dorset.[95] Having lived to see the defeat of the Axis, he died of natural causes at the age of 68 at Bournemouth, England on 21 August 1945, remembered as an ambassador who had prepared the way for the Anglo-American collaboration of World War II. Had Lindsay enjoyed greater influence in shaping British policy toward Europe, his name would be more readily recalled today. Yet it is difficult to disagree with Sir Frederick Leith-Ross who regarded Lindsay as one of the "wisest and best balanced" British diplomats of the thirties and considered it a tragedy that his practicality and realism were not given greater weight in the formation of British foreign policy.[96]

¹Ray Atherton to Henry L. Stimson, 15 November 1929 (enclosing letter from Sir Ronald Lindsay to Atherton, 13 November 1929), 701.4111/698, U.S. State Department records, RG 59, National Archives, Washington, D.C. (hereafter cited as D/S File #).

²Understandably, historians of Anglo-American relations in the thirties have concentrated upon the outbreak of World War II and the Roosevelt administration's policy of support for Britain. There is no detailed study of Anglo-American relations during the decade, although the general background is surveyed from a British perspective in H. C. Allen, Great Britain and the United States: A History of Anglo-American Relations (1783-1952) (New York, 1969), pp. 762-80, and H. G. Nicholas, The United States and Britain (Chicago, 1975), pp. 84-89. The most comprehensive account, presented from an American viewpoint, is Richard N. Kottman, Reciprocity and the North Atlantic Triangle, 1932-1938 (Ithaca, N.Y., 1968). See also Benjamin D. Rhodes, "The British Royal Visit of 1939 and the 'Psychological Approach' to the United States," Diplomatic History 2 (Spring 1978): 197-211.

³During one particularly frustrating incident in December, 1932, the Hoover administration indicated that it might accept a reduction in the British war debt through a complicated scheme involving the issuance of bonds by Britain to reduce the schedule of payments required by the Anglo-American debt agreement of 1923. Lindsay asked Assistant Secretary of State Harvey Bundy whether the Hoover administration could guarantee that Congress would approve the plan should Britain accept. Bundy replied negatively, stressing that any reduction of Britain's payments was contingent upon favorable action by Congress. "Well," Lindsay stated tartly, "Damn your American Constitution. You Americans can threaten but you can never promise." Harvey Bundy memoir, Columbia Oral History Collection, 114, Columbia University, New York, N.Y.

⁴Thomas E. Hachey, ed., "Winning Friends and Influencing Policy: British Strategy to Woo America in 1937," Wisconsin Magazine of History 55 (Winter 1971-1972): 124. Hachey's article is primarily a reproduction of Lindsay's 22 March 1937 telegram to Foreign Secretary Anthony Eden, in which Lindsay replied to Eden's request for suggestions on how to retain American goodwill should a major crisis arise in Europe. Anthony Eden, Facing the

Dictators (Boston, 1962), p. 598, contains a highly edited version of Lindsay's dispatch which deletes the ambassador's stylistic flourishes.

[5]Hachey, "Winning Friends and Influencing Policy," p. 120; New York Times, 29 March 1930, 23 August 1945; Washington Star, 21 May 1939.

[6]Atherton to Stimson, 15 November 1929 (Lindsay to Atherton, 13 November 1929, enclosed), S/D File #701.4111/698.

[7]New York Times, 29 May 1930.

[8]Lindsay to Arthur Henderson, 14 May 1939, FO 371/14282/A3741, British Foreign Office records, Public Record Office, London (hereafter cited by FO volume and document file number).

[9]Lindsay to Henderson, 10 July 1930, FO 371/14282/A4976.

[10]Lindsay to Henderson, 14 May 1930, FO 371/14282/A3741.

[11]Lindsay to Henderson, 26 March 1930, FO 414/265/A2538.

[12]Lindsay to Henderson, 14 May 1930, FO 371/14282/A3741.

[13]Lindsay to Henderson, 3 July 1930, FO 414/266/A4769.

[14]Lindsay to Henderson, 10 November 1930, FO 371/14283/A7668.

[15]Lindsay to Henderson, 10 March 1931, FO 414/267/A1955.

[16]Lindsay to Sir John Simon, 20 November 1931, FO 414/268/C8903.

[17]Lindsay to the Marquis of Reading, 28 October 1931, FO 414/268/C8359, and Lindsay to the Marquis of Reading, 4 November 1931, FO 414/268/C8360. Hoover told Stimson that Wells had lectured him. Stimson's impression was that Wells had "pulled a string which had unwittingly turned loose facts which possibly had been made for others." Memorandum of a conversation between Lindsay and Stimson, 4 November 1931, D/S File #711.40/49.

[18]Lindsay to Simon, 10 December 1931, FO 414/268/A7433.

[19]Lindsay to Simon, 17 December 1931, FO 414/268/A7539.

[20]Lindsay to Simon, 31 December 1931, FO 414/269/A187.

[21]Lindsay to Simon, 15 January 1932, FO 414/269/A488; Lindsay to Simon, 5 February 1932, FO 414/269/A1019.
[22]Lindsay to Simon, 12 February 1932, FO 414/269/A1164.
[23]Lindsay to Simon, 4 March 1932, FO 414/269/A1589.
[24]Lindsay to Simon, 24 March 1932, FO 414/269/A2014.
[25]Lindsay to Simon, 27 April 1932, E. L. Woodward and Rohan Butler, eds., Documents on British Foreign Policy, 1919-1939 (London, 1948), second series, 3:131.
[26]Lindsay to Simon, 25 February 1932, FO 414/269/A1410.
[27]Lindsay to Simon, 27 April 1932, Documents on British Foreign Policy, second series, 3:133.
[28]Lindsay to Simon, 21 April 1932, FO 414/269/A2641.
[29]Lindsay to Simon, 12 May 1932, FO 414/269/A3087.
[30]Lindsay to Simon, 22 June 1932, FO 414/270/A3992.
[31]Memorandum of a conversation between Stimson and Lindsay, 23 June 1932, D/S File #800.51/W89/528.
[32]Lindsay to Simon, 6 July 1932, FO 414/270/A4318.
[33]Lindsay to Simon, 8 July 1932, FO 414/270/A4329.
[34]Lindsay to Simon, 21 July 1932, FO 414/270/A4756.
[35]Lindsay to Simon, 15 November 1932, FO 414/270/A8010.
[36]Lindsay to Simon, 15 March 1933, FO 414/271/A2336.
[37]Lindsay to Simon, 9 March 1933, FO 414/271/A2141.
[38]Lindsay to Simon, 1 January 1934, FO 414/272/A420.
[39]Lindsay to Simon, 25 October 1933, FO 414/272/A7983.
[40]Lindsay to Simon, 15 March 1933, FO 414/271/A2336.
[41]Lindsay to Simon, 1 January 1934, FO 414/272/A420. See also Thomas E. Hachey, ed., "Profiles in Politics: British Embassy Views of Prominent Americans in 1939," Wisconsin Magazine of History 54 (Autumn 1970): 18. The article is a collection of biographies of prominent American personalities written by Lindsay. But contrary to Hachey's title, the majority of the sketches were composed between 1933 and 1938 and then reprinted in 1939.
[42]Hachey, "Profiles in Politics," p. 54.
[43]Lindsay to Simon, 3 May 1933, FO 414/271/A3705.
[44]Lindsay to Simon, 1 January 1934, FO 414/272/A420.
[45]Lindsay to Simon, 3 May 1933, FO 414/271/A3705.
[46]Lindsay to Eden, 1 January 1936, FO 414/273/A308.
[47]Lindsay to Simon, 30 January 1933, Documents on British Foreign Policy, second series, 5:748-52. Frank Freidel, Franklin D. Roosevelt: Launching the New Deal

(Boston, 1973), p. 105, contends that Lindsay confused Roosevelt's supposed economic ignorance with what was in fact a considerable degree of political awareness. Perhaps the most judicious conclusion is that Roosevelt's view in early 1933 was a blend of political awareness and some economic ignorance.

[48]Raymond Moley, After Seven Years (New York, 1939), p. 220.

[49]Lindsay to Simon, 8 June 1933, Documents on British Foreign Policy, second series, 5:823.

[50]Lindsay to Simon, 11 June 1933, FO 371/16671/C5255; Lindsay to Hull, 13 June 1933, U.S. Department of State, Foreign Relations of the United States (hereafter cited as FRUS), 1933 (Washington, 1950-1952), 1:839-41.

[51]Lindsay to Simon, 15 June 1933, FO 794/17.

[52]Lindsay to Simon, 27 July 1933, FO 414/272/A5782.

[53]Ibid.

[54]Leith-Ross to Sir Warren Fisher, 3 November 1933, FO 371/16675/C9617; Lindsay to Simon, 4 November 1933, Documents on British Foreign Policy, second series, 5:856-57.

[55]Lindsay to Simon, 11 January 1934, FO 414/272/A685.

[56]Herbert Feis, 1933: Characters in Crisis (Boston, 1966), p. 338. Press Conferences, 12 January 1934, 3:60, President's Personal File, Franklin D. Roosevelt Papers, Roosevelt Library, Hyde Park, New York.

[57]Lindsay to Simon, 1 January 1935, FO 414/274/A234.

[58]Department of the Treasury, Annual Report of the Secretary of the Treasury 1934, (Washington, 1935), pp. 238-42.

[59]Lindsay to Simon, 18 May 1934, Documents on British Foreign Policy, second series, 5:926-28.

[60]Lindsay to Leith-Ross, 21 May 1934, FO 371/17586/A4602.

[61]Lindsay to Simon, 31 January 1934, FO 414/272/A1411.

[62]Lindsay to Simon, 26 October 1934, FO 414/272/A8741.

[63]Lindsay to Simon, 16 November 1934, FO 414/272/A9368.

[64]Lindsay to Simon, 7 March 1935, FO 414/272/A2603.

[65]Lindsay to Simon, 28 May 1935, FO 414/272/A5079.

[66]Lindsay to Sir Samuel Hoare, 2 August 1935, FO 414/272/A7584.

[67]Lindsay to Anthony Eden, 28 July 1936, FO 414/273/A6436.

[68]Lindsay to Eden, 9 November 1936, FO 414/273/A9111.

[69]Lindsay to Eden, 23 January 1937, FO 414/274/A986.

[70]Lindsay to Eden, 12 February 1937, FO 414/274/1421.

[71]Lindsay to Eden, 2 March 1937, FO 414/274/A1893.

[72]Lindsay to Eden, 28 May 1937, FO 414/274/A4108.

[73]Lindsay to Eden, 19 July 1937, FO 414/274/A5352.

[74]Lindsay to Eden, 27 July 1937, FO 414/274/A5509.

[75]Lindsay to Eden, 11 December 1937, FO 414/275/A174.

[76]Lindsay to Eden, 30 July 1937 (notations by Vansittart and Eden attached), FO 794/17.

[77]F. R. Hoyer Millar to Sir Alexander Cadogan, 27 October 1938, ibid.

[78]Viscount Halifax to Neville Chamberlain, 16 November 1938, ibid.

[79]Lindsay to Halifax, 25 October 1938, ibid.

[80]Lindsay to Halifax, 12 September 1938, FO 414/275/C9711.

[81]Hachey, "Winning Friends and Influencing Policy," pp. 127-29. For the negotiation of the trade agreement, see Arthur W. Schatz, "The Anglo-American Trade Agreement and Cordell Hull's Search for Peace 1936-1938," Journal of American History 57 (June 1970): 85-103.

[82]Lindsay to Simon, 13 May 1933, Documents on British Foreign Policy, second series, 5:803-804.

[83]Lindsay to Halifax, 16 August 1938, FO 414/275/A6602.

[84]Cordell Hull, The Memoirs of Cordell Hull (New York, 1948), 1:380.

[85]Lindsay to Halifax, 8 October 1938, FO 414/275/A7645.

[86]Lindsay to Halifax, 16 November 1938, FO 414/275/A8878.

[87]Lindsay to Halifax, 16 November 1938, FO 414/275/A8877.

[88]Lindsay to Halifax, 2 March 1939, FO 414/276/A1919.

[89]Lindsay to Halifax, 27 July 1939, FO 414/276/A5381; Lindsay to Halifax, 3 July 1939, FO 414/276/A4794.

[90]Lindsay to Halifax, 27 July 1939, FO 414/276/A5381.

[91]Lindsay to Oliver Harvey, 27 June 1939, FO 794/17.

[92]Lindsay to Halifax, 10 September 1939, FO 794/17.

[93]Halifax to Lindsay, 12 September 1939, FO 794/17.

[94]Lindsay to Eden, 16 August 1937, FO 414/274/A6188.

[95]Notation by Vansittart written in the margin of Lindsay to Eden, 30 July 1937, FO 794/17.

[96]Sir Frederick Leith-Ross, Money Talks: Years of International Finance (London, 1968), p. 112.

SIR JOHN SIMON'S WAR WITH
HENRY L. STIMSON: A FOOTNOTE
TO ANGLO-AMERICAN RELATIONS
IN THE 1930's

Michael Holcomb

"My general report," wrote British Foreign Secretary Sir John Simon to Prime Minister Ramsey MacDonald in the autumn of 1934, "is that in the international field we stand high.   Everybody, I think, is impressed with the steadiness of Britain, all the more so because of the unsteadiness of most other people.   If there is no great achievement to record there is no serious lapse to deplore. . . ."[1]   This smug assessment would not have been agreeably received in certain quarters where considerable discontent lingered as a consequence of British Far Eastern policy during the Manchurian and Shanghai crises of 1931 and 1932.[2]   Still, by 1934, those troublesome episodes had largely run their course: Japan controlled Manchuria (renamed Manchukuo), while Imperial Japanese troops had evacuated Shanghai in May, 1932.

Even before these events had been relegated to history, the question of Anglo-American cooperation over Manchuria and Shanghai became embroiled in controversy. The essence of the American charge was noted in a letter written to Simon in 1940:   "I see that John Kennedy (the American Ambassador's son), in his book, "Why England Slept." [sic], refers to Manchuria, and repeats the fable that you turned down Stimson's offer of co-operation . . . and describes this as one of the great blunders of post-war British diplomacy."[3]

It is important to understand that this controversy occurred against a backdrop of considerable acrimony and strained Anglo-American relations.   Serious problems caused by the world-wide Depression weighed heavily upon both nations.   The question of World War I debt repayment, with the United States in the role of impatient creditor, seemed to defy amicable solution.   Further, while Americans became self-indulgently isolationist, many Britons were awakening to Great Britain's lack of security and the hopelessness of disarmament.   Nor was there any lack of provocation to

weaken the spirit of accord. Surely the American performance at the World Economic Conference, held in London in June, 1933, was enough to convince many Englishmen of Yankee perfidy. It is hardly surprising that Sir Robert Vansittart, Permanent Undersecretary of State, penned an acerbic note on the future of Anglo-American relations in which he concluded that "the U.S.A. will always disappoint us."[4] Particularly in the Far East, Vansittart felt Britain should be skeptical of American suggestions for cooperation against Japan; British policy toward Japan, Vansittart believed, ought rather to be pre-occupied with keeping the Japanese "as friendly i.e. non-dangerous, as possible, than in endeavouring to better our existing relations with the USA, which are as good as that unreliable country will or can allow them to be."[5]

When the State Department intimated the following year that the sympathy and understanding and "readiness to consult and collaborate" which formerly characterized Anglo-American relations were somehow lacking, Vansittart sneered that "Their policy, from the moment the war closed became one of precipitate egotism, and it has never varied, except to increase." In Vansittart's view, all the English attempts to accommodate the Americans--from termination of the alliance with Japan to agreement on naval parity--appeared to have been in vain. The London Economic Conference was the capstone, the American handling of which he found "nauseatingly disloyal." For the State Department "to lay at our door any short-coming in Anglo-American relations" required considerable complacency, if not effrontery.[6]

A situation was fast approaching when it would be necessary for America to undertake some initiative. "The days of our long and sterile courtship" were over, wrote Vansittart, and "I do not believe we shall ever get any-where by the way that has already been tried to the full." Among the English, he perceived a growing disillusionment with America that, if it became general, could be disastrous. Seeing no signs either of cordiality or cooperation, he feared the growing American tendency to reduce its responsibilities everywhere. "It is really up to the U.S. Government to make a move," he wrote, "--otherwise than to the rear."[7]

It was against this background that the Simon-Stimson controversy (as it was indexed in Foreign Office files) began to take a definite form in 1934. Former Secretary of State Henry Stimson now actively undertook the task of revealing what appeared to him the various means by which the Foreign Office had undermined Anglo-American cooperation during the Manchurian imbroglio. So successful was he in this effort that by the end of the decade it had become, in the eyes of the newly appointed British ambassador to Washington, "the universal conviction in America that Manchuria would have been saved if it had not been for Simon's opposition."[8]

Stimson appeared at once to have given currency and refutation to a charge arousing concern in Anglo-American diplomatic circles that the Foreign Office had declined an American proposal to join in calling a conference under the Nine Power Treaty of 1921-1922. The entire business, Stimson explained in a call to the State Department, had been part of a "systematic effort to rally world opinion against Japanese sabotage of postwar multilateral peace treaties to which she was a party." His nonrecognition note of 7 January 1932 was conceived as the "first step" in this process. The British Foreign Office, however, had reacted not only by refusing to follow it but actually belittling it in a press release.[9]

Amplifying the story, Stimson said that it was after the Japanese attack on Shanghai that he had tried to draw the British into a joint invocation of the Nine Power Treaty. By this means, the Secretary of State had hoped that "perhaps eventually a conference of the powers" could be called "to conciliate the issue between Japan and China as to Manchuria." With no intention of "crossing wires" with the League, he expected that his efforts in this regard would "support and invigorate League action. . . ." When Simon made Anglo-American collaboration contingent upon favorable responses from the other signatories to the Nine Power Treaty, Stimson felt his proposal effectively blocked.[10] Consequently, he chose to make an appeal to world public opinion through a more informal device. In a public letter on 24 February to Senator William E. Borah, Chairman of the Senate Committee on Foreign Relations, Stimson asserted the integrity of United States treaty rights in the Far East and, in drawing attention to the principle

of nonrecognition of changes wrought in violation of the Washington treaties of 1922, invited other nations to join in its support.[11] While he had <u>not</u>, in fact, proposed holding a conference, Stimson wrote that to argue over this was quite unimportant. What really mattered was that he had "proposed a joint course which might to advantage have been followed," to which the British responded negatively.[12]

This was the opening salvo in the controversy and it elicited a prompt response from Sir John Simon and the British Foreign Office. Simon drafted a lengthy memorandum refuting Stimson and establishing to his own satisfaction the reality of Anglo-American cooperation and agreement.[13] Meanwhile, Sir John Pratt, a Far Eastern specialist and principal polemicist for British foreign policy in the region, reached a similar conclusion. Satisfied with their version of events, the only remaining concern of the two Englishmen was that Stimson might repeat his charge in a forthcoming autobiography.[14]

Rather than waiting for his book to be published, Stimson returned to the attack and shifted the basis for his charge of British coolness toward cooperation. In a conversation with Sir Ronald Lindsay, the British ambassador in Washington, he referred to earlier developments surrounding the publication of his nonrecognition note of 7 January 1932. Had he been joined "quickly and cordially" by other governments (especially Great Britain) in his advocated policy, "the inevitable result would have been a Conference of the Nine Powers by which the Japanese would inevitably have been paralysed." According to Lindsay, Stimson believed that his note "might well have been . . . construed" as an invitation to a conference.[15]

Simon's response to Stimson's tenacity was more one of contempt than anger. "I am afraid that the further [he] gets away from the events on which he meditates," wrote the British Foreign Secretary, "the more confused his recollection becomes." Continuing his criticism of the former Secretary of State, Simon said that his preoccupation with the past was a "further example of self-hallucination" and living proof that "retired statesmen should not write their reminiscences if much reflection of their own efforts

leads them to explain their own want of success by other people's treachery."[16]

Simon's rebuttal to what he labeled this "champion example of Mr. Stimson's confusion of mind" rested upon two arguments. First, he could not have desired that his note of 7 January be construed as an invitation to a conference. Undersecretary of State William Castle indicated as much in a conversation with Lindsay three days later when he said the State Department had concluded that to consult with the Nine Power Treaty signatories would mean too much delay. Furthermore, within another few days, American representatives in China were saying that there appeared to be no occasion for calling a conference. Secondly, Stimson wrote his letter to Senator Borah on 24 February "because the other Powers had adopted the policy of the note of January 7th and not because they had not done so." Disturbed and perplexed by Stimson's attack, Simon remembered "the principal part" he had taken at Geneva in securing League adoption of the Stimson Doctrine, for which he had received warm American thanks.[17]

The main task of arguing and defining the British position from 1934 to 1940 fell upon Sir John Pratt. As a senior adviser and specialist on Far Eastern matters in the Foreign Office, he had had a direct hand in shaping and articulating British policy throughout every stage of the disputes over Manchuria and Shanghai. Because of his knowledge and experience, he took a near-proprietary interest in defending the policies that he had advocated. For most occasions, old or revised Pratt memoranda provided the basis for official responses, if any were desired. After 1940, he was joined by others in the defense of British Far Eastern policy during the crises of 1931-1933.

Pratt reacted even more strongly than Simon to Stimson's charges with a memorandum averring that the former secretary scarcely realized the ineffectiveness of nonrecognition by a few powers. Indeed, in the Englishman's eyes, but for British action the American note of 7 January would have been as impotent as the Wilson administration's response to Japanese demands against China in 1915.[18] "It was we," he wrote immodestly, "who

94

saw that the proper way of handling the note [of 7 January] was to get the so-called Stimson Doctrine adopted by the League." In support of this claim, he pointed to the two League declarations of 29 January and 16 February 1932 that substantially incorporated the principle of non-recognition and concluded, "the idea had by this time dawned up[on] Mr. Stimson's mind that this adoption of his note by the League had given it a force and effect of which he never dreamed when he first drafted it."[19]

To one outspoken English critic who echoed Stimson's claims, Pratt maintained that the United States government had suddenly and "without any diplomatic preparation" suggested British cooperation against Japan. Considering Great Britain's membership in the League and Japanese assurances before that organization, the Foreign Office had thought it improper to go along. Nevertheless, "His Majesty's Government had very skillfully made their close cooperation with America an instrument for reinforcing the action and the moral authority of the League."[20]

What Pratt defended as virtue, Stimson dismissed as guile: the British had "preferred to take refuge in the inconspicuousness of League action among the flock of European nations." Stimson maintained that on three different occasions he had conferred by transatlantic telephone with Sir John Simon in mid-February, 1932 in a fruitless effort to secure a joint invocation of the Nine Power Treaty. As a result, he had published his informal letter to Senator Borah. Its success at home and abroad in rallying public opinion confirmed his impression "of the powerful effect the joint official action of Britain and America would have had if it had been taken along the same line." Great Britain had clearly breached "the great policy of Anglo-American cooperation."[21]

Stimson's tenacious opinion and persistent attack were not welcome in London. "With characteristic dishonesty," Pratt asserted Stimson had again taken up cudgels even after having been shown the Foreign Office memoranda refuting his earlier charges. In response, Pratt composed another closely reasoned memorandum. The portrayal of events that emerged from his narrative was one of American insensitivity to political and military reality, and policy direction by the personal whim of Stimson. For example,

the Foreign Office feared that a strongly worded note to Japan might provoke Japan "into going further than she otherwise would."[22] Yet the Secretary of State had closed the door to negotiations which if pursued might have brought an end to hostilities.

According to Pratt, it was through the efforts of Sir John Simon that a nonrecognition clause based upon the Nine Power Treaty and the Pact of Paris was inserted in the appeal adopted by the League on 16 February that fore-shadowed its later formal adoption of the Stimson Doctrine. "One might have expected," Pratt intoned with dry under-statement, "that in due course there would have been further recensions of the draft and that at the appropriate moment it would have been issued as an Anglo-American or Nine Power declaration. In fact no further communication on the subject was received from Mr. Stimson."[23] The conclusion to be drawn was that the other powers obviously regarded the League appeal as a satisfactory adoption of the Stimson Doctrine. Stimson himself had expressed gratification; his public letter to Senator Borah was intended merely to provide a purely American complement. Consequently, Stimson's latest charges were "entirely without foundation."[24]

In July, 1935, Pratt reviewed the entire Sino-Japanese dispute, taking swipes at "idealists" who had thwarted reason. The American attitude from the beginning was hostile to Japan. Clearly, both before and after the American note of 7 January, "Mr. Stimson never had the slightest intention of proceeding from words to deeds, and his policy was doubly harmful for while irritating Japan it confirmed China in the false belief that material aid would be forthcoming."[25]

In June, 1936, dismayed members of the Foreign Office noted that the Simon-Stimson misunderstanding persisted. Consequently, to counteract erroneous interpretations and to set the record straight, Pratt prepared a new paper especially for a British delegation planning to attend the August conference of the Institute of Pacific Relations in California.[26] Then the Simon-Stimson controversy surfaced again with the publication of Stimson's book, The Far Eastern Crisis: Recollections and Observations. The Foreign Office had for some time suspected that the former

Secretary would publicly reveal his complaints against the British government, so the publication was hardly surprising. "Mr Stimson can be remarkably acid and untruthful for so lovable a man," mused Sir Robert Vansittart, "and remarkably stupid for so intelligent a man."[27]

Alive to the challenge and undaunted by repetition, Pratt came forward with yet another memorandum. This time he addressed himself to a review not only of the controversy as it had developed, but also to some specific charges made in Stimson's book. The brunt of Pratt's argument focused upon a new Stimson variation of an old theme: that British reluctance to join in the démarche of mid-February, 1932 caused him to press the idea no further. As Stimson claimed, "the British disclaimer obviously killed the possibility of any such démarche."[28] In Pratt's view, however, Secretary Stimson had been "both impulsive and impatient" throughout the period of the Shanghai crisis. Indeed, Sir John Simon had successfully maneuvered the League into adopting nonrecognition on 16 February and, except for Stimson's ineptness, "he would probably have been equally successful in securing in due course a joint invocation of the Nine Power Treaty."[29] Pratt excoriated Stimson for claiming that Far Eastern affairs might have been altered by invoking the Nine Power Treaty and trying to induce Japan to discuss its dispute with China before an impartial conference or, if that approach failed, imposing economic sanctions against Japan. "There is no evidence that he ever advanced either of these propositions, nor is it at all probable that he would at any time have found anyone to concur in them," Pratt wrote. "As regards a conference, from first to last Japan firmly refused to hold a conference over Manchuria with third parties present. That was the obstacle which prevented a settlement of the dispute."[30]

In Stimson's March efforts to secure a League resolution on nonrecognition, Pratt charged him with acting on the basis of erroneous press reports and with employing dubious tactics to reach his objective. As for Stimson's disappointment that the British government did not follow his lead of 7 January, Pratt questioned his timing: "Certain ideas which came into Mr. Stimson's mind in February would appear . . . to have been transferred in

the book to the earlier period, November and December."[31] The Briton also parried one of Stimson's own arguments into a defense of the British position on the necessity of acting with the League; Stimson had commented favorably on the League's vital role in the Sino-Japanese dispute. Because the League had employed its machinery to seek a solution, the issue became one between Japan and the entire world rather than between Japan and the United States. Recognizing the value of this distinction, Stimson had realized the importance of America furnishing "independent support to the League rather than play[ing] a role of leadership." Pratt believed that Stimson scarcely comprehended how completely this view justified British actions and attitudes throughout the dispute. Similarly, Stimson failed to realize "how greatly his own impatience, impulsiveness and unfounded suspicions contributed to the difficulties he describes."[32]

Pratt's memorandum, dated 1 October 1936, had a receptive audience, and the Foreign Office ordered it (and the attached documents) printed.[33] Significantly, these were not made public, although copies were sent to the House of Commons, to the British embassies in Washington and Tokyo, and, from time to time, to persons who might discreetly use its contents to good effect.

If Sir John Pratt expected this latest effort to provide a definitive answer to Stimson's allegations, he was disappointed. During the next four years, evidence mounted that Stimson's version of history had embedded itself in the public mind and, as long as the Foreign Office refrained from making its private refutations public, Stimson's points were destined to prevail.

From sources as far afield as Manila and Peking, New York and Chicago, came repeated examples of repetition and embellishment of Stimson's story.[34] Some of these were so pernicious and damaging in the Foreign Office's view that Pratt wondered "whether it would now be desirable to try to secure publicity for our view in the U.S. press."[35] Although the British decided not to counterattack Stimson, concern over this question spawned a fresh memorandum by Pratt, copies of which were sent to the British embassy in Washington and the British Library of Information in New York.[36] Finally, late in 1937, the Foreign Office tried

unsuccessfully to encourage an independent, unofficial history of the Far Eastern situation. Pratt briefed Cambridge scholar and diplomatist Professor Edward H. Carr about the project, but Carr was too overworked to assume the task.[37]

A year later, Pratt launched a personal campaign to destroy the legend of British perfidy in 1932. Although by this time he had returned to private life, he carefully cleared each stage of his program with the Foreign Office before proceeding. He was spurred to action by a (London) Times lead article of 5 November 1938, reporting the remarks of Secretary of State Cordell Hull on American relations with Japan, that contained the now familiar charges of noncooperation.[38] Pratt responded with a letter offering a straightforward but subdued rebuttal. In a second letter, Pratt proposed to make apology for a poorly drafted Foreign Office communiqué of 9 January 1932, to which he attributed the "real cause of America's grievance."[39] The projected publication of this letter, which attempted to placate Stimson by admitting culpability to a lesser charge, produced extended discussion and lengthy debate in the Foreign Office. Despite an unsympathetic reception in the Far Eastern Department, both letters were approved for publication.[40]

Pratt's strenuous efforts to lay the matter to rest did not work. Instead, the effect of his public airing of the controversy was to stimulate further discussion. Over the next two years, this became increasingly evident; Foreign Office records for this period reveal a steady interest in the issue. In the United States, the British consulate in San Francisco and the British Library of Information in New York frequently rebutted Stimson's charges.[41] Meanwhile, the Foreign Office continued its active support of Pratt (whose letters had been published in the Times) and other campaigns challenging the well-established American view that Manchuria was lost for want of British support for Stimson's efforts.

During the summer of 1939, the ever-busy Pratt sent an eleven-page article in the form of a letter to the editor of the American journal, Amerasia, under a title suggested by the Foreign Office, "Did Britain fail to back America over Manchuria?"[42] Regarding it as "a most useful paper"

for replying "to the frequent enquiries which we receive on this subject," the Far Eastern Department ordered fifty copies of the communication. The primary American complaint against British Far Eastern policy, mused one official from an end-of-the-decade perspective rich with parallel, was

> not so much that Sir John Simon rebuffed Mr. Stimson as that we did not give a lead. St. George, whose business it is to fight dragons, refused on this occasion to do so. He followed up this refusal by a failure to fight dragons in Abyssinia, in Spain and in Czechoslovakia. When heroes fail to fight the public turns against them. I think therefore that our present European policy, if it is successful, will prove the most effective silencer of the Simon-Stimson controversy.[43]

Hereafter, discussion of the controversy moved predominantly on a level of public debate. From Sir John Pratt's prolific pen there continued to flow a torrent of articulate briefs for the British position. Far from flagging in interest, his determination to represent a good cause seemed indeed to increase with age. To Lord Lothian, he wrote in rage and frustration that "the most serious aspect of this matter is that our own intellectuals and idealists (God forgive them for all the evil they have brought upon us!) eagerly accept American calumnies as the truth."[44]

Publicists other than Pratt recognized the same necessity for keeping up the good fight. In August, 1939, for example, Sir Roland Evans of the Liberal National Organization, assisted by Pratt, supervised the printing of a pamphlet on "The Truth about Britain, the League and Manchuria." Due to the outbreak of war, however, its circulation was restricted, and thus the pamphlet was not generally available until 1941.[45] The Royal Institute of International Affairs, meanwhile, had already announced its intention to publish a review of British Far Eastern policy, with a section devoted to clearing up misunderstanding over the Simon-Stimson controversy.[46] In April, 1940, the British Library of Information in New York prepared a twelve-page mimeographed memorandum entitled "The Japanese Conquest of Manchuria: British and American

Policies." Completed with the assistance of Lord Lothian, His Majesty's ambassador in Washington, the memorandum was given a "very limited distribution among friendly and interested persons," with perhaps a second, abbreviated edition reaching a slightly wider audience.[47]

However pressed by other business, Sir John Pratt continued to expend effort on the Simon-Stimson controversy. He indefatigably answered critics in the press when they dared allude to the Stimson allegations, including one caustic letter to the editor of the New York Herald Tribune.[48] This letter he produced in mimeographed form, together with his two Times letters of November, 1938 and the Amerasia article of 1939, for distribution by the Foreign Office as it thought fit. Pratt also submitted the draft of another article for publication.[49]

Only when the Simon-Stimson controversy became stale and rather tiresome did the interest of the Foreign Office wane. With World War II in progress, to combat the Stimson myth any longer would have seemed a quixotic digression against "a psychological fact which no amount of explaining will wipe out."[50] The Foreign Office noted in December, 1940, that given American sentiment, "the Simon-Stimson controversy [had] lapsed into greater obscurity than usual."[51]

Sir John Simon himself, although he professed to harbor no bitterness, regarded Stimson's version as one "now unhappily crystallized in American history." One new development had given him some satisfaction, however. Lord Lothian revealed in November, 1940, that during a recent conversation with Stimson, after he had brought up the old story of British noncooperation in 1932, the former Secretary of State "was highly apologetic and all but ashamed of himself."[52]

Back in government as Secretary of War, Stimson's repentance appeared all the more evident the following January when he gave testimony before the Senate Foreign Relations Committee. He explained that his book on the Far Eastern crisis "was not at all in the shape of such a sweeping condemnation of Great Britain's Government as has been commonly . . . bandied about in our Press." Some clarification seemed necessary, for the British "did not

wholly refrain from making an effort to back us up." For the most part, they had exerted themselves effectively in the League of Nations. His only cause for mentioning this now, Stimson told the Senators, was to indicate that many who had not read his book had "mistakenly criticized" Great Britain "with my apparent authority."[53]

Despite the weakness of this recantation, which in reality was little more than a friendly gesture in wartime emergency, Sir John Simon cited it with victorious delight in several pieces of correspondence. Just as Sir John Pratt had done, he wrote regularly to correct the authors of erroneous views that appeared in various newspapers and books. He usually sent along as well a copy of Sir Roland Evans' pamphlet, "The Truth about Britain, the League and Manchuria."[54]

Not all of Simon's correspondents pliantly accepted his personal efforts at historical revisionism, and simply regarded the Evans' tract for what it was--a case of special pleading. One of these, Lord David Davies, not only held his ground in arguing that the British government had let the Americans down, but cited as authority a recent interview with Stimson. Any apparent change in the Secretary of War, Simon should realize, had as its purpose the inducement of his fellow Americans to join in the fight against the fascist dictators.[55]

Sir John Pratt finally addressed the problem of "Manchuria and Some Myths" in a long-contemplated book on War and Politics in China, published in 1943. Henry Stimson also kept alive the substance of his original complaint against Great Britain. Although stated more moderately than he had in The Far Eastern Crisis, he presented his arguments anew in 1947 in On Active Service in Peace and War, an account co-authored with McGeorge Bundy.[56] Until the end of his life, one correspondent informed Sir John Simon, Stimson maintained that he had been correct, and that "the essential truth was in his book The Far Eastern Crisis."[57]

In an autobiographical record of his own career published a year before his death in 1953, Simon produced a very brief and rather bland statement of the British position during the Manchurian crisis.[58] He doubted

102

whether further public challenge to the Stimson myth, especially by himself, would serve any useful purpose. Nevertheless, he was much enheartened by the appearance a few months later of a book by Professor Reginald Bassett of the London School of Economics. Entitled Democracy and Foreign Policy: A Case History, The Sino-Japanese Dispute, 1931-33, Bassett's book covered the troublesome history of the Simon-Stimson controversy in England and its effects upon public opinion.[59] Although written without access to official Foreign Office archives, the study amounted to a vindication of Sir John Simon's personal role in shaping British Far Eastern policy in the early 1930's, and of the larger policy itself.

If Bassett's book revived Simon's hope that something had been "gained for the cause of historical truth," there remained the apprehension that Stimson's allegations against the British had become firmly believed by this time, especially in the United States.[60] Ample evidence that this was indeed the case came in a letter to Simon in October, 1952. The writer found that whatever the occasion or audience, Americans were convinced that the British government had rejected Stimson's offer of full cooperation. "I never met anyone, even among the professors and others working on League matters, who had faced the fact of the unqualified isolationism of the Hoover Administration." This illustrated "the unchanging demand, in relation to international policy, that Britain should not only take the initiative but also be ready to shoulder the burden!"[61]

Throughout this protracted controversy, Henry Stimson appears to have appreciated fully the fact that historical judgment would favor those who sought to check aggression over those who temporized. If this view is correct, then his complaint against the British in The Far Eastern Crisis stands out as a premeditated historical coup. A more charitable explanation would be that Stimson combined a predilection to complain with an incomplete recollection of facts and details when he wrote his book. In either case, Stimson's viewpoint prevailed in the United States and in England. As one writer observed in 1939, Stimson seemed to be "the one American official since the war who was willing to break the isolation policy and to share with Britain the responsibility of naval power in preserving the orderly process," and this explained the

tendency to blame Britain for not taking advantage of the tentative steps toward cooperation.[62]

Beyond any doubt, Stimson in 1936 magnified any feelings he actually held in 1932 about British refusal to follow his lead in the note of 7 January. Even as he invited Anglo-American cooperation, he confided in his diary that England's preoccupation with its many troubles might dampen its enterprising spirit. His later complaint that the "British let us down" on the 7 January note appears on examination of the documentary record more in the nature of pejorative reflection than accurate recollection. Contemporary evidence indicates that Stimson believed that Great Britain had passed over an excellent opportunity for winning friendship with China, but that is all. Even after the onset of the Shanghai crisis late in January, 1932, Ambassador Sir Ronald Lindsay observed that Stimson had not complained when Great Britain failed to associate itself with his recent note to Japan.

As for the 7 January note being a first step in a "systematic effort to rally world opinion against Japanese sabotage of [the] post-war multilateral peace treaties to which she was a party," it is difficult to verify that such a plan actually existed and, granting that one did, it was far from systematic. The more durable impression is one of Stimson groping for the most expedient measures to censure Japan and articulate nonrecognition. Before the Cabinet, he was an ardent advocate of diplomatic bluff, notwithstanding American naval weakness in the Far East. One observes in Stimson's behavior more determination than system and more eloquence than action.

During February, 1932, Stimson became increasingly suspicious of the British government and to a lesser degree of Sir John Simon. Yet his criticism of their refusal to associate with his Nine Power declaration seems unjustified. By 16 February Stimson himself recognized that it was not the most desirable means for handling the problem. There is scant evidence to support the thesis that he really expected the cumulative effect of these efforts to produce a conference. Finally, it is difficult to understand Stimson's dissatisfaction with the wording of any but the 11 March resolution of the League supporting a policy of nonrecogni-

tion. Even this final version took on every appearance of a Pyrrhic victory of polemic virtue.

During the course of the Simon-Stimson controversy, the Foreign Office proclaimed itself the champion of the doctrine of nonrecognition before the League, and therefore of complete cooperation with the United States. Yet Stimson's pique at having been spurned was justifiable. The Foreign Office was demonstrably biased in favor of Japan, fault-finding in its estimation of China, and lukewarm toward cooperation with America in the Far East. It could defend, as Pratt and others did repeatedly, its policies which were narrowly correct and proper but which otherwise appeared transparently benevolent and cautious toward a Japan it was loathe to antagonize. As one author has suggested, the Foreign Office suffered from a tendency to search for constraints while looking for a decision.[63]

The principle of close Anglo-American cooperation, repeatedly stressed as an imperative need, seemed to the Foreign Office one most applicable to some other area promising tangible results, as in Europe. More often than not, the Foreign Office disdainfully regarded the eccentric Stimson as a problem quite as embarrassing as the fact of Japanese aggression itself. Consequently, it often acted in a manner calculated to threaten rapport. In the Foreign Office more than in the American State Department there was divided counsel, but its predominant and characteristic expression was one of contempt for China and friendship at any cost for Japan. In tension between the two, Anglo-American cooperation became an object of manipulation for the purpose of neutralizing the moral fervor of the United States. British policy toward the League, at least after some of its initial blunders of excessive zeal in the early stages of the Manchurian crisis, was substantially the same.

The protracted Simon-Stimson controversy must be taken as an index of the importance of the events upon which it focused. Earlier than most in the troubled 1930's, Stimson tried to mend his historical fences--not to prove his innocence but to demonstrate his prescience. If today his arguments can no longer be accepted completely, he must at least be credited with making them part of the common historical conscience.

[1]Sir John Simon to Ramsey MacDonald, 3 October 1934, Sir John Simon Papers, British Foreign Office records, 800/291, Public Record Office, London (hereafter cited by FO volume and document file number).

[2] For background, consult Robert H. Ferrell, American Diplomacy in the Great Depression: Hoover-Stimson Foreign Policy, 1929-1933 (New Haven, 1957); A. Whitney Griswold, The Far Eastern Policy of the United States (New Haven, 1938); William R. Lewis, British Strategy in the Far East, 1919-1939 (London, 1971), pp. 171-205; Dorothy Borg, The United States and the Far Eastern Crisis of 1933-1938: From the Manchurian Incident through the Initial State of the Undeclared Sino-Japanese War (Cambridge, 1966), pp. 1-45; Christopher Thorne, "The Shanghai Crisis of 1932: The Basis of British Policy," American Historical Review 75 (October 1970): 1616-39.

[3]Evans to Simon, 17 October 1940, Sir John Simon Papers (Private Collection), Institute of Historical Research, University of London, London (hereafter cited as Simon Papers [Private Collection]); John F. Kennedy, Why England Slept (New York, 1961 [1940]), pp. 33-34.

[4]15 December 1933, FO371/16612/A9235.

[5]Ibid.

[6]Vansittart to Sir Ronald Lindsay, [?] September 1934, vol. 109, Stanley Baldwin Papers, Cambridge University Library, Cambridge, England.

[7]Ibid.

[8]Lord Philip Lothian to Sir John Pratt, 31 May 1939, FO371/23474/F6578.

[9]Stanley K. Hornbeck to Norman Davis, 13 December 1934, "'Far Eastern Crisis' Manuscript and Notes," Henry L. Stimson Papers, Sterling Memorial Library, Yale University, New Haven, Connecticut (hereafter cited as Stimson Papers).

[10]Ibid.

[11]Armin Rappaport, Henry L. Stimson and Japan, 1931-33 (Chicago, 1963), pp. 140-42, presents the Borah letter as something of a "diplomatic masterpiece."

[12]Hornbeck to Davis, 13 December 1934, "'Far Eastern Crisis' Manuscript and Notes," including Diary No. 27, pp. 96-99, Stimson Papers.

[13]Memorandum by Simon, 11 December 1934, Simon Papers, FO800/289.

[14]Memorandum by Pratt, 10 December 1934, FO371/18156/F7488; Sir Victor Wellesley to Lindsay, 10 January 1935, FO371/18156/FO800/290.

[15]Lindsay to Simon, 13 February 1935, Simon Papers, FO80/290; Stimson's notes to Japan and China on 7 January 1932 took the position that "in view of the present situation and of its own rights and obligations..., the American Government deems it to be its duty to notify both the Government of the Chinese Republic and the Imperial Japanese Government that it cannot admit the legality of any situation de facto nor does it intend to recognize any treaty or agreement entered into between those Governments, or agents thereof, which may impair the treaty rights of the United States or its citizens in China, including those which relate to the sovereignty, the independence, or the territorial and administrative integrity of the Republic of China, or to the international policy relating to China, commonly known as the open door policy; and that it does not intend to recognize any situation, treaty or agreement which may be brought about by means contrary to the covenants and obligations of the Pact of Paris of August 27, 1928, to which Treaty both China and Japan as well as the United States, are parties." Stimson to Peck, 7 January 1932, U. S. Department of State, Foreign Relations of the United States (hereafter cited as FRUS), 1932 (Washington, 1948), 3:7-8.

[16]Simon to Lindsay, 12 March 1935, Simon Papers, FO800/290.

[17]Ibid.

[18]Taking advantage of the unstable conditions produced by World War I, Japan followed its seizure of German Far Eastern possessions and holdings with a group of Twenty-One Demands upon China. Accepted as presented, they would have seriously impaired Chinese sovereignty. The more objectionable ones were withdrawn, but China under duress acquiesced to the others. The United States responded with a note insisting upon maintenance of an "open door" policy, the political and territorial integrity of China, and its own treaty rights in China. Thus, to some extent, Stimson's "doctrine" of nonrecognition in 1932 was adumbrated in 1915.

[19]Memorandum by Pratt, 25 February 1935, Simon Papers, FO 800/290.

[20]Draft letter by Pratt to Sir Arthur Salter, 18 April 1935, FO371/19324/ F2631.

[21]Stimson to Lord Lothian, enclosure in Austen Chamberlain to Sir Robert Vansittart, 3 April 1935, FO371/19324/F2767.

²²Minute [internal departmental marginalia, critiques, and opinions], 26 April 1935, FO371/19324/F2767; Memorandum by Pratt, 12 April 1935, ibid.

²³Memorandum by Pratt, 12 April 1935, ibid.

²⁴Ibid.

²⁵"The Sino-Japanese Dispute," 15 July 1935, FO371/19261/F4961.

²⁶Parliamentary Question, 29 April 1936, FO371/20275/F2412.

²⁷Minute, 10 October 1936, ibid.

²⁸"Memorandum concerning Allegations by Mr. Stimson that His Majesty's Government failed to cooperate with the United States Government in 1932 in connection with the Sino-Japanese Dispute," 1 October 1936, ibid.; Henry L. Stimson, The Far Eastern Crisis: Recollections and Observations (New York, 1936), pp. 161-65.

²⁹"Memorandum concerning Allegations. . .," 1 October 1936, FO371/20275/F6485.

³⁰Ibid.

³¹Ibid.

³²Ibid.

³³Minute by Pratt, 19 July 1936, ibid. The obvious fact that Pratt wrote this memorandum two or three months before it was printed on 1 October accounts for the discrepancy in dates.

³⁴W. P. W. Turner to Lindsay, 23 September 1937, FO371/20275/F8421; Cowan to Far Eastern Department, 19 September 1937, FO371/20275/F6719; Robert Wilberforce, of the British Library of Information, to R. A. Leeper, in the Foreign Office, 1 November 1937, enclosing a copy of an article appearing in Forum, by Norman Angell, entitled "The Triumph of Lawlessness: The Peaceful Nations Take it Lying Down," FO371/20275/F9278; Agnus Fletcher, of the British Library of Information, to the Far Eastern Department, 30 August 1937, FO371/20955/F6237.

³⁵Draft letter from Anthony Eden to C. T. Culverwell, [n.d.], FO371/21022/F10311.

³⁶Minute by Pratt, 9 December 1937, FO371/21022/F10718.

³⁷Minutes by Pratt, 16 September and 20 October 1937, FO371/20955/F6237.

³⁸Clippings of Times articles, FO371/22158/F11896.

³⁹Minute by Howe, 19 November, and Pratt to Howe, 16 November 1938, FO371/22158/F12629.

[40]Minute by [indecipherable initials], 10 November 1938, FO371/22158/F12223; Minute by Howe, 19 November 1938, FO371/22158/F12629.

[41][Unsigned] minute, 6 January 1939, FO371/23474/F154; British Library of Information to News Department, Foreign Office, 7 March 1939, FO371/23474/F2762.

[42]11 July 1939, FO371/23474/F2762. For an unamended copy, see Simon Papers (Private Collection). It was written in answer to Ian F. G. Milner, "Anglo-American Cooperation in the Far East," Amerasia 3 (May 1939): 124-27. Pratt's article appeared in the August, 1939 issue.

[43]Minute by A. A. Dudley, 22 July 1939, FO371/23474/F7456.

[44]Pratt to Lord Lothian, 29 August 1939, ibid.

[45]FO371/23474/F9906; copy also in the Simon Papers (Private Collection) together with bibliographic information in the "General Notes: of the Liberal National Organization, April 10, 1941."

[46]S. A. Heald to C. F. Warner, 12 April 1939, FO371/23474/F2762.

[47]Enclosure, British Library of Information to News Department, Foreign Office, 29 April 1940, FO371/24693/F3257.

[48]Pratt to the editor of the New York Herald Tribune, 27 August 1939, FO371/24673/F1365.

[49]Pratt to D. J. Scott, 23 February 1940, ibid.

[50]Minute by J. N. Whitehead, 1 April 1940, FO371/24724/F2334.

[51]Draft letter from the Far Eastern Department to the British Library of Information, 2 December 1940, sending copies of Evans' pamphlet, FO371/ 24693/F5329.

[52]Lord Lothian to Simon, 19 November 1940, Simon Papers (Private Collection).

[53]"Extract from minutes of United States Senate Committee on Foreign Relations, January 29th, 1941," ibid.

[54]Simon to Lord David Davies, 4 April 1941, ibid.

[55]Davies to Simon, 11 June 1941, ibid.; see also correspondence between Lord Cecil and Lord Davies in 1939, Viscount Cecil of Chelwood Papers, No. 51138, British Museum, London.

[56]Henry L. Stimson and McGeorge Bundy, On Active Service in Peace and War (New York, 1948).

[57]S. K. Ratcliffe to Simon, 9 October 1952, Simon Papers (Private Collection).

[58]John A. Simon, Retrospect: The Memoirs of Viscount Simon (London, 1952).

[59]Reginald Bassett, Democracy and Foreign Policy: A Case History, the Sino-Japanese Dispute, 1931-1933 (London, 1952).

[60]Simon to Bassett, 5 February 1953, Simon Papers (Private Collection).

[61]Ratcliffe to Simon, 9 October 1952, ibid.

[62]Bruce C. Hopper to Captain Taylor, 22 February 1939, FO371/ 23474/F2762.

[63]Thorne, "The Shanghai Crisis of 1932," pp. 1616-17.

SOVIET-AMERICAN RELATIONS AND THE EAST-ASIAN IMBROGLIO, 1933-1941

Judith Papachristou

For more than a quarter of a century after World War II, a debate about prewar American policy toward Japan dominated the writings of American diplomatic historians who alternately attacked and defended President Franklin D. Roosevelt's response to Japanese expansion.[1] Recent scholarship reveals the minor role of the United States in influencing Japanese history during the 1930's, and the debate is losing its relevance.[2]

There were few American alternatives that could have had dramatic impact on Japan in those years. One such choice was for the United States to acquiesce in Japan's expansionist goals in China, a position the Roosevelt administration never seriously considered.[3] Another option, judged equally unfeasible during most of the isolationist decade, was to oppose Japan in China by military means. A third possibility--alliance or collaboration with the Soviet Union to deter Japan--was possibly the most practicable of these alternatives. Yet American historians have generally neglected the importance of the Soviet Union in the development of United States-Japanese policy during the prewar era. In fact, little is known about the halting steps taken by President Roosevelt toward cooperation with the Russians against Japanese expansion in East Asia. This paper is concerned with those steps and the course of American-Soviet relations in East Asia.

Roosevelt understood and appreciated the potential of the interrelations of the United States, the Soviet Union, and Japan; and he attempted to use Soviet-American relations to influence Japan. Moreover, he seriously explored cooperation and collaboration with the Soviet Union and on several occasions made specific diplomatic moves in that direction. But powerful forces operated against cooperation with the Russians: American public opinion, Roosevelt's own political considerations, rigid distrust of and opposition to the Soviets within the American government, and, finally, Roosevelt's interpretation of the balance of power in East Asia.

Assuming the Presidency in 1933, Roosevelt inherited long-standing attitudes and policies about the American role in East Asia. Fundamental to these was the belief that East Asia, especially North China, was a region of major concern to the United States because of economic and political interests in the area. The United States, Japan, and Russia had been major protagonists in North China since the late nineteenth century. Indeed, when Russo-Japanese rivalries in East Asia flared into war in 1905, President Theodore Roosevelt observed that Japan was "playing our game" by challenging Russia's ambitions.[4] "Our game," as Theodore Roosevelt understood it, meant preventing any one power from dominating North China and preserving economic opportunity in that area of China for Americans. The United States pursued this "Open Door" policy at least until Franklin D. Roosevelt's time. During these decades, World War I, the Russian Revolution, and the turmoil of the 1920's had severely restricted Russia's role in East Asia; and Japan emerged as the threat to the balance of power and the Open Door.

The Japanese made threatening moves against China in the late 1920's. In 1931 they seized Manchuria, and in 1933 Japanese troops began to advance into China's northern provinces. Russian guards and Japanese soldiers faced each other along the lengthy Soviet-Manchurian border; disagreements and border clashes occurred. Even as Franklin D. Roosevelt was inaugurated for his first term as President, the Russians and the Japanese were preparing for war.

One of Roosevelt's first steps in office was to prepare for the resumption of diplomatic relations with the Soviet Union. To the new President, recognition of Russia was long overdue; the communist leadership had controlled the Russian landmass for over a decade and other nations had established relations with the Soviet regime. In establishing diplomatic contact, Roosevelt also hoped a Soviet-American rapprochement would restrain Japan, prevent war in the Far East, and maintain the existing balance of power.[5]

The implications of a Soviet-American rapprochement were apparent to all three protagonists. The Russians predicted that war was inevitable without some cooperation

with the United States, and they suggested that recognition would enable both countries to help each other in East Asia. The Japanese, for their part, worried that diplomatic recognition presaged Russian-American collaboration and possible American financial aid to the Soviets.[6]

The resumption of diplomatic ties was widely interpreted as a move toward preserving peace in the Pacific, although few observers understood how the two powers would act to keep the peace. Discerning onlookers noted, though, that the first Soviet ambassador to the United States, Alexander Troyanovsky, was considered a Japanese expert. Similarly, the appointment of William C. Bullitt as American ambassador suggested cooperation between the two powers since Bullitt had long favored closer Soviet-American ties.[7]

Both American and Soviet observers credited recognition with being "the largest single deterrent" to a Russo-Japanese war.[8] Nonetheless, the psychological effects of establishing diplomatic relations did not satisfy Soviet security needs. During and after recognition negotiations, the Soviets urged the United States to take specific steps toward cooperative actions and policies. In keeping with their suggestion, special envoy Maxim Litvinov proposed a Soviet-American nonaggression pact to Roosevelt.[9] In Moscow, Ambassador Bullitt noted two themes pervading his talks with Joseph Stalin and other top Soviet leaders: the imminence of a Japanese attack on Russia and the necessity for American cooperation to preserve a Pacific peace. Meanwhile, the Soviets urged the United States to send army, navy, and air attachés to Moscow to establish close working relations with their Russian counterparts. These American personnel, the Soviets hoped, would provide military advice, particularly on air defenses. Other Soviet requests were for steel rails for double-tracking the Trans-Siberian Railroad; support for a nonaggression pact between the United States, the Soviet Union, China, and Japan; the visit of an American squadron or warship to Vladivostok or Leningrad; and a commitment from the United States, France, and Britain that Japan would not get loans or credits for military uses.[10]

The United States spurned these Soviet overtures and Russian offers of cooperation were never tested.[11]

Fortuitously for the Soviets, American rejection of collaboration coincided with a decrease in the likelihood of Japanese aggression. Then in March, 1935, the Russians sold the Chinese Eastern Railroad, a move tantamount to Soviet withdrawal from Manchuria and a step toward improving Russo-Japanese relations. Although conflict with Japan continued along the Manchurian-Mongolian border and disagreement persisted over the implementation of the Chinese Eastern sale agreement and the ownership of small islands in the Amur River, the danger of a second Russo-Japanese war had lessened.[12]

Meanwhile, Soviet-American relations were deteriorating rapidly. Roosevelt's decision to recognize the Soviet Union had evoked both skepticism and opposition within his administration, especially from influential members of the State Department such as Robert Kelley, chief of the department's Russian Division, and William Phillips, Under-secretary of State, whose distrust and antagonism to the Soviets were not tempered by the President's Realpolitik arguments. On their insistence, recognition was accompanied by a series of mutual commitments concerning Soviet propaganda activities in the United States and a memorandum of intent to settle outstanding debts and claims against the Soviet Union.[13]

For many Americans the most persuasive argument for recognition had been the promise of increased trade between the two nations and its resulting economic benefits to the American economy. Hampered by the Soviets' lack of credits, however, and because of American claims against Russia, trade did not grow appreciably. A further roadblock to trade appeared in April, 1934, when Congress passed the Johnson Act prohibiting government loans to nations in default of World War I obligations. This meant that the United States could not legally extend a loan to the Russians until they repaid outstanding debts; they, in turn, would not compromise on payment of the debts without compensatory loans. While diplomats wrestled with these issues through 1934, they were unable to agree on a mutually acceptable solution.

As talks continued into 1935, American irritation and impatience increased until 31 January when Secretary of State Cordell Hull ended the discussions. The embassy in

Moscow was informed that the government was contemplating a variety of actions to demonstrate its disappointment and annoyance at the failure of the debt discussions: the Export-Import Bank, founded to aid trade with Russia, would be abolished; American military attachés in Moscow would be called home; and the number of diplomatic and consular personnel in Russia would be decreased.[14]

Relations deteriorated further during the summer of 1935 when the Third International held its world-wide meeting in Moscow. To many Americans, discussion at the conference of a Comintern program for the spread of propaganda in the United States constituted a brazen violation of the Roosevelt-Litvinov agreements accompanying recognition, and several government officials publicly labelled it as such. A disappointed and disillusioned Ambassador Bullitt accused the Soviet government of treachery; his harsh statements received enthusiastic applause in Congress where irate politicians spoke of breaking diplomatic relations with the Soviet Union, deporting radical agitators, and curtailing immigration. Public opinion appeared to approve the hardening tone in official statements and the decision to terminate the debt discussions.[15]

During this time, policymakers within the administration were "at the Oriental crossroads of decision," as Secretary Hull put it. Faced with Japanese advances, the United States could withdraw from East Asia to avoid conflict, accepting the loss of what it deemed its treaty rights and acquiescing in Japanese expansion. The Roosevelt administration never considered withdrawal seriously, however. As ambassador to Japan Joseph C. Grew wrote in December, 1934, "Our government has not the slightest intention of relinquishing the legitimate rights, vested interest, non-discriminatory privilege for equal opportunity and healthful commercial development of the United States in the Far East."[16]

Though committed to the maintenance and defense of American interests, the administration was severely limited in its actions by isolationism in Congress and the country. In addition, disagreement among government officials hampered the development of a clear-cut program toward Japan. Policymakers sought means of deterring Japanese

expansionism while encouraging and supporting her moderate politicians to seek an accommodation of Japanese ambition and American interests. The result was a compromise policy that included unyielding opposition to Japanese expansion in East Asia, insistence on American rights and interests, increased naval construction, as well as diplomatic efforts to minimize friction between Japan and the United States.[17]

Cooperation with the Soviets was one obvious means of demonstrating opposition to Japanese expansion. Realizing this, Stanley K. Hornbeck, a State Department adviser on Asian affairs and a stern opponent of Japanese expansionism, pointed out early in 1935 that American commercial and economic cooperation with the Soviet Union could increase Soviet strength and discourage reckless moves by the Japanese. It was to our advantage, Hornbeck claimed, to reach a settlement of financial issues with Russia and increase trade between the two nations.[18]

Hornbeck's suggestion was impractical in light of domestic and international affairs, however. In Russia the sensational purge trials of 1936 and 1937 confirmed the widespread view that Russia was barbarous and treacherous. Furthermore, Roosevelt, a candidate for re-election in 1936, was susceptible to political attack for association with the Soviet Union. During the election campaign, he was repeatedly accused of leaning to the political left, and influential newspapers owned by William Randolph Hearst labelled Roosevelt the unofficial candidate of the Comintern. Father Charles Coughlin, the radio priest from Detroit, Michigan, challenged Roosevelt to repudiate the support of the American Communist party, and the New York Times advised him to do so.[19] On the international scene, there were fears that Soviet-American action might be threatening and provocative to Japan. Consequently, Soviet requests to participate in both the preliminary talks and the regular meetings of the London Naval Conference met with American opposition.[20]

Still, American policymakers did not forget the significance of Soviet power in East Asia, and threatening events in Europe also made them aware of the need for improvement in Soviet-American relations. Thus, President Roosevelt and State Department officials told Joseph E.

Davies, leaving for Moscow as Bullitt's successor, that good relations with the Russians were of "real importance" in view of the world situation. Departing for the Soviet capital at the height of the publicized purge trials, the new ambassador was cautioned to act with reserve, to restrain his friendliness, and to take the position that the Soviets must initiate any negotiations of the debt issue.[21]

While there was no resolution of the debt-loan issue, the United States late in 1936 began considering Russian requests to purchase ships and airplanes from American manufacturers. State Department officials had approved the talks, and the President personally intervened with American businessmen and other government officials on behalf of Soviet purchasers.[22] Then in November, 1936, the German-Japanese Anti-Comintern Pact was signed, accompanied by disturbing rumors of a secret alliance to partition the Pacific between the two nations. Evaluating the agreement, Far Eastern experts concluded that neither Germany nor Japan was ready for war against Russia. Noting that Japan might fight either with Britain, the United States, or the Soviet Union, the specialists urged continued and increased Anglo-American cooperation. They warned that war between Russia and Germany and Japan was hazardous to American interests and recommended that the United States also seek to prevent a Japanese-Soviet war.[23]

Prevention of a Russo-Japanese war, which had earlier influenced Roosevelt's recognition of the Soviets in 1933, remained a constant component of American policy in the Pacific throughout the thirties. Even some of the staunchest anti-Soviets agreed that such a conflict would not be in America's interest. Bullitt, for example, recommended that the United States do everything possible to prevent a Russo-Japanese war, which he feared would upset the balance of power in East Asia and result in China's loss of independence.[24] Thus, despite strong and antagonistic reactions to the purge trials and continuing irritation at the unresolved issue of debts and loans, American policy in 1936 was governed by the same interest as in 1933.

The outbreak of the Sino-Japanese war in July, 1937, provoked a critical examination of American policy.[25] Those

117

State Department men who had persistently opposed cooperation with the Soviets before and after recognition again challenged the advisability of any kind of agreement with them in East Asia. Worried about Soviet influence in China, they called attention to the dependent relation between Russia and Outer Mongolia, to links between Russian and Chinese communists, and to the increase of Soviet influence in Sinkiang. When the Chinese announced a Sino-Soviet nonaggression pact on 29 August, the State Department critics interpreted the pact as a portent of increasing Soviet influence in China. J. Pierrepont Moffat, chief of the department's Division of European Affairs and son-in-law of Ambassador Grew, argued that if Japanese advances in East Asia were stopped by United States pressure, "China would merely fall prey to Russian anarchy." We would, Moffat predicted, "have the whole job to do over again and a worse one."[26]

Moffat, who claimed to and probably did represent the views of the anti-Soviet bloc in the State Department, said, in effect, that Japanese ascendancy in China was preferable to Soviet domination.[27] The remark reveals serious differences between the President and an important segment of the State Department; the President did not want domination of China by either Japan or Russia, but Japan was the immediate threat. Without the anti-Soviet outlook of these State Department officials, and fearful of Japan's increasing naval strength, Roosevelt was inclined to cooperate with the Soviets. It was a policy that involved risk, but one less dangerous than the threat of Japanese expansion.[28]

Despite reservations within the State Department, as well as anti-Soviet feeling in Congress and the public, the Japanese attack on China drew the United States and the Soviet Union closer together, and, largely because of its determination to take a stronger stand against Japanese advances, the United States moved to improve Russian relations. In mid-July, 1937, negotiations for renewal of the Soviet-American commercial treaty proceeded with little trouble, and the agreement was amended to expand and facilitate certain trade.[29] At the end of July, the two countries indulged in an unusual display of friendliness when vessels of the American fleet visited Vladivostok for four days and were greeted with effusive hospitality: croquet, football games, baseball, a circus, musicals,

receptions, and dances testified to the American welcome. In <u>Pravda</u> and <u>Izvestia</u>, the visit evoked a rash of friendly articles.[30]

A new threat to stability in East Asia soon strengthened Roosevelt's inclination toward closer relations with the Russians. In July, 1938, the Russians clashed with the Japanese at Changkufeng, near the borders of Manchuria, Korea, and the Soviet Union. For weeks heavy fighting raged between well-prepared troops equipped with bombers, tanks, and artillery. The specter of a Russo-Japanese war hung over Asia again. Only after weeks of negotiations was a committee formed to resolve the border controversy that had set off the explosion.[31]

Earlier in 1938, the administration had taken a dramatic step when the President authorized Ambassador Davies to explore an exchange of Asian military and naval information with the Russians. It seemed wise, Roosevelt told Davies, to share intelligence considering the similar objectives the two countries had in that part of the world. Early in June, Davies discussed the proposal with Stalin and Foreign Minister V. M. Molotov. He assured the Russians that the information exchanged would be limited to four men in the United States: the President, the Secretary of State, the Undersecretary, and a liaison officer. To Davies' surprise, both Stalin and Molotov responded favorably, but they insisted that their interest in the proposal be kept confidential. The Russians expressed concern about the identity of the liaison officer; they had no confidence in certain Americans. When Davies mentioned Lieutenant Colonel Philip R. Faymonville, the American military attaché in Moscow, both Stalin and Molotov reacted favorably. Their response would not have surprised many of the anti-Soviet bloc in the State Department who considered Faymonville to have a "pro-Russian" bias. At the least, he was notably more sympathetic to the Soviet experiment than many diplomats.[32]

Davies returned home toward the end of June on department orders. In addition to the positive response to Roosevelt's military exchange program, he brought back a Soviet proposal for partial solution of the nagging debt controversy, which Stalin claimed he was eager to resolve. According to Davies, the Russians agreed to pay the debt

119

of the Kerensky Provisional Government, up to $50 million, contingent upon the granting of a ten year, $200 million line of credit at the prevailing interest rate. As for the debts of Russia's Tsarist regime and claims against that government, the Soviets adamantly refused to recognize any obligation. In Davies' view, "The Soviet Government [had] . . . reversed its position in connection with the debt settlement" and was sincerely endeavoring to end the bad feelings engendered by the failure of earlier debt negotiations.[33] The President was pleased with the Soviet attitude and instructed Davies to work out details with State Department personnel and with Russian commercial representatives in the United States so that the debt proposal could be presented to the Senate.[34]

Despite these hopeful signs, the proposal was never sent to the Senate. After Congress had rejected an administration recommendation for partial settlement of the Hungarian debt in the fall of 1938, Roosevelt decided to drop the Soviet agreement rather than risk another embarrassing defeat.[35] Davies never returned to Moscow, and one of his last official acts before assuming the ambassadorship to Belgium was to write to the Russian commercial representatives apologizing for the delay in resolving the debt issue and conveying his hope that someday an agreement would be reached.[36]

In January, 1939, Faymonville was recalled from his post as military attaché in Moscow. The President, who had previously extended the colonel's assignment for a year, decided to follow War and State Department recommendations to recall Faymonville despite Davies' suggestion that he remain in Moscow. No equivalent liaison officer replaced him, and Roosevelt's military information exchange proposal came to naught.[37]

Soviet attempts to purchase battleships also proved abortive. At the end of 1936, the Russians formed the Carp Export and Import Corporation to act as purchasing agent for American-built warships and aircraft. The State Department approved the contemplated sales, and in 1937 a contract was drawn up between the Russians and the Bethlehem Shipbuilding Corporation for the construction of a battleship destined, according to the Soviets, for service in the Pacific. Roosevelt approved the contract, as did

120

Chief of Naval Operations William Leahy, but from the beginning there was strong and unflagging opposition to the transaction within the Navy Department.[38] Through 1938 the Russians energetically pursued the purchase despite almost two years of frustration. Although Secretary Hull reiterated the administration's support and the President personally recommended speed, the sale was thwarted. The navy attributed delays to what it described as complications, while ship designers spoke of technical difficulties; then builders, concerned about losing favor with the navy, joined the public and succeeded in frustrating the sale. American manufacturers sold small arms and ammunition and airplanes to the Russians, but battleships for the Soviet Pacific fleet remained on the drawing boards.[39]

Soviet-American relations in Asia, like every other aspect of American foreign policy, were twisted into a new perspective by the world-shaking events of 1939. Peace ended in March when Hitler moved into Czechoslovakia; in September, Britain and France declared war on Germany when the Reich invaded Poland. Shortly before that, the Germans and the Soviets signed a nonaggression pact. Events in Europe underlined the link between Europe and Asia more clearly than ever before for American policy-makers: if Russia were entangled in East Asia, Germany was more free in Europe; if Russia were occupied by European affairs, Japan was less restricted in Asia. The Nazi-Soviet pact appeared to free both Germany and the Soviet Union from concern about each other's intentions. Consequently, some officials speculated that the pact would inhibit Japan and increase the chance of a peaceful settlement in the Pacific; some optimists even thought the pact might frighten Japan and lead her to renounce military ties with Germany and Italy.[40] The British, worried that a Russo-Japanese rapprochement would leave the United States alone against Japan and divert American interest and involvement from Europe, raised the possibility of an American settlement with Japan. Convinced that Japan and Russia would never reach a workable accommodation, however, Secretary Hull rejected out-of-hand an acceptance of any Japanese territorial gains.[41]

Despite Hull's certainty, American complacency concerning a Russo-Japanese settlement was shaken first by the Nazi-Soviet pact and then by a truce ending the

121

Soviet-Japanese border war and the creation of a commission to prevent such incidents by negotiating a boundary agreement. Cables from Grew in Tokyo and rumors of Russo-Japanese agreement over China, long a major stumbling block to Russo-Japanese friendship, further challenged American assumptions about Russia and Japan.[42] While a Far Eastern Division Memorandum prepared early in November concluded that any Soviet-Japanese rapprochement would be short-lived, a second memo only a few weeks later questioned whether American refusal to recognize or condone Japanese gains in China was not driving Japan toward the Soviet Union.[43] Despite such misgivings, the State Department adhered to its original position: Japanese-Soviet friendship was improbable. No matter what agreements were reached, Japan's distrust of the Soviets was so deep that she would neither reduce her forces in Manchuria or China nor feel free to move against American or English interests in East Asia. In sum, the United States need make no concessions to forestall a Russo-Japanese agreement.[44]

Soviet-American relations eroded rapidly after the Nazi-Soviet pact. Russia's attack on Poland in mid-September, the conclusion of Soviet pacts with Estonia, Latvia, and Lithuania, and finally the attack on Finland in November, 1939, worsened the situation. Steps initiated earlier for closer ties were reversed. The Navy Department, shipbuilders, and technical personnel resisted with renewed vehemence any battleship construction for the Russians. In November, 1939, the administration reversed its position and advised six leading shipbuilders not to obligate their facilities, now deemed necessary for national defense.[45] Soviet efforts to buy airplanes also collapsed: American manufacturers, outraged at the invasion of Finland, proposed to cancel all existing contracts.[46] On 2 December, with sympathies for the Finns running high, Roosevelt called for a moral embargo on the shipment of planes or equipment to nations carrying on "unprovoked bombing and machine-gunning of civilian populations from the air."

The anger behind demands from the public and many congressmen for a break in diplomatic relations with Russia did not obscure the administration's view of international relations. Roosevelt and Hull, aware that the Russo-

122

German agreement was fraught with difficulties and hopeful of preventing a Russo-Japanese understanding, sought to check further erosion of Soviet-American relations; early in 1940, they sought to prevent punitive legislation aimed at the Soviets.[47] Meanwhile, Soviet Ambassador Constantine Oumansky and Undersecretary Sumner Welles were holding talks through the spring and summer of 1940.[48] These conversations were unpleasant exchanges. Yet, given the perilousness of the international situation, neither side chose to end the talks.[49]

Momentous events took place in 1940. Germany's defeat of Holland and France exposed the bases and resources of Indo-China and the Netherlands East Indies to Japan. A Russo-Japanese boundary agreement was finally signed, raising once again the specter of a Russo-Japanese rapprochement. Then, Japan, Germany, and Italy signed the Tripartite Pact on 27 September, an agreement aimed ostensibly at the United States and Britain. Some Americans feared the alliance contained secret provisions for Soviet-Japanese ties or plans for Russo-Japanese cooperation in China.[50]

In light of these unsettling events, the United States moved quietly to eliminate friction with the Soviet Union. At the end of June, the administration seriously entertained Chinese suggestions for a three-way loan involving the United States, China, and the Soviet Union. Designed primarily to aid China, the program insinuated an improvement in Russo-American relations, which Roosevelt deemed desirable in order to "keep Russia on the fence so we can keep peace in the Pacific." The proposal foundered in the fury following Soviet incorporation of the Baltic states in June, 1940, but it was postponed not discarded.[51] The Welles-Oumansky talks continued through the summer of 1940 and into 1941 despite the Soviet takeover of Estonia, Latvia, and Lithuania. In fact, American concessions enabled resolution of several disputes concerning trade; the commercial treaty was amended and renewed; and in August, 1940, the United States gave the Soviets permission to charter tankers for use in the Pacific.[52] In the same month, over Hull's objections, Roosevelt authorized Secretary of the Treasury Henry Morgenthau to begin discussions concerning the three-way loan agreement with Oumansky.[53] As 1941 began, the United States ended the

moral embargo against Soviet trade and announced the opening of a consulate in Vladivostok to facilitate trade at that port. Behind the administration's actions lay the knowledge of Germany's plan to attack Russia (information Roosevelt shared with Stalin) and the President's concern for the impact on East Asia of a Russo-German war.[54]

On 13 April 1941, Russia and Japan signed a pact calling for peaceful relations and neutrality in case of an attack on one of them. Soviet eagerness to reach agreement seemed to reflect concern over Germany, and most members of the administration interpreted the pact as the result of German pressure on Russia.[55] But the treaty appeared also to increase the likelihood of an American-Japanese conflict. Accordingly, Soviet requests for machine tools and other materials were not filled, and the atmosphere of the Welles-Oumansky talks suggested a changing mood.[56] In reality, there was no substantive change in American policy in view of Hitler's imminent attack on Russia, which was expected to minimize if not destroy the significance of the Russo-Japanese agreement and to foster American-British-Soviet cooperation. When war actually occurred, Japan seemed more likely to move against Russia, preoccupied and weakened by the attack on her western front, than against European colonies in Southeast Asia.[57]

American statesmen dreaded a Russo-Japanese war not only because it would weaken the Soviets in Europe but also for its consequences in the Pacific. Such a conflict was likely to result in Japanese victory and occupation of the Siberian coast, giving Japan strategic advantages over the Aleutian Islands, the North Pacific, and Alaska.[58] Thus, a Far Eastern Division Memorandum noted that "Moves or gestures by the United States which would render Japan uncertain in regard to the intentions of the United States in the South Pacific would operate in the direction of preventing Japan from becoming involved in Siberia."[59] In keeping with this thinking about a Russo-Japanese war, the government considered actions such as direct aid to Russia and increased aid to Britain and China.[60]

The German attack on Russia on Sunday, 22 June 1941, plunged Japanese policymakers into debate about Japan's course. On 2 July 1941, an Imperial Conference set

Japan's future course, rejecting war against the Soviet Union in favor of an advance southward into Indo-China. Preparations were begun for fighting the United States and Britain. Although Roosevelt soon learned about the Japanese decision from intercepted and decoded messages, his attitude toward a possible Russo-Japanese confrontation did not change.[61] On 6 July, the President sent a message to Japanese Premier Fumimaro Konoye expressing "earnest hope" that Japan would not enter into hostilities against the Soviet Union. The Japanese responded with a warning that the situation in East Asia would change radically if the Soviet Union allied with Britain or if the United States sent war supplies to Russia via Vladivostok.[62] Undeterred by this threat, the United States announced its intention to ship supplies to the Soviet Union, and the first American gasoline shipment left for Vladivostok on 1 August amid much speculation about Japan's reactions when the ships entered Asian waters. Japan officially requested that the United States recall the tankers; they received no response.[63]

While the decision to aid Russia originated in the military needs of the European front, the State Department hoped that the threat of Anglo-American-Soviet cooperation would deter Japan.[64] Thus, no effort was made to conceal the decision in order to minimize friction with Japan. It was, instead, well publicized as were the mission to Moscow of presidential aide Harry Hopkins in late July and the Atlantic Conference proposal for a meeting of the three powers in Moscow.

In addition to sending aid to the Soviets via Vladivostok and dropping hints of Soviet-American collaboration in the Pacific, the administration took its most direct step toward confrontation with Japan by freezing all Japanese assets in the United States in the summer of 1941. This move, along with the decisions to cut off Japan's supply of oil and to stand firm against her drive south, had enormous consequences for the United States. The administration ignored the warnings of some State Department and Foreign Service officials that economic pressure on Japan would provoke an attack, and it also overrode the objections of American military advisers who cautioned the President that the country was unprepared for war.[65] Aware of these dangers, the administration

hoped economic pressure would intimidate rather than provoke Japan; it also calculated that the threat of Soviet-American collaboration and the danger of a war with both the United States and the Soviet Union would reinforce Japan's hesitation.[66] The course set during the summer of 1941 was followed in the fall. Close relations and cooperation with the Soviets were seen as a means of applying pressure on Japan while continuing friction between Russia and Japan seemed to ensure that Japan, though provoked by American pressure, would not risk retaliation against the United States or Britain.[67]

During the fall, the situation deteriorated steadily. A growing quantity of American material was shipped by way of Vladivostok despite Japanese protests and threats to close off the Sea of Japan and blockade the Soviet port. The administration believed the pronouncements were aimed primarily at the Japanese public.[68] Fresh border skirmishes between Russia and Japan stirred up war rumors, but with their knowledge from decoded messages, top administration officials were certain that Japan would not attack Russia.[69] On 30 November, the government received a decoded message in which Foreign Minister Shigenori Togo instructed Ambassador Hiroshi Oshima in Berlin to inform the Germans of grave danger of war between Japan and the United States and Britain. The administration turned its attention to military preparation; war with Japan seemed all but inevitable.[70]

The events of the 1930's in East Asia present a bewildering scene as Soviet-American relations changed constantly, veering in one direction and then another, responding to forces in Asia, Europe, and within the United States. Nonetheless, important elements of American policy can be discerned in the confusion.

One of these elements was the consistent appreciation by Roosevelt and most of his advisers of the interrelation-ship between the United States, the Soviet Union, and Japan in East Asia and the implications of this situation for East Asian diplomacy. Closely following this was the fundamental assumption of American policymakers that Russian and Japanese interests in East Asia were basically in conflict. Consequently, the administration believed a substantial and long-lasting Russo-Japanese rapprochement

was improbable and need not be feared by the United States. In effect, American thinking about East Asia took Russo-Japanese antagonism for granted.

Another element of American policy was the administration's realization that Japan regarded Soviet-American friendship and cooperation with foreboding. The three powers knew that such cooperation could bring considerable pressure to bear upon Japan to halt her expansion on the Asian mainland.

On several occasions, starting with recognition in 1933, the President took action toward the Soviet Union that exploited Japan's fear of Soviet-American collaboration. He also explored means of cooperation and took steps toward military and economic cooperation with the Russians. The United States, however, never developed the potential of cooperation with the Russians in Asia.

Many factors lay behind the failure of Soviet-American collaboration, as this study has revealed. Part of the explanation can be found in the nature of American policy toward Japan, a complex, confusing, and often contradictory response to Japanese expansion. While the President was determined to oppose and deter Japan, much of the country was equally determined to preserve American isolation from events in Asia and Europe. Moreover, there were serious disagreements among executive, State Department, and Foreign Service officials concerning the most effective response to Japan. Some officials feared that opposition would antagonize Japan and encourage her most expansionist politicians and militarists; they advocated a policy that tempered disapproval with caution and friendship. They hoped to encourage moderates within Japan and deter further aggression. Other American officials argued that only a strong stand would intimidate Japan; they believed such a stand would not lead to war but would force the Japanese to face the consequences of their actions in Asia. The policy that resulted reflected both of these viewpoints. Its contradictory and vague nature was rationalized by some who maintained that keeping Japan guessing about American intentions might also deter her.

In this context, working with the Soviets excited suspicions among those who feared antagonizing Japan.

Throughout the thirties, such officials blocked the development of cooperation. It was not until military considerations in Europe necessitated supplying the Russians and when efforts to persuade Japan to desist from her adventuring had been abandoned that a spirit of cooperation developed.

Another explanation for the failure of cooperation lies in the diplomatic relations between the two nations. Recognition in 1933 provided only a temporary improvement in Soviet-American affairs. Throughout the thirties, misunderstanding and distrust characterized Soviet-American diplomacy. There was disagreement over Russia's debts, unfulfilled expectations of trade, criticism of the International, the Soviet purge trials, the Nazi-Soviet pact, the Russian invasion of Poland, the Russo-Finnish war, and the Russian advance into the Baltic states. Not until Hitler's attack on Russia in 1941 did the United States and Russia even contemplate a policy of cooperation in Asia.

Most important, there existed within the State Department and other parts of the government influential and determined men who had opposed recognition in 1933 and who continued to oppose and obstruct steps toward the resolution of differences between the two countries throughout the 1930's. These officials constituted a serious impediment to the policy of cooperation in East Asia. They not only argued against working with the Soviets, but they actively tried to prevent it with their insistence on the primacy of the debt issue, with their opposition to Faymonville's extended term in Moscow, and by their obstruction of battleship construction.

The domestic political scene also presented a formidable obstacle to Soviet-American cooperation as Roosevelt's political opponents and some of the press criticized his domestic reforms for being socialistic and accused the President of leaning too far to the political left to be a loyal American. Finding his domestic policies increasingly controversial, Roosevelt was clearly not prepared to risk further political damage by fostering Soviet-American friendship, that is, until the dangers of international war outweighed domestic political considerations.

Yet another factor helps explain the failure of the Roosevelt administration to pursue cooperation with the Soviet Union in East Asia: Roosevelt's belief that the interests of the United States were best served by a continuation of the existing balance of power there, a balance in which the conflicting interests of the United States, Russia, and Japan prevented any one power from altering the situation radically. From this attitude followed the administration's opposition to Japanese expansion in China as well as its view that war between Russia and Japan jeopardized American interests in Asia.

At first glance, the United States might have been expected to welcome if not promote a Russo-Japanese war that would divert Japan from conflict with American interests and allow the United States to stand by while its competitors fought and weakened each other. In fact, whenever Russo-Japanese disagreement threatened to turn into war, the Roosevelt administration used its influence to discourage such conflict. This was the pattern of American policy well before Hitler's attack on Russia made a Russo-Japanese war undesirable from a European perspective. To Roosevelt, war between the Soviet Union and Japan was objectionable because, as Bullitt succinctly stated, "someone might win it."[71] The President also rejected the proposition that Japanese domination in China was preferable to Soviet hegemony, a view held by the anti-Soviet bloc within the State Department.

Basic to Roosevelt's thinking was the goal of preserving the stalemate of American, Russian, and Japanese ambitions that had resulted in the continued independence of China and the maintenance of an open door in East Asia for some fifty years. With the benefit of hindsight, the President's commitment to this traditional goal seems to have overlooked major changes occurring in Asia, most conspicuously the rise of Japanese and Chinese nationalism and the growing strength of the communists in China. Roosevelt's viewpoint narrowed his alternatives, limited his flexibility, and, as we have seen, prevented his forging a substitute for a balance of power that could not work in the middle of the twentieth century.

[1]For examples, see William L. Neumann, America Encounters Japan (Baltimore, 1963) and Dorothy Borg, The United States and the Far Eastern Crisis of 1933-1938 (Cambridge, 1964).

[2]See Dorothy Borg and Shumpei Okamoto, eds., Pearl Harbor as History: Japanese-American Relations, 1931-1941 (New York, 1973).

[3]Description of the movement for withdrawal can be found in Judith Papachristou, "An Exercise in Anti-Imperialism: The Thirties," American Studies 15 (Spring 1974): 61-77.

[4]Edward H. Zabriskie, American-Russian Rivalry in the Far East (Philadelphia, 1946), p. 104.

[5]Robert Browder, The Origins of Soviet-American Diplomacy (Princeton, 1953), p. 165; Edward M. Bennett, Recognition of Russia (Waltham, Mass., 1970), p. 137; Beatrice Farnsworth, William C. Bullitt and the Soviet Union (Bloomington, 1967), p. 91.

[6]Fullerton to Stimson, February, 1932, 760 N. 00/23, U.S. State Department records, RG 59, National Archives, Washington, D.C. (hereafter cited as D/S File #); Grew to Hull, 9 March 1933, D/S File #761.94/95; Grew to Hull, 9 March 1933, U.S. Department of State, Foreign Relations of the United States (hereafter cited as FRUS), 1933 (Washington, 1949), 3:228-30; Cordell Hull, The Memoirs of Cordell Hull (New York, 1948), 1:276.

[7]Browder, Origins of Soviet-American Diplomacy, pp. 154, 165; The Nation 137 (November 1933): 607.

[8]Grew to Hull, 23 March 1934, FRUS, 1934 (Washington, 1950-52), 3:85-88; Bullitt to Hull, 16 April 1934, D/S File #761.94/734.

[9]Bullitt to Hull, 13 March 1934, FRUS, 1934 3:74.

[10]Bullitt to Hull, 4 January 1934, FRUS, The Soviet Union, 1933-1939 (Washington, 1952), pp. 59-62.

[11]Browder, Origins of Soviet-American Diplomacy, p. 194; Bullitt to Hull, 13 March 1934, FRUS, 1934 3:74; Hull to Bullitt, 17 March 1934, ibid., p. 78; Phillips Memorandum, 20 November 1933, ibid., pp. 463-65; Bullitt to Hull, 4 January 1934, FRUS, The Soviet Union, 1933-1939, pp. 59-62.

[12]Jane Degras, ed., Soviet Documents on Foreign Policy (London, 1935), pp. 120-21; Joseph Clark Grew, Ten Years in Japan (New York, 1944), p. 117; Phillips

Memorandum, 7 February 1936, FRUS, 1936 (Washington, 1953-54), 4:40-41.

[13]Browder, Origins of Soviet-American Diplomacy, pp. 101, 105-106, 131-37; Martin Weil, A Pretty Good Club: The Founding Fathers of the U.S. Foreign Service (New York, 1978), pp. 68-70. For examples, see Far Eastern Division Memorandum, undated, D/S File #861.01/1872; Donald G. Bishop, The Roosevelt-Litvinov Agreements: The American View (Syracuse, 1965), p. 17; Herbert Feis, 1933: Characters in Crisis (Boston, 1966), p. 308; William Phillips, Ventures in Diplomacy (Boston, 1953), p. 156.

[14]Browder, Origins of Soviet-American Diplomacy, p. 188.

[15]Farnsworth, Bullitt, pp. 89, 145-56; Communist International 7/99, 114, D/S File #861.00 Congress; New York Times, 27 August 1935; Literary Digest 120 (September 1935): 12.

[16]Hull, Memoirs 1:290-301; Grew, Ten Years in Japan, p. 145.

[17]See, for example, Hull, Memoirs 1:290-91 and D/S File #711.94/1004, 1005, 1026, 1034.

[18]Hornbeck Memorandum, 3 January 1935, FRUS, 1935 3:829-30.

[19]New York Times, 20 and 21 September 1936.

[20]Hull to embassy in Moscow, 27 June 1934, D/S File #500A15 A5/98; Bingham to Hull, 26 June 1934, FRUS, 1934 1:276.

[21]Davies to Hull, 19 January 1937, FRUS, The Soviet Union, 1933-1939, pp. 357-360; see Moore to Roosevelt, 16 January 1937, quoted in William Appleman Williams, American-Russian Relations, 1781-1947 (New York, 1952), p. 340, 69n; Joseph E. Davies, Mission to Moscow (New York, 1941), p. 4.

[22]Kelley Memorandum, 24 March 1937, FRUS, The Soviet Union, 1933-1939, pp. 465-66; Green Memorandum (Office of Arms and Munitions Control), 13 May 1937, ibid., pp. 472-73; Green Memorandum, 30 August 1937, ibid., p. 479.

[23]Chargé in Japan to Hull, 3 October 1936, FRUS, 1936 4:335; Grew to Hull, 4 December 1935, ibid., pp. 404-465, 398, 400; William E. Dodd, Jr. and Martha Dodd, eds., Ambassador Dodd's Diary (New York, 1941), p. 366; Far Eastern Division Memorandum, 28 November 1936, D/S File #762 93/149.

[24]Bullitt to Hull, 20 April 1936, FRUS, The Soviet Union, 1933-1939, pp. 294-95. Bullitt wrote:

> If war comes between Japan and the Soviet Union, we should not intervene but should use our influence and power toward the end of the war to see to it that it ends without victory, and that the balance between the Soviet Union and Japan in the Far East is not destroyed, and that China continues to have at least some opportunity for independent development.

[25]Within the State Department, debates ensued about the relative effectiveness of applying sanctions against Japan or seeking ways to help solve Japan's problems and decrease Japanese-American differences. See, for example, Far Eastern Division Memorandum, 12 October 1937, FRUS, 1937 (Washington, 1954), 3:596-600. New ideas were also brought forth. Roosevelt's quarantine speech in October may well have grown out of a protean plan for neutral cooperation against the belligerents. See Borg, The United States and the Far Eastern Crisis, pp. 385-86. The inconclusiveness of American policy was well illustrated at the Brussels Conference. See, for example, Hull, Memoirs 1:554; British embassy to Department of State, 19 October 1937, FRUS, 1937 4:89-91; and Sumner Welles, Seven Decisions That Shaped History (New York, 1950), pp. 75-76.

[26]D/S File #861.01/2120; Bullitt to Hull, 5 August 1937, FRUS, 1937 3:326-27; Chargé in Germany to Hull, 28 August 1937, FRUS, 1937 3:489-90; Nancy H. Hooker, ed., The Moffat Papers (Cambridge, 1956), p. 156.

[27]Weil, A Pretty Good Club, p. 59.

[28]Ibid., pp. 68-69.

[29]William L. Langer and S. Everett Gleason, The Challenge to Isolation: The World Crisis of 1937-1940 and American Foreign Policy (New York, 1952), pp. 44-45. The original commercial agreement was signed in 1935, one of the few tangible results of earlier efforts to bridge the gap between the United States and the Soviet Union.

[30]Izvestia article, D/S File #711.61/62; Henderson to Hull, 20 August 1937, FRUS, The Soviet Union, 1933-1939, pp. 388-90; State Department to Navy Department, D/S File #811.3394/255 and 811.3361; Bullitt to Hull D/S File #811.3361/30.

[31]See Japanese-Soviet border clashes, FRUS, 1938 (Washington, 1954-56), 3:441-88. For more detail, see Alvin D. Coox, The Anatomy of a Small War: The Soviet-Japanese Struggle for Chang Kufeng/Khom 1938 (Westport, Cn., 1977), and Hosoya Chihiri, "Japan's Policies Toward Russia," in James Morley, ed., Japan's Foreign Policy, 1868-1941: A Research Guide (New York, 1974), pp. 399-401.

[32]Davies to Hull, 17 January 1938, FRUS, The Soviet Union, 1933-1939, pp. 596-98; D/S File #800.51W89 USSR/237; Davies, Mission to Moscow, pp. 341-54; Charles Bohlen, Witness to History (New York, 1973), p. 45.

[33]Davies, Mission to Moscow, pp. 370-72; D/S File #800.51W89 USSR/247; Henderson to Hull, 29 September 1937, FRUS, The Soviet Union, 1933-1939, pp. 594-600.

[34]Davies, Mission to Moscow, pp. 371-72.

[35]Ibid., pp. 323, 371-72, 432-35.

[36]Davies Memorandum, 5 July 1938, FRUS, The Soviet Union, 1933-1939, p. 599.

[37]On Faymonville's recall, see 200AR, Miscellaneous, Box 5, Franklin D. Roosevelt Papers, Roosevelt Library, Hyde Park, N.Y. (hereafter cited as Roosevelt Papers).

[38]Green memoranda, 13 May, 21 August, and 11 October 1937, FRUS, The Soviet Union, 1933-1939, pp. 472-73, 478-81, 486; Hull Memorandum, 18 May 1938, ibid., pp. 686-87.

[39]Hull Memorandum, 26 March 1938, ibid., pp. 678-79; Green Memorandum, 24 May 1938, ibid., p. 692; Hull and Edison (Acting Secretary of the Navy) to Roosevelt, 8 June 1938, ibid., pp. 697-98; Green Memorandum, 4 November 1938, ibid., p. 705.

[40]Langer and Gleason, Challenge to Isolation, p. 188; Herbert Feis, The Road to Pearl Harbor (New York, 1963), p. 28.

[41]Hull to Dooman (Chargé in Japan), 30 August 1939, FRUS, 1939 (Washington, 1955-57), 3:60; Langer and Gleason, Challenge to Isolation, p. 194. In February, four days of hard fighting occurred. In May, Russian and Japanese troops along the Mongolian border were fighting with aircraft, artillery, and tanks.

[42]Hooker, The Moffat Papers, p. 265; Steinhardt (ambassador to the Soviet Union) to Hull, 1 November 1939, FRUS, The Soviet Union, 1933-1939, p. 789; Grew to Hull, 27 November 1939, FRUS, 1939 3:85; Grew to Hull, 28 November 1939, ibid., pp. 602-604.

[43]Far Eastern Division memoranda, 6 November 1939, FRUS, 1939 3:76-88, and 20 November 1939, D/S File #761.94/1172.

[44]Grew, Ten Years in Japan, pp. 295-97; State Department Memorandum, undated, FRUS, 1939 3:92-94; Grew to Hull, 27 November 1939, ibid., pp. 83-84, and 6 December 1939, D/S File #761.94/1176.

[45]Hull to Gibbs and Cox, 17 August 1939, FRUS, The Soviet Union, 1933-1939, pp. 894-95; Green Memorandum, 6 September 1939, ibid., pp. 895-96; Green Memorandum, 16 September 1939, ibid., pp. 896-98; Hull to Gibbs and Cox, 3 October 1939, ibid., pp. 898-99; Green Memorandum, 9 October 1939, ibid., p. 899; Hull to International General Electric Co., 8 November 1939, ibid., pp. 899-900; Hull to Gibbs and Cox, 18 November 1939, ibid., p. 900; Hull to International General Electric Co., 21 November 1939, ibid., p. 901; Green memoranda, 28 November, 1 and 4 December 1939, ibid., pp. 901-903.

[46]See above.

[47]Hull, Memoirs 1:702, 709.

[48]See New York Times, 9 February, 13 January, and 17 January 1940; John M. Blum, From the Morgenthau Diaries (Boston, 1965), 2:130; Langer and Gleason, Challenge to Isolation, p. 339.

[49]Langer and Gleason, Challenge to Isolation, pp. 388-89, 11, 640-42.

[50]Steinhardt to Hull, 28 November 1940, FRUS, 1940 (Washington, 1959-61), 1:676, 679-80; Johnson (ambassador in China) to Hull, 20 July 1940, ibid., 4:404; Blum, Morgenthau Diaries 2:362; New York Times, 28, 30, and 29 September 1940; Grew, Ten Years in Japan, p. 333; Grew to Hull, 2 October 1940 and Johnson to Hull, 3 October 1940, FRUS, 1940 1:657-59.

[51]Blum, Morgenthau Diaries 2:347.

[52]New York Times, 9 August 1940.

[53]Hornbeck Memorandum of Conversation, 15 August 1940, FRUS, 1940 4:663; Blum, Morgenthau Diaries 2:357-62; Langer and Gleason, Challenge to Isolation, p. 727. Morgenthau and Oumansky reached no agreement and the project died.

[54]Blum, Morgenthau Diaries 2:335; British embassy to Department of State, 12 September 1940, FRUS, 1940 4:112.

[55]Robert J. Butow, Tojo and The Coming of The War (Princeton, 1961), p. 207; Hull, Memoirs 2:909; Harold Ickes, Secret Diary, The Lowering Clouds (New York, 1954), 3:484-85.

[56]Grew to Hull, 14 April 1941, FRUS, 1941 (Washington, 1956-62), 4:945-47; Henderson Memorandum of Conversation, 10 April 1941, ibid., 1:741; Hull, Memoirs 2:971; FRUS, 1941 1:866-914.

[57]Grew to Hull, 23 June 1941, FRUS, 1941 4:979; Far Eastern Division memoranda, 23 and 24 June 1941, ibid., pp. 981-85; D/S File #740.0011 European War 1939/16502.

[58]D/S File #740.0011 European War 1939/16502; FRUS, 1941 4:289.

[59]Memorandum by Assistant Chief Adams, 25 June 1941, FRUS, 1941 4:279.

[60]Ballantine to Hull, 18 June 1941, ibid., pp. 270-71; Far Eastern Division Memorandum, 2 July 1941, ibid., pp. 288-89; D/S File #740.0011 European War 1939/13723.

[61]U.S., Congress, Joint Committee on the Investigation of the Pearl Harbor Attack, Report (Washington, 1946), Part 12, Text of Intercepted Messages, pp. 1-2.

[62]Hull, Memoirs 2:1012; FRUS, 1941 2:502-504. Throughout the summer, the idea of a Japanese attack on the Soviet Union found credence within the State Department. Only at the highest levels within the administration was there almost certainty, based on decoded information, that Japan would move against Indo-China before she moved against the Soviet Union. Blum, Morgenthau Diaries 2:375; Far Eastern Division Memorandum, 4 July 1941, FRUS, 1941 4:288.

[63]New York Times, 6, 8, and 24 August 1941; FRUS, 1941 2:568-69, 569-79 and 4:397, 403.

[64]New York Times, 6 July 1941; Raymond Dawson, The Decision to Aid Russia, 1941 (Chapel Hill, 1959), p. 122.

[65]Feis, Road to Pearl Harbor, pp. 232, 240; Paul W. Schroeder, The Axis Alliance and Japanese-American Relations, 1941 (Ithaca, 1958), p. 178.

[66]Far Eastern Memorandum incorporating ideas of Hull and Hornbeck, 31 July 1941, Cordell Hull Papers, Library of Congress, Washington, D.C.; Ickes, Secret Diary, entry of 3 August 1941, 3:592; Hornbeck Memorandum, 2 September 1941, FRUS, 1941 4:419.

[67]Ballantine Memorandum, 23 September 1941, FRUS, 1941 4:470-75.

[68]Hull Memorandum of Conversation, 4 September 1941, ibid., 1:827, 44; New York Times, 25 September 1941.

[69]New York Times, 28 October and 6 November 1941, 3 December 1945. See Pearl Harbor Attack, Report, pp. 51-53.

[70]Letter from Grew, 22 September 1941, and also memorandum, 17 March 1941, describing views of Admiral William Pratt, Japan, Box 11, President's Secretary's File, Roosevelt Papers; Steinhardt to Hull, 24 March 1941, FRUS, 1941 4:921-23; Gerow (Acting Chief of Staff) to Hull, 21 November 1941, ibid., 4:630; William C. Bullitt, "How We Won the War and Lost the Peace," Life 25 (30 August 1948): 82.

[71]Bullitt to Hull, 20 April 1936, FRUS, The Soviet Union, 1933-1939, p. 294. Roosevelt, of course, did not believe he was choosing between a Japanese-American war and a Russo-Japanese war since his policy was promulgated on the assumption that it would succeed without either. By the time it became obvious that America and Japan were on a collision course, the alternative of a Russo-Japanese war was totally unacceptable: Japan had decided to move south and Russia had become an indispensable ally against Germany.

FRANKLIN D. ROOSEVELT AND THE PROBLEM OF
NAZI GERMANY

Brooks Van Everen

American foreign policy is affected by many factors, including the prejudices and preconceptions that our presidents hold about other countries. These prejudices are often overlooked when historians explain the foreign policy of individual chief executives. Franklin D. Roosevelt, for example, held strong views about Germany and the German people, and throughout his adult life he believed that the Germans epitomized everything that was anti-democratic and totalitarian in the international world. As a young man he acquired a sharp dislike of the autocratic nature of the German government and the militarism that seemed to permeate its internal and external behavior. These views conditioned and shaped many of his reactions to Nazi Germany and, in turn, Roosevelt's perception of Germany influenced and shaped the American response to Hitler's Third Reich. Roosevelt saw the Nazi state as he had seen the Germany of Kaiser Wilhelm II, a dictatorial regime run by an evil clique of criminals who were directly supported by a self-seeking group of "war-breeding militarists" in the German army.[1] Throughout the war, the American President equated the Nazi party with the German army, and he was convinced that the war could end only when both of these groups were totally defeated.

Generally, historians have seen President Roosevelt's prewar foreign policy toward Europe as very cautious and timid because he was preoccupied with domestic policy and rather indifferent to the wave of anarchy engulfing Europe.[2] The general thrust of the literature on Roosevelt's pre-1941 policy has clearly established that he was hesitant, confused, and vacillating on the proper response to the threat posed by Nazi Germany.[3] Yet, if one can judge the President by what he felt and said in private, rather than by what he did in public, it is clear that his animosity toward Germany was very strong and that it influenced his policies and attitudes toward that country.

Roosevelt insisted that unconditional surrender should be the sole basis for ending the Second World War with Germany. This demand for complete and total surrender

revealed much about his perception of Germany, just as it indicated something of his thinking about how he hoped to resolve the "German problem" after the termination of hostilities. The unconditional surrender concept, reflecting Roosevelt's thinking on the armistice terminating the First World War and the inadequacies of the Versailles peace, was retained with remarkable tenacity by the American leader because it was central to his thinking about what must be done with Germany after hostilities ceased. Indeed, Roosevelt resisted all efforts to alter or modify the meaning of the doctrine despite very substantial pressure for change because he considered it crucial to postwar stability in Germany and world peace.[4]

Once the United States was in the war, President Roosevelt would be closely associated with much of the planning for the postwar treatment of Germany. He favored, as he had after the First World War, a harsh and punitive settlement with the great European power. He wanted to see Germany dismembered and disarmed, and he argued that extensive controls should be imposed on German life for many years after the war. His attitude was further revealed in the summer and fall of 1944 with his initial acceptance of the punitive Morgenthau Plan for the postwar treatment of Germany. The President felt an obligation to future generations to end the German threat to the peace and security of the world.

Franklin Roosevelt's early life and his experiences as a young adult played an important role in conditioning his later reactions to international relations generally and to Germany in particular. His family traveled frequently to Europe as he was growing up, and often these journeys were for prolonged periods. His father especially enjoyed visiting Germany, and young Franklin made eight trips there before he was fourteen.[5] It has been argued that Roosevelt developed a lifelong dislike for German arrogance and provincialism as a result of his early contacts with the Central European people.[6] Certainly by 1914 he had acquired a view of the Germans that was significant in shaping his later actions and perceptions. Like many of his contemporaries, he focused on the evil nature of the German autocracy, the persistent influence of Prussian militarism, the absence of democracy, and government by intrigue and suspicion.[7] It is reasonable to assume that by

the First World War Roosevelt's view of Germany was one that would remain unchanged until his death in 1945.

Roosevelt's only year in public school was in Baden in southern Germany, and his exposure to German schools was the source of many of his impressions of that land. To be sure, his later experiences influenced his memories of the adventure; for example, two months before his death the President told reporters that he remembered when railroad employees and school children throughout Germany suddenly had to start wearing uniforms when the "militaristically minded" German Emperor Wilhelm II came to the throne. As Roosevelt recalled, "railroad employees all over Germany were in uniform, and they were all taught to march."[8] Thereafter, he asserted, the German people became very militaristic, displaying a real love for uniforms and marching. Until his death, he was convinced that peace was impossible with the Germans if they were allowed to march and wear uniforms.[9]

As Assistant Secretary of the Navy under Woodrow Wilson, Roosevelt made trips to Europe in 1918 and 1919. Unhappy with the armistice ending World War I, he believed that unless Allied troops entered and occupied Germany a "conditional settlement" would give the German militarists the impression that they had not really lost the war on the battlefield.[10] Roosevelt was confident that a premature ending of the war, prior to a decisive military victory, would lead to an excessively generous peace that would simply sow the seeds of a future conflict. Furthermore, an easy settlement would not strike at the heart of the German problem, militarism. Based on his expressions about the inadequacies of the armistice and the peace thereafter, it is clear that Roosevelt favored a stern settlement with the Germans which the victors would enforce and police when World War II ended.[11]

The President left no doubt where his sympathy lay once the European war began in September, 1939. He was not neutral in thought or action and he had no intention of being so. A year before the outbreak of war, Roosevelt said that "the situation here will be very different from 1914. In that year," he told his ambassador in Italy, William Phillips, "while the great majority of Americans were inclined to sympathize with the Allies, there was an honest

effort, led by the President, to remain neutral in thought. . . . Today I think 90% of our people are definitely anti-German and anti-Italian in sentiment and incidently [sic], I would not propose to ask them to be neutral in thought."[12] Roosevelt told an audience at Queen's University in Kingston, Ontario, that there was nothing he could do to prevent people from having opinions about "wanton brutality, undemocratic regimentation and massive violations of human rights."[13] Harboring such views, it is not surprising that the President's proclamation of neutrality in September, 1939, implied that Americans need not be disturbed by being pro-Allied in their sentiments. According to Samuel Rosenman, a presidential speech writer, such partiality in the proclamation reflected the President's true sentiments.[14] Indeed, long before the war, Secretary of State Cordell Hull and Roosevelt had concurred that it would be in the national interest to assist Britain and France, first in the effort to keep war from starting, and second, to win the war with Germany if it came.[15]

As war approached, Roosevelt speculated about German ambitions in Europe. In April, 1939, he asked at his press conference: "What if the totalitarian powers win? . . . Heavens, if they were to win a large European war, they would want domination of Europe and the things that go with Europe."[16] The American leader believed that Germany's aims and ambitions involved more than redressing alleged injustices; he feared that Germany sought hegemony over all of Europe. This, in turn, would directly threaten the vital political, military, and economic interests of the United States.

During the fall of 1939, the President was often mentioned as a possible mediator between the warring states. Ambassador Joseph Kennedy cabled from England that the President had the opportunity to save the world; and the American chargé in Germany told the State Department that only a direct offer of mediation by the President could bring positive results from the German government.[17] At home, a public opinion poll found that over one-third of the populace favored having the President mediate the war in Europe.[18] Despite these sentiments, Roosevelt resisted the pressures that were placed upon him. He told the American minister to Belgium, his friend Joseph Davies,

that he would not support anything less than a real settlement.[19]   He was convinced that a lasting peace was impossible, however, since compromise and negotiations were alien and foreign terms to the German leadership. Consequently, at the President's direction, Hull cabled Kennedy that "this government . . . sees no opportunity, nor occasion, for any peace move to be initiated by the President of the United States."[20]   Roosevelt felt a negotiated settlement with the Germans was impossible: "How can one speak of a negotiated peace in this war," he asked, "when a peace treaty would be as binding upon the Nazis as the bond of gangsters and outlaws."[21]

Militarism loomed very large in Roosevelt's perception of the German problem, and he believed the militarist tradition of Prussia had directly affected the internal and external behavior of the Nazi state.   The papers of the President are full of letters, pamphlets, books, and articles on the continuity of the militarist tradition in Germany, and all the evidence suggests that he was strongly influenced by this material.[22]   Roosevelt perceived this trait as perverting and destroying the very ideals making democratic civilization possible and worthwhile.   The President believed that the military in Germany determined the citizen's place in society and the limits of individual freedom.   Once in uniform, he felt the German citizen acquired a "herd mentality" allowing him to trample over other people and their rights.[23]   The President believed that the defeat of Germany would involve something more than simply the elimination of Hitler and his Nazi party.   Traditions that were embedded deeply in German history would have to be destroyed, and a pattern of behavior practiced for generations would have to be altered.

Once the United States entered the war, the President devoted considerable attention to the problem of what should be done with a defeated Germany.   Closely associated with proposals for the disarmament, dismemberment, and the policing of the German state, during the period from 1942 to 1945, were such policies as "unconditional surrender," the Morgenthau Plan, and the occupation zones for the military government in postwar Germany.   In his view, these policies would secure the victory long after the final shots had been fired.

During the Second World War, virtually all American planners agreed that Germany must be disarmed after the war. Much of the unanimity achieved on this issue resulted from the President's blunt comments and his active leadership of this cause. In May, 1942, Roosevelt told visiting Russian Foreign Secretary Vyacheslav Molotov that disarmament would have to be enforced throughout Germany for many years after the war.[24] Six months later, the President wrote the South African statesman, Jan Christian Smuts, "I am convinced that disarmament of the aggressor nations is an essential first step, followed up for a good many years to come by day and night inspection of that disarmament and a police power to stop at its source any attempted evasion of the rules."[25] Roosevelt's proposals to disarm Germany after the war were favorably received by the American public; a January, 1943 poll indicated that seventy-seven percent of citizens surveyed favored the Reich's total disarmament after hostilities ended.[26]

Closely connected to Roosevelt's plans for the disarmament of Germany were his proposals for regular inspection of the defeated state to ensure compliance with the peace imposed by the victors. Military occupation had several purposes, but a central objective was to have sufficient forces stationed in Germany to police and supervise the populace. After Canadian Prime Minister Mackenzie King visited Washington in December, 1942, he told the American minister to Canada, Jay Pierrepont Moffat, that the President wanted the four major Allies to act as a police force to guarantee German compliance with the disarmament terms.[27]

As the Italian mainland was invaded in September, 1943, Roosevelt told Senator George Norris of Nebraska that he had "been visualizing a superimposed--or if you like it, superassumed--obligation by Russia, China, Britain and ourselves that we will act as sheriffs for the maintenance of order during the transitional period" after the war.[28] Finally, in his report on the Teheran Conference, Roosevelt announced to the Congress that there was unanimous agreement among the Allies that Germany must be garrisoned and strictly controlled for many years after the war.[29]

While substantial agreement existed on the need to disarm and police Germany, major differences of opinion

142

emerged over the desirability of partitioning or dismembering the German state. Appalled at the excesses of the Nazis, many observers argued that Germany should be reduced in size so that the Germans no longer endangered their neighbors. As Roosevelt explained at the Teheran Conference, Germany had been less dangerous to civilization in 1810 when it was divided into 107 provinces, and perhaps it would be wise to return Germany to that state.[30] Few discerning experts approved Roosevelt's number, but many favored dividing the Reich into three to seven parts.

Genuinely intrigued with the idea of partitioning the Reich, Roosevelt was not reluctant to discuss it.[31] En route to the Teheran Conference, for example, the President told the Joint Chiefs of Staff that he favored dividing Germany into three states.[32] On 1 December 1943, however, Roosevelt presented a plan to Prime Minister Winston Churchill and Marshall Joseph Stalin for the separation of Germany into five distinct states: (1) a smaller and weaker Prussia; (2) Hanover and the northwest; (3) Saxony and Leipzig; (4) Bavaria, Baden, and Wurtenberg; and (5) Hesse-Darmstadt, Hesse-Kassel, and the area south of the Rhine.[33] No decision was reached on the President's plan, but according to his personal Chief of Staff, Admiral William Leahy, it was well received by the British and the Russians.[34] Almost a year later, during the debate over the Morgenthau Plan in September, 1944, Roosevelt was still referring to this plan, so it was obviously an important part of his thinking about the future of Germany.[35]

Roosevelt's views about Germany were also revealed in the "unconditional surrender" policy announced at a press conference at the conclusion of the Casablanca Conference in January, 1943.[36] Many historians have pointed out that the President had in mind the problems plaguing Woodrow Wilson in 1918. They argue that Roosevelt wanted it understood that there would be no negotiated peace or compromise settlement, no Fourteen Points or promises made to the Germans about what might happen after the war was over. The war would end only when the Germans agreed to unconditional surrender.[37]

Over the next two years, the President reaffirmed his pledge to continue the war until unconditional surrender

was achieved, and he resisted all efforts to alter or modify the policy. In Ottawa in August, 1943, he told the Canadian Parliament that the Allies were determined to make sure the Germans knew they had lost.[38] During the same month, Roosevelt responded to a Congressional resolution asking him to define the meaning of unconditional surrender by answering that the policy would allow the Allies to accomplish essential goals in Germany.[39] In the first half of 1944, great pressure was placed on the American government generally, and on President Roosevelt specifically, to define the phrase "unconditional surrender." The Soviet government in particular favored announcing the exact conditions to be imposed upon Germany after the war. While the Soviets claimed to be concerned with the negative impact the undefined slogan was having on German forces, it is probable that the Russians, favoring a very harsh treatment of Germany, were interested in getting the Americans to commit themselves to some detailed proposals.[40] Roosevelt, however, was wary of being specific, and on 24 January 1944, the State Department instructed Ambassador W. Averell Harriman to inform the Russians that the United States thought it prudent not to discuss either the terms which Germany should expect or the meaning of unconditional surrender.[41] Privately the President was not so hesitant, and he disclosed some of his ideas in a letter to an old friend, Charles Burlingham.

> We seek not merely to prevent the Germans from ever overwhelming all of Europe and us all now, but we seek to prevent them from trying to repeat it twenty years later. . . . Better than Wilson, who said 'This is the war to end all wars.' That went too far. We are not omniscient but we ought to set up machinery that has a reasonable chance to prevent a similar war happening for a long time--say a couple of generations.[42]

To the president of Boston University, Roosevelt repeated the same idea: "We must not allow the seeds of the evils we shall have crushed to germinate underground and reproduce themselves in the future."[43]

As plans developed for the Normandy invasion in the spring of 1944, military authorities in Great Britain and Washington sought clarification of the unconditional

surrender formula. Many of these men believed that the concept hindered Allied propaganda appeals that might help shorten the war, and these officials thought that the conflict could be ended early if only the unconditional surrender doctrine were altered.[44] Thus, the American Joint Chiefs of Staff sent a series of memoranda to the President on 25 March 1944, suggesting that the time had come to modify the unconditional surrender policy because the term had allowed Nazi leaders to invoke the specter of annihilation which, in turn, had stiffened the German will to resist.[45] Roosevelt rejected this suggestion by the Joint Chiefs and asserted that future peace hinged on the resolution of the German problem; to change Germany would take many generations and that was why unconditional surrender was necessary.[46] It was obvious to many officials in the American government that the President was, in Cordell Hull's words, "holding very strongly to the principle of unconditional surrender for Germany."[47] Consequently, William Phillips, serving as political adviser at the Supreme Headquarters of the Allied Expeditionary Force in London, was instructed in mid-April that the President wanted no further discussion or comment on unconditional surrender by military or political authorities in England.[48]

The President was deeply concerned at the short memories that people seemed to have about the Germans and especially about the circumstances at the end of the First World War. "There has been a good deal of complaint among some of the nice, high-minded people, about unconditional surrender, that if we changed the term 'unconditional surrender,' Germany might surrender more quickly," he told a press conference near the end of July, 1944. Roosevelt pointed out, "Practically every German denies the fact they surrendered in the last war, but this time they are going to know it."[49] In August the President complained to Senator Kenneth McKellar of Tennessee that people were suddenly becoming lenient on the peace terms for Germany.[50] He was convinced that Germany had been able to wage war again because too many people had gone "soft" on the Germans between 1919 and 1935, and he confessed that he had little sympathy for these individuals.

By the middle of 1944, Franklin Roosevelt and the officials in his administration had devoted considerable time

and discussion to the problems of postwar Germany, but few specific decisions had been made and no detailed plans for postwar policy in Germany existed. Roosevelt had been hesitant to define a specific program for the treatment of Germany, although he clearly held strong ideas about the goals that should be pursued. Once the invasion of France established the Allies in northwest Europe, it was obvious that specific proposals for Germany would have to be made, and in the late summer of 1944 increasing pressure was placed on Roosevelt to accept final plans for the Nazi state. Responding to this pressure, Roosevelt encouraged those around him to direct their attention to the future treatment of Germany. Among those heeding the President's call was the Secretary of the Treasury, Henry Morgenthau, Jr.

A longtime neighbor and a close friend of Roosevelt's near Hyde Park, New York, Morgenthau proved to be a trustworthy companion and Roosevelt asked him to serve the New Deal. Morgenthau loved and admired the President and obtained great satisfaction from serving him loyally, and Roosevelt came to depend on his neighbor for advice and help. The bond between the two men was unique within the Roosevelt administration, and the President respected Morgenthau's advice, especially admiring the "intuitive understanding" the Treasury Secretary seemed to have. Roosevelt often entrusted programs and duties to Morgenthau that he would not give to others in his official family.[51] It was Morgenthau's intuition rather than his expertise that the President appealed to when he asked for Morgenthau's thoughts on the treatment of Germany. As we have seen, Roosevelt favored a harsh settlement with Germany, and there was much in Morgenthau's own thinking which coincided with the President's deepest instincts. Much of the President's subsequent acceptance of the Morgenthau Plan, as the Treasury Secretary's proposals were known, derived from the fact that it conformed to his own pattern of thinking about Germany. The weight of the evidence, including the President's previous statements on the German problem, suggests that Roosevelt favored the Morgenthau Plan and that he continued to favor it after he was forced to repudiate publicly the most Draconian provisions of the plan.[52] Certainly, historians who have examined Roosevelt's contradictory behavior over the Morgenthau Plan have portrayed him as a confused and badly informed President who "wavered among his

contending advisers."[53] Some of this confusion derives from the peculiar circumstances of the presidential election of 1944 and the manner in which critics of the proposal emphasized Morgenthau's plan for the de-industrialization of the Ruhr Valley. For political and administrative reasons, the President disowned the plan because of the heavy criticism that the radical proposal generated, yet he supported many other parts of the program.

Like Roosevelt, Morgenthau believed that a harsh and punitive settlement with Germany was the prerequisite to security in the postwar world. Like the President also, he felt that the entire German nation was involved in a broad criminal conspiracy against the civilized world. Morgenthau was convinced that the Germans would cultivate plans and carry out future assaults unless they were contained after the war.[54] Consequently, Morgenthau wished to see Germany dismembered and partitioned, and he felt it would be necessary to have rigid controls over the economic and military life of Germany to prevent that nation from disturbing the peace. Because Morgenthau, like Roosevelt, thought of the Germans as incurable militarists, he had little faith in the possibility that the German people would change their behavior after the war. As he observed,

> The Nazi regime is essentially the culmination of the unchanging German drive toward aggression. German society has been dominated for at least three generations by powerful forces fashioning the German state and nation into a machine for military conquest and self-aggrandizement. Since 1864, Germany has launched five wars of aggression against other powers, each war involving more destruction over larger areas than the previous ones.[55]

During August, 1944, Morgenthau became aware of the preliminary plans developed by the State and War Departments for the postwar treatment of the Reich. Generally, these plans emphasized a moderate treatment for Germany, with few controls over its postwar economic, political, and military life; and the Secretary of the Treasury became concerned that these agencies were preparing what he considered "easy" and "soft" terms for Germany.[56] On 19 August, Morgenthau told his chief that

147

from what he could see nobody was making plans to treat Germany rigorously "along the lines you wanted."[57] Roosevelt expressed fear that Morgenthau was right, and he told his friend, "We have got to be tough with Germany and I mean the German people not just the Nazis. We either have to castrate the German people, or you have got to treat [them] in such a manner so they can't just go on reproducing people who want to continue the way they have in the past."[58]

After a trip to England, Morgenthau gave the President an army occupation manual or Handbook that had been tentatively prepared for possible use by an occupying American military government in Germany. In a memorandum, he drew the President's attention to those parts of the manual which suggested that the German people and their country should be treated gently after the war.[59] On the same day, the President confided to Secretary of the Navy James Forrestal that he was most unhappy with the lack of "toughness" in the manual, telling Forrestal that for a number of years after the war the Germans should only have a subsistence level of food rations equal to the lowest level of the people they had conquered.[60] The following day, the President sent Secretary of War Henry Stimson a memorandum on the Handbook in which he criticized its proposed measures as well as the general thinking implicit in the document. Roosevelt disliked the impression conveyed by the Handbook that Germany would be quickly restored to its prewar status, and he lectured Stimson that

> . . . every person in Germany should realize that this Germany is a defeated nation. I do not want them to starve to death, but as an example, if they need food to keep body and soul together, beyond what they have, they should be fed three times a day with soup from army soup kitchens. That will keep them perfectly healthy and they will remember that experience all their lives. The fact that they are a defeated nation, collectively and individually, must be so impressed upon them that they will hesitate to start any new war. . . . The German people, as a whole, must have it driven home to them that the whole nation has been engaged in a

148

lawless conspiracy against the decencies of modern civilization.[61]

Meanwhile, the Morgenthau Plan was largely completed. It proposed de-industrializing the centers of heavy industry in the Ruhr Valley and called for the dispersal of industrial workers throughout Germany. The primary purpose of the plan was the elimination of the industrial base for German warfare.[62] The Morgenthau Plan also called for the dismemberment of the Reich, with large transfers of territory to Germany's neighbors; the land remaining would be divided into two separate and independent states.[63] These two states would be subject to military control and occupation for many years after the war. In essence, Morgenthau believed that a military occupation, disarmament, and dismemberment were not enough; to him, future international peace and security demanded an industrially weakened Germany.

At the Quebec meeting in 1944, both Roosevelt and Churchill endorsed and approved the Morgenthau Plan when it was presented by its author. Less than a month later, however, the same two leaders rejected the Morgenthau program. This repudiation was largely the result of intense pressure from lower level officials within the American and British governments who feared the economic consequences of the plan on Germany and Europe.[64]

Roosevelt was in the midst of a campaign for his fourth term. His opponent, Governor Thomas Dewey, appeared to be making some telling points with his criticism of an administration divided about Germany. On 27 September, the President told Henry Stimson that he had no intention of making Germany a purely agricultural country, and he implied that his underlying motive in accepting the Morgenthau proposal was to help England financially after the war, giving her the opportunity to compete for German markets.[65] Continuing to disassociate himself from the Morgenthau Plan, Roosevelt claimed that "No one wants to make Germany a wholly agricultural nation again, and yet somebody down the line has handed this out to the press. . . ." He added, however, "I just cannot go along with the idea of seeing the British Empire collapse financially, and Germany at the same time building up a potential rearmament machine to make another war possible in twenty

years."[66] On the same day, the President discarded the Morgenthau Plan and returned the responsibility for planning the postwar treatment of Germany to the State and War Departments.[67]

Neither Henry Morgenthau nor the Treasury Department officials who collaborated with him were discouraged by the President's reaction. Certainly the Treasury Secretary lost some ground as a result of Roosevelt's apparent repudiation of the Morgenthau Plan, but this did not mean that he had lost his influence with the President. As Morgenthau recorded in his diary:

> I asked the President if he wanted me to interest myself in the future treatment of Germany. He didn't answer me directly. I said, 'Look, Mr. President, I am going to fight hard, and this is what I am fighting for. . . . A weak economy for Germany means that she will be weak politically, and she won't be able to make another war. . . . I have been strong for winning the war, and I want to help win the peace.' The President said, 'Henry, I am with you 100%!'[68]

Morgenthau believed that the President subscribed to the general outlines of his program for Germany to the end, even though he could not publicly demonstrate his support. Discussing Germany in Warm Springs, Georgia, the night before the President died, Roosevelt told Morgenthau that he was determined not to allow sentimental considerations to interfere with the need to prevent the Germans from again becoming aggressors.[69] In her book, This I Remember, Eleanor Roosevelt confirmed that her husband believed in the Morgenthau program for Germany because he felt it would prevent the Germans from having the economic base to wage modern warfare.[70] Similarly, the President's eldest son, Elliot, verified Morgenthau's assertion in his book, As I Saw It.[71] It might be argued that Eleanor and Elliot Roosevelt are not credible witnesses because they were not really that close to the President and his thinking. Yet there is much in the Morgenthau program that duplicates Roosevelt's thinking about Germany throughout his entire life.

Franklin Roosevelt's attitude toward postwar Germany related closely to his views on international relations generally and America's relations with Russia specifically. The President was convinced that Germany must be contained, a goal he believed the Soviets shared. Throughout the war, the Russian leader Josef Stalin argued for the most ruthless treatment of Germany; he seemed sincere in his belief that unless Germany was dealt with harshly there would be another war in twenty years.[72] Stalin and Roosevelt established an important "community of trust" in the similarity of their views about the Germans and what should be done with them. It is clear that the American leader and the Russian dictator reached substantial agreement on the need to dismember and disarm Germany after the war, and they were often far ahead of Winston Churchill and many of their advisers on these questions. The course Soviet-American relations might have taken had the President lived is unknown, but it seems reasonable to believe that if Roosevelt could have followed his lifelong instincts about Germany, there would not have been such equivocation and confusion in American policy regarding the postwar treatment of Germany. We will never know what part American equivocation over the postwar treatment of Germany played in the Russian decision to act alone in East Germany, nor can we know what relationship existed between Truman's hesitancy about German policy and Stalin's decision to erect a security sphere in Eastern Europe.

Roosevelt's relationship with Stalin is the subject of much historical debate. It may be, as many of Roosevelt's critics have asserted, that the President was naive and unrealistic about Stalin and Soviet intentions, and that he was foolish to believe that Soviet-American relations would remain harmonious after the war ended. Many close observers fault Roosevelt for ignoring the vast ideological gap between the Bolshevik leader and himself, and they assert that no action by Roosevelt could overcome the enmity and suspicion of Stalin.[73] Yet some of the same critics note that Stalin was both an ideologist and a pragmatist and that Roosevelt's attempts to reach the practical side of the Soviet leader were not as foolish as they once appeared to be. As Arthur Schlesinger, Jr. observed, "With the extraordinary instinct of a great political leader, Roosevelt intuitively understood that Stalin

was the only lever available to the West against the Leninist ideology and the Soviet system. If Stalin could be reached, then alone was there a chance of getting the Russians to act contrary to the prescriptions of their faith."[74]

Looking back at those postwar years, it is tempting to argue that the wartime alliance would inevitably collapse and the Cold War ensue. In this sense it does not make much difference if one blames the Cold War on Soviet imperialism, Bolshevik ideology, Stalin's paranoia, American capitalist and democratic missionary ideology, or Harry Truman, for the result is the same. Yet it is possible that Franklin Roosevelt might have been able to avert the worst suspicions and tensions of the Cold War era and agree with Stalin on the resolution of the German question.

During the last months of Roosevelt's life, he appeared to be retreating from making any specific program for Germany, but there is no reason to believe that his animosity toward the Germans had changed. Roosevelt continued to speak of both the evil criminals who led Germany and the cowardly people who followed them. He believed in the collective responsibility of the German people for the crimes of the Nazi regime. The President persisted in his attacks on the militarists in the German army, and he renewed his pledge to banish the criminal forces that had corrupted Germany for generations. He wanted the German people to know that they had been following sinister leaders and that they were responsible for the deeds of those leaders.[75] As Roosevelt explained to the Congress following his return from Yalta,

> Our objective in handling Germany is simple. It is to secure the peace of the future world. Too much experience has shown that that objective is impossible if Germany is allowed to retain any ability to wage aggressive war. That objective will not harm the German people. On the contrary, it will protect them from a repetition of the fate which the General Staff and Kaiserism imposed upon them again hundred fold. It will be removing a cancer from the German body which for generations has produced only misery and pain for the whole world.[76]

During his last days, the President knew that Germany posed a serious problem to the future of world peace, and he was convinced that German power had to be contained. When he died on 12 April 1945, his fundamental attitude toward Germany was not appreciably different from what it had been in 1914 or in 1939. His conception of what was possible in the resolution of the "German problem" had undergone considerable modification, however, as a result of the complexities introduced by Hitler's war.

[1]George F. Kennan, Memoirs, 1925-1950 (Boston, 1967), p. 123.

[2]Arnold A. Offner, The Origins of the Second World War: American Foreign Policy and World Politics, 1917-1941 (New York, 1975).

[3]William Langer and S. Everett Gleason, The Challenge to Isolation, 1937-1940 (New York, 1952), pp. 38-39; Warren Kimball, The Most Unsordid Act: Lend-Lease, 1939-1941 (Baltimore, 1969), p. 239; T. R. Fehrenbach, F.D.R.'s Undeclared War, 1939 to 1941 (New York, 1967), pp. 16, 330; Selig Adler, The Uncertain Giant: American Foreign Policy Between the Wars (New York, 1965), p. 221; Wayne Cole, "American Entry Into World War II: A Historiographical Appraisal," Mississippi Valley Historical Review 43 (March 1957): 595-617; Robert Divine, The Reluctant Belligerent: American Entry Into World War II (New York, 1965), p. 158.

[4]Raymond G. O'Connor, Diplomacy for Victory: FDR and Unconditional Surrender (New York, 1971), passim.

[5]James Roosevelt, Affectionately F.D.R. (New York, 1959), p. 21.

[6]John Snell, Wartime Origins of the East-West Dilemma Over Germany (New Orleans, 1959), pp. 30-31.

[7]William Hassett, Off the Record with FDR, 1942-1945 (New Brunswick, N.J., 1958), p. 199.

[8]Press Conferences, XXV, 23 February 1945, President's Personal File, Franklin D. Roosevelt Papers, Roosevelt Library, Hyde Park, N.Y. (hereafter cited as PC, PPF, Roosevelt Papers).

[9]John Gunther, Roosevelt in Retrospect (New York, 1950), p. 116.

[10]Frank Freidel, Franklin D. Roosevelt (Boston, 1952-1956), 1:33-34.

[11] Ibid., 2:13; William Leuchtenburg, Franklin D. Roosevelt: A Profile (New York, 1967), p. 81; Sumner Welles, Seven Decisions that Shaped History (New York, 1950), p. 174; Willard Range, Franklin D. Roosevelt's World Order (Athens, 1959), p. 1; PC, XV, 8 April 1940, PPF, Roosevelt Papers; Adolf Berle to Roosevelt, 1 September 1938, "State Dept.-A.A. Berle" folder, President's Secretary's File, Franklin D. Roosevelt Papers, Roosevelt Library, Hyde Park, N.Y. (hereafter cited as PSF, Roosevelt Papers).

[12]Elliot Roosevelt, F.D.R.: His Personal Letters (New York, 1948-50), 4:810.

[13]Samuel Rosenman, The Public Papers and Addresses of Franklin D. Roosevelt (New York, 1938-1950), 7:493.

[14]Samuel Rosenman, Working with Roosevelt (New York, 1952), p. 189.

[15]Cordell Hull, The Memoirs of Cordell Hull (New York, 1948), 2:684.

[16]PC, XIII, 20 April 1939, PPF, Roosevelt Papers.

[17]Kennedy to Hull, 11 September 1939, 740.011/258, U.S. State Department records, RG 59, National Archives, Washington, D.C. (hereafter cited as D/S File #); Kirk to Hull, 18 October 1939, D/S File #740.0011/810.

[18]Hadley Cantril, Public Opinion, 1935-1946 (Princeton, 1951), p. 760.

[19]Roosevelt, Personal Letters 3:938-39.

[20]Hull to Kennedy, 11 September 1939, D/S File #740.0011/258.

[21]Rosenman, Public Papers 9:xxx.

[22]Congressman A. J. Sabeth to Roosevelt, 25 June 1941, folder 955, PPF, Roosevelt Papers; Leopold Amery to Myron Taylor, 19 December 1941, "Vatican: Myron Taylor, 1939-1944" folder, PSF: Diplomatic, ibid. Arthur Murray to Roosevelt, 8 February 1940, "Arthur Murray" folder, PSF: Great Britain, ibid.

[23]PC, XV, 5 June 1940, PPF, Roosevelt Papers.

[24]Memorandum of Conference held at the White House by Mr. Harry L. Hopkins, Special Assistant to President Roosevelt, 29 May 1942, U.S. Department of State, Foreign Relations of the United States (hereafter cited as FRUS), 1942 (Washington, 1961), 3:572-74.

[25]Roosevelt, Personal Letters 3:1372.

[26]Office of War Information, Bureau of Intelligence, to Oscar Cox, 6 March 1943, Lend-Lease Files, Box 76, Oscar Cox Papers, Roosevelt Library, Hyde Park, N.Y.; Cantril, Public Opinion, p. 170.

[27]Nancy Hooker, ed., The Moffat Papers (Cambridge, 1948), p. 388.

[28]Roosevelt, Personal Letters 4:1445.

[29]Louise Holborn, War and Peace Aims of the United Nations, 1943-1945 (Boston, 1948), 3:255.

[30]Bohlen minutes of Tripartite Meeting, 1 December 1943, FRUS: The Conferences at Cairo and Teheran, 1943 (Washington, 1961), p. 603; FRUS, 1942 3:520.

[31]Hooker, Moffat Papers, p. 388.

[32]Minutes of President's Meeting with Joint Chiefs of Staff, 19 November 1943, FRUS, The Conferences at Cairo and Teheran, 1943, p. 253.

[33]Ibid., p. 600.

[34]William Leahy, I Was There (New York, 1950), p. 210.

[35]Roosevelt Memorandum, "Safe File: Germany" folder, PSF, Roosevelt Papers.

[36]Hopkins Log of Casablanca Trip, Book 7: Casablanca, 24 January 1943, Harry Hopkins Papers, Roosevelt Library, Hyde Park, N.Y. (hereafter cited as Hopkins Papers); PC, XXI, 24 January 1943, PPF, Roosevelt Papers.

[37]Robert Sherwood, Roosevelt and Hopkins (New York, 1950), p. 697; Robert Murphy, Diplomat Among Warriors (Garden City, N.Y., 1964), p. 240.

[38]Address by President Roosevelt to Canadian Parliament, Department of State Bulletin 9 (25 August 1943): 123.

[39]Holborn, War and Peace Aims 3:232-34.

[40]Hull to Roosevelt, 14 January 1944, FRUS, 1944 (Washington, 1966), 1:493.

[41]Hull to Harriman, 24 January 1944, S/D File #740.0011/32571.

[42]Roosevelt to Charles C. Burlingham, 29 May 1944, folder 1169, PPF, Roosevelt Papers.

[43]Roosevelt to Daniel Marsh, 6 March 1944, folder 1090, ibid.

[44]Stettinius to Hull, 10 March 1944, S/D File #740.00119/2330.

[45]Joint Chiefs of Staff to Roosevelt, 25 March 1944, FRUS, 1944 1:501.

[46]Ibid., pp. 501-502.

[47]Hull to Roosevelt, 17 April 1944, "State Dept.: 1944-1945" folder, PSF, Roosevelt Papers.

[48]Hull to William Phillips, 17 April 1944, ibid.

[49]PC, XXIV, 29 July 1944, PPF, ibid.

[50]Roosevelt to Senator Kenneth McKellar, 21 August 1944, folder 3715, PPF, ibid.

[51]John Blum, From the Morgenthau Diaries (Boston, 1965-1967), 2:3.

[52]Eleanor Roosevelt, This I Remember (New York, 1949), pp. 333-35; Elliot Roosevelt, As I Saw It (New York, 1946), p. 238; Henry Morgenthau, Jr., Germany Is Our

Problem (New York, 1945), p. xi; Henry Morgenthau, Jr., "Postwar Treatment of Germany," Annals of the American Academy of Political and Social Science 246 (July 1946): 126; Range, Roosevelt's World Order, p. 83.

[53]James MacGregor Burns, Roosevelt: Soldier of Freedom (New York, 1970), p. 520.

[54]Blum, Morgenthau Diaries 3:565.

[55]Committee on the Judiciary, Morgenthau Diary (Germany) (Washington, 1967), 1:599.

[56]Ibid., 1:13.

[57]Blum, Morgenthau Diaries 3:342.

[58]Ibid.

[59]Morgenthau Diary 1:18; Blum, Morgenthau Diaries 3:18.

[60]Walter Millis, The Forrestal Diaries (New York, 1951), p. 10.

[61]Roosevelt to Stimson, 26 August 1944, FRUS, 1944 1:544-46; John Chase, "The Development of the Morgenthau Plan Through the Quebec Conference," The Journal of Politics 16 (May 1954): 337.

[62]Morgenthau Diary 1:4-5.

[63]Blum, Morgenthau Diaries 3:357-58.

[64]Morgenthau Diary 2:39.

[65]Henry Stimson and McGeorge Bundy, On Active Service In Peace and War (New York, 1948), p. 580.

[66]Roosevelt to Hull, 29 September 1944, FRUS: The Conferences at Malta and Yalta, 1945 (Washington, 1955), p. 155.

[67]Fred Israel, ed., The War Diary of Breckinridge Long (Lincoln, Nebraska, 1966), pp. 385-86.

[68]Blum, Morgenthau Diaries 3:419.

[69]Roosevelt, This I Remember, pp. 333-34.

[70]Ibid., p. 335.

[71]Roosevelt, As I Saw It, p. 238; Morgenthau, Jr., "Postwar Treatment of Germany," p. 125.

[72]Bohlen Memorandum on dinner meeting, Teheran Conference, 29 November 1943, Box 32, Hopkins Papers; Harriman notes on conversation with I. M. Maiski, Background to Yalta, 20 January 1943, Box 10, ibid.

[73]Charles E. Bohlen, Witness to History, 1929-1969 (New York, 1973), p. 211; Kennan, Memoirs, p. 229; Arthur Schlesinger, Jr., "Origins of the Cold War," Foreign Affairs 46 (October 1967): 48-50.

[74]Schlesinger, Jr., "Origins of the Cold War," p. 48; Robert Divine, Roosevelt and World War II (Baltimore, 1969), pp. 72-73.

[75]Roosevelt to Stettinius, 3 January 1945, FRUS: The Conferences at Malta and Yalta, 1945, p. 401.

[76]President's Report to Congress on Crimea Conference, Department of State Bulletin 12 (1 March 1945): 323.

THE WRINGER IN POSTWAR GERMANY:
ITS IMPACT ON UNITED STATES-GERMAN
RELATIONS AND DEFENSE
POLICIES

James M. Erdmann

During the height of the Cold War, a large-scale United States Air Force intelligence-collection operation resulted in the voluntary interrogation in West Germany of over 300,000 former Wehrmacht prisoners of war repatriated from Russia after the Second World War. Called the WRINGER, it attempted to determine the military capabilities and intentions of the Union of Soviet Socialist Republics. Directed principally by a diversified military intelligence organization under the operational direction of the Headquarters, United States Air Force Europe (USAFE), and with the assistance of several hundred German citizens, it sought to obtain current information about the resurgent industrial and military power of the Soviet Union and the Soviet-dominated states in Central and Eastern Europe. From more than one million intelligence information reports produced in five years of debriefings, USAFE widely disseminated significant data on Soviet activities among United States armed forces in Europe, the responsible ministries of the German Federal Republic, and various operational staffs of the emergent North Atlantic Treaty Organization (NATO) to guide them in developing national estimates and defense measures.

WRINGER reports provided NATO commanders with sufficiently detailed strategic and tactical information about Soviet political and military strength to enable them to work out adequate and feasible contingency plans to meet the confrontations of the Cold War. Should deterrence fail, the air intelligence information furnished by WRINGER reports gave the United States Air Force's Strategic Air Command (SAC) vital data for carrying out its contemporary strategic bombardment missions: descriptions of urban areas and targeting diagrams of key Soviet military installations, as well as analyses of the air defense systems around those power centers.

Carried on in nearly one hundred refugee camps or urban interrogation centers throughout the territory of the German Federal Republic, the field operations of the WRINGER program made a significant contribution to the improvement of German-American relations that characterized the postwar period in Germany. The willingness of German citizens to come to the debriefing centers and relate their experiences in Russia swept aside the cynicism of the immediate post-surrender years and the resentment often shown by the defeated soldiery toward their military occupiers. They were joined by millions of refugees who could describe from painful, firsthand experience the political coercion and expulsion of Germans from Eastern European lands. To the Americans and their German countrymen now serving as interrogators and translators in the WRINGER centers, the refugees expressed their abhorrence of communism. In helping the debriefing teams gather information about the new Soviet military-industrial power bases, as well as the build-up of Soviet military forces in Central Europe, they came to share the American apprehension of the growing threat of Soviet expansionism.

The recognition of the Soviet threat and the realization that the United States was prepared to defend Germany, projected as NATO's forward area in the event of a general war in Europe, generated a new confidence in American actions and policies. Many of Germany's future leaders worked for or passed through the WRINGER in the days of reconstruction: politicians, businessmen, industrialists, Bundeswehr officials, or simply parents of the next generation. Their friendly reception by WRINGER teams may account in part for their willingness after 1954 to see their country rearmed and to contribute major military forces to NATO for the defense of the West.

Genesis of the WRINGER Program

The WRINGER program was born during the winter of the 1948-1949 Berlin blockade, a time when the manifest threat of the Soviet Union to take control of Germany, if not to bring all of Central Europe under its domination, made it imperative for the United States and its NATO allies to prepare their military forces for general war in Europe. Its function was to provide the Department of Defense and the military establishments of the other NATO nations with

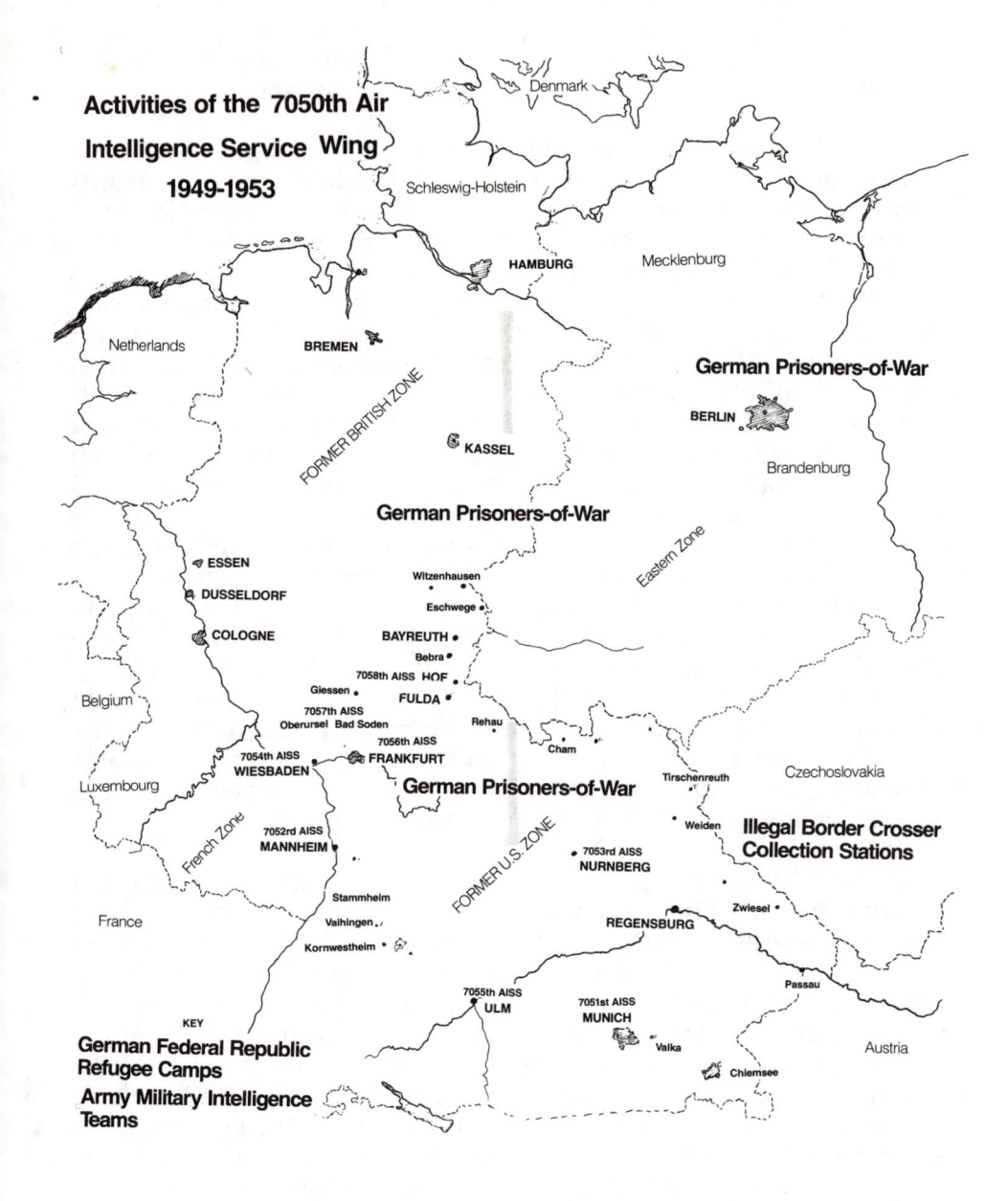

Activities of the 7050th Air Intelligence Service Wing 1949-1953

Denmark

Schleswig-Holstein

HAMBURG

Mecklenburg

Netherlands

BREMEN

FORMER BRITISH ZONE

German Prisoners-of-War

BERLIN

Brandenburg

KASSEL

German Prisoners-of-War

Eastern Zone

ESSEN

DUSSELDORF

COLOGNE

Witzenhausen

Eschwege

BAYREUTH

Bebra

7058th AISS HOF

Giessen

FULDA

7057th AISS
Oberursel Bad Soden

Rehau

Cham

Belgium

7056th AISS
FRANKFURT

Tirschenreuth

Czechoslovakia

7054th AISS
WIESBADEN

German Prisoners-of-War

Luxembourg

French Zone

FORMER U.S. ZONE

7052rd AISS
MANNHEIM

Weiden

Illegal Border Crosser Collection Stations

7053rd AISS
NURNBERG

France

Stammheim

Vaihingen

Kornwestheim

REGENSBURG

Zwiesel

Passau

7055th AISS
ULM

7051st AISS
MUNICH

Valka

Austria

Chiemsee

KEY

German Federal Republic Refugee Camps

Army Military Intelligence Teams

The WRINGER in Postwar Germany

enough information about the political moves and military strength of the Soviet Union to enable them to develop a strategy to prepare for such a conflict. The initial, somewhat hesitant and exploratory operations of the first WRINGER teams and their later incorporation into a fully manned and well-financed field collection agency can be understood only in the context of contemporary NATO strategy, the progenitor of the WRINGER program.

The purpose of the Allied Command Europe (ACE)--the international military structure established in the months following the signing of the North Atlantic Treaty in April, 1949--was to defend the territories and political integrities of the NATO signatories, including their rights in the occupation zones of Germany and Berlin. Conceived of at the dawn of an era in warfare that might well include intercontinental attacks by fleets of bombers carrying atomic weapons, ACE's mission was, first, to raise and deploy sufficient military forces to prevent a general war and, second, if war came despite the deterrent, to achieve victory. A combination of factors favored the adoption of what has been termed a "traditionalist"[1] doctrine of alternative responses to aggression by the Soviet Union in Central Europe: the nature of earlier military alliances and arrangements among the major NATO powers; their common experience in waging the Second World War in Europe-- particularly the lessons learned by the American strategic air forces and the British Royal Air Force Bomber Command in their joint strategic bombing offensive against Germany; and the preponderance of Soviet military manpower in Europe, coupled with the development of nuclear weapons in Western arsenals during the war.

This traditionalist doctrine called for the defensive positioning of the conventional military forces of the Western European nations from the boundaries of Western Germany back to the Rhine River, or, failing that, the launching from the United States and special air bases in England of a nuclear striking force against targets in Russia and its forward area. While relying on NATO's conventional forces and weapons to contain the Red Army in the opening days of hostilities, the United States would also be prepared to wreak such devastation on the society and war-making potential of the Soviet Union by air attack against the interior zones, that the Soviet leaders would

recoil from total war. To implement this strategy, the United States Strategic Air Command, designated as the primary force for any NATO counteroffensive operations, would be ordered to destroy the military forces, bases, and war-related industries in Russia itself, while ACE subordinate commands, provided with nuclear-armed fighter-bombers employed in an attack role, would strike at mobile targets in the aggressor's invasion force. NATO tactical aircraft, assigned to support the main ground armies, would defend the alliance bases coming under attack in NATO's area of responsibility.[2] Organized into a United States European Command (U.S. EUCOM),[3] all United States military forces in Europe were then assigned to NATO. The Commander-in-Chief, U.S. EUCOM, serving also as the Supreme Allied Commander Europe, would thus be able to employ against Russia all the Alliance forces in Europe. To do so, he would require carefully integrated war plans and complete military data on the Soviet Union.

As the confrontations of the Cold War culminated in the Berlin crisis during the winter of 1948-1949, the commander of United States forces in Europe set to work with his main subordinate commands to develop these war plans in detail and to assign missions to the few combat forces at his disposal.[4] It soon became apparent that neither a current military order-of-battle of the Soviet forces in Europe nor a comprehensive estimate of their possible modes of attack was available. Since the Soviet Union had been a wartime ally just four years before, only routine intelligence collection operations on the forces in the Soviet bloc had been conducted by Western nations. Now, to the dismay of American leaders still conditioned by the general euphoria following the defeat of Germany and the establishment of the United Nations, the 27 partly mechanized and highly mobile Red Army divisions in garrison status in or near the Soviet zone of occupation, recently augmented by Eastern European militia-type armies, loomed as possible invasion forces. If general war broke out over control of Berlin or the future of Germany, it was a foregone conclusion that the 175 to 250 Soviet divisions still mobilized in the interior of Russia, if employed as combined forces in a sustained offensive, had the combined might to overrun Germany and reach the Rhine River barrier within two weeks.[5] Only one combat-ready ground division had been assigned to NATO by the embryonic

Western Union Defense Organization (established by the Brussels Treaty in March, 1948), and the only American unit with a field-combat capability, the First Constabulary Division, was dispersed throughout the American zone of occupation in Germany and responsible only for maintaining civil order. Furthermore, there were few reserve forces left in the nations that had fought World War II. In their rush to disarm following the German surrender, the three principal combatants in the European Theater of Operations--the United States, Great Britain, and Canada--had reduced their troop strength from a combined total of 4,720,000 men to garrison forces of 391,000, 488,000, and none, respectively. Scattered around the globe for occupation duties, these troops on the average were poorly equipped; they had no combat supply, engineer, or artillery units; and in Europe they had no prepared positions from which to fight. There was not enough ammunition in the whole theater to last more than a few weeks.[6] The Soviet Union, meanwhile, had kept the bulk of its wartime veterans--an estimated 5,000,000 men in combat-ready divisions well supported by 6,000 modern aircraft--ready for immediate attack. A centralized Red Army command net now linked the forces in the Central European area with those in the military districts of the Soviet Union.

If general war should come to Western Europe in this period of ominous imbalance of military forces and the United States and other Alliance commanders were forced to use air attacks to stem a Soviet invasion, they would have to know the answers to certain important operational questions: which Red Army targets should be destroyed and in what order of priority? Which bases and war industries in the Central European area or in the Russian heartland fueled and propelled Red Army combat divisions? Should the ground armies debouching from the Soviet zone of occupation in Germany be attacked first or their support installations and their auxiliary forces? Which logistic arteries were most critical for the Soviet forces? Which were the most vulnerable? In this context, the main problem for later WRINGER interrogators and air force analysts was to determine where the vital Soviet military bases were and how they were defended against air attack. The information available to the small planning staffs in the U.S. EUCOM and SHAPE was obsolescent, sparse, and conflicting in nature. "The inadequacies of our intelligence were

recognized to be so extreme," an early historian of the 7050th Air Intelligence Service Wing (AISW) recounts, "that the initiation of spontaneous collection efforts [by Headquarters, USAFE] was ordered."[7]

By the summer of 1949, the Allied military services engaged in the build-up of the first combat-ready NATO divisions (there were only fourteen by the outbreak of the Korean War in June, 1950) were at work filling the intelligence gaps. The headquarters of the United States Air Force directed USAFE to provide the details from which to construct target maps on fifty main Soviet cities.[8] Officials in the Air Intelligence Directorate of the Office of the Assistant Chief of Staff, A-2, USAFE, acting on the directive, were thrown into a state of consternation because they had little cartographic data on the Soviet Union and no current intelligence describing the military installations in or adjacent to the key Russian cities. Their "Background USSR" files in the Air Vulnerabilities Section were dated and, when they appealed to the Aerial Reconnaissance Branch of the Collections Directorate for current photography, they were told that there had been no "recce" missions over Russia since the autumn of 1944, when German Luftwaffe reconnaissance flights had supported the Wehrmacht operations on the eastern front. The data collected on these missions was recognized as obsolete.[9] The collectors further noted that there was virtually no way to get a look at the vital centers in Russia from either the air or the ground. Russia had forbidden all foreign flights over its territory, and even the Allied diplomatic-mission flights to Moscow that the Soviets infrequently permitted were always routed by the Soviet navigators along courses which skirted the urban complexes by hundreds of kilometers. Similarly, Allied military attachés assigned to Moscow normally were denied travel permits to visit other areas in the Soviet Union. Few European businessmen were being admitted to the country, and German scientists working in the Soviet Union at the end of the war were usually kept in protective custody for an average of five years before being allowed to return home.

The Decision to Exploit the POWs

At this juncture, some Air Intelligence Information Reports that had been routinely compiled in the Air

165

Vulnerabilities Section of the Air Intelligence Directorate, USAFE A-2, from background investigations of some of the first repatriated POWs from Russia, were read with renewed interest.[10] The POWs, it was noticed, had been incarcerated in labor camps all over Russia and put to work repairing Russia's bomb-damaged installations or constructing new factories. Most of them had been used as common laborers, clearing away rubble, erecting buildings, or digging ore from mines; but a small portion had worked inside the new factories. Most important, many of them had come from the very urban areas listed in the priority targets.[11]

USAFE intelligence analysts who were assigned the task of compiling data on the key Soviet cities soon realized that the repatriated POWs--many of whom had experience in the fields of engineering and the skilled trades before receiving technical training in the Wehrmacht--possessed a surprisingly accurate and detailed knowledge about the new steel mills, chemical plants, power and communications facilities, and military installations that the Russians were now building behind their war-devastated zones. How could their knowledge be exploited? It was gradually perceived that possibly an air force target chart for one of the new military or industrial complexes could be produced by a trained interrogator directing all the ex-POWs who had labored in that same area to describe in detail the factories on which they had worked. Their individual memory sketches could be later fitted together like the pieces of a jigsaw puzzle to form a composite installation diagram. Similarly, if questioned by experts familiar with the emerging mosaic of Soviet power centers, refugees daily fleeing the Russian-controlled areas of Central and Eastern Europe often were able to confirm from their own observations or by means of correspondence with friends and relatives living in the Soviet bloc the existence of the installations in the Soviet's forward area.

Pursuant to the exploitation of those they categorized as "Human Intelligence" sources, staff planners in the responsible offices of the air force intelligence hierarchy down to the only field unit in existence in USAFE, the small First Air Intelligence Service Organization,[12] went to work to develop adequate operations to carry out their formidable mission. Their initial problem, that of estimating the size

of the pool of knowledgeable sources, was four-fold: to determine how many refugees and POWs were already present in West Germany or would become available in the future, where they came from, what their value was as informants, and how they could be contacted.

How many POW camps were there in the vastness of Russia between Moscow and the Urals, and had their inmates really learned anything of military-intelligence value? An 11 January 1949 report from the 7707th EUCOM Intelligence Center, entitled "List of PW Camps in the USSR" and summarizing all information available to the end of 1948, listed only 116 camps as "frequently confirmed by PW's," 41 camps as confirmed "once or twice," and 46 as "possibly in existence." This same study reported a total POW population in the camps of 11,059 officers and 141,640 enlisted men.[13]

Western Allied officials in Germany realized that these figures were probably much lower than the actual numbers of camps and the POWs housed in them, but until the 1950 national registration instigated by Chancellor Konrad Adenauer in the German Federal Republic[14] there were no reliable official numbers. The military offices and quasi-official agencies in Germany authorized to assist in the care and relocation of the overwhelming flood of demobilized soldiers and destitute people moving back and forth across Europe had often grouped together such categories as: "Members of Former German Armed Forces Missing"; "Civilians Carried Off to the Soviet Union"; and "Civilian Prisoners in Custody in Eastern States."[15] In the 23 April 1947 "Agreement of Foreign Ministers at Moscow, Regarding Repatriation of German War Prisoners," Soviet Deputy Premier Vyacheslav Molotov stated that there were currently only 890,532 POWs left in the Soviet Union, of whom 252,395 would be returned before March, 1948. In January, 1949, however, the Western Allies called attention to some major discrepancies between the numbers of POWs who had come into their custody and the Soviet claims. They insisted that 1½ million persons were still unaccounted for, in addition to those listed on their rosters as "dead" or "released."[16] The Adenauer government sent a commission to the United Nations the next year with voluminous documentation to appeal for assistance in ascertaining the fate of 1,156,663 members of the "former German Armed Forces

missing in the Eastern Theater of War," a number that included 118,507 POWs known by name to be in the custody of the Soviet Union, Czechoslovakia, and Poland.[17] Through the TASS news agency in Frankfurt on 4 May 1950, the Soviets claimed that they had returned 1,939,163 "prisoners" after the end of the war and that the repatriation of German POWs was now completed. Germans in both the Eastern and Western zones were stunned, and the Allies now combined their protests with those of the German government in what was becoming a major issue in the Cold War.

Value and Availability of POWs as Air Intelligence Sources

WRINGER planners early in 1949 did not have access to all the records giving rise to this dispute, but informal talks with German refugee-camp commanders, officials from the German Red Cross, and church-sponsored relief agencies convinced them that large numbers of knowledgeable sources would soon become available in Western Germany. The flow of refugees encountered in screening camps in Austria and on the zonal borders of West Germany was expected to fluctuate widely, depending on political conditions in Eastern Europe. Aware of the general attitude of the Russians with regard to the justice of holding and working the POWs ("of course we have more than 890,000 prisoners, but we need them more than Germany does," said one Russian officer in Berlin[18]), intelligence planners estimated that between 4,000 and 6,000 POWs a month would be arriving. They further calculated that approximately 50 percent of the POWs released in 1949 and 1950 would possess information of value, giving them a pool of at least a million informants to interrogate immediately, with the prospect of hundreds of thousands in the future.[19]

During the confrontation that accompanied the Berlin blockade, WRINGER advocates justified expanding their role by emphasizing the worth of the air intelligence already collected from refugees and POWs coming from Central Europe. They also predicted that as the Soviet bloc became increasingly isolated from the West, POWs might be the only intelligence informants of the future. There was already much evidence that the Soviets and their East German allies

were making the Berlin and zonal borders to the West impassable with barbed wire, land mines, and armed patrols by the Volkspolizei, and that soon the only point of exodus for refugees would be the western sectors of Berlin and its airfields.

Many officers of the respective air staffs were skeptical of the POWs as intelligence sources. The issue involved two considerations: first, the physical condition of men who had spent years at hard labor, and second, the political attitudes of Germans permitted to go home. The efforts of the Soviets to indoctrinate captured German officers and enlisted men were well known. The shocking debilitation of the first returning servicemen from the Soviet Union in the summer of 1948 had convinced many officials that, with very few exceptions, POWs might be physically incapable of undergoing any kind of extended interrogation. To cite one example, one news report from Hamburg described the condition of a trainload of 450 German war prisoners and 60 women forced laborers returning to the British zone: "ten of the women and forty-five men were transferred immediately to hospitals suffering from heart and lung problems; most of the women had worked in Siberia and the Ural Mountains."[20]

Furthermore, should some POWs happen to be returned early and in good health, would it not be because they had been converted to the socialist cause and provided with better food and living conditions in return for their new allegiance? Debriefers in the West German receiving camps had become aware that the Soviet authorities had started an intensive campaign to segregate the POWs. Alternating techniques of persuasion and intimidation, Soviet prison officials identified and collected for repatriation only those POWs who showed a political awakening. The results of this program became evident in early 1949 when a group of the selected POWs arrived in Augsburg: "It is not the fault of the USSR if so many PW's return to Germany in a pitiable state," one of them said. "It is the fault of the PW's themselves if they do not recover politically."[21] Ominously, other members of this group had declared that the Russians "had no more patience" with the POWs still in their custody and would discharge henceforth only those considered reliable anti-fascists and democrats. Russian officials confirmed this view in East Berlin on 21 September

1950 when they announced the repatriation of the first contingent of thousands of German engineers and technicians who had been working in the Soviet Union over the previous five years "to repair the damage done by the Fascist German invaders." One of those repatriated explained to news correspondents at a hastily arranged press conference, "We are locked in friendship with the Soviet people; now we are pledged to fight for peace and the unification of Germany."[22]

Opposite conclusions were drawn by the daring British reporter Werner Knop, one of the first Westerners to penetrate the Soviet zone of occupation in Germany and investigate conditions there. Stealing across the zonal boundary into the area of the Harz Mountains early in 1948, he spent several months investigating such developments as the communists' virulent propaganda campaign against their former allies, the new forced-labor camps for political dissidents, the Soviets' efforts to collectivize agriculture, and their methods of converting German workers into proletarians. Anxious to know German war prisoners' true feelings toward the Soviet Union and communism, he returned to West Germany and visited the federal camp at Moschendorf:

> I watched the arrival of two thousand men and thirty women--ten thousand years of captivity in Siberia behind them, and upon their faces ten times as many years of wretchedness. Fifteen minutes before, they had gone through the Russian border station and had seen the last of the tawdry paraphernalia of Bolshevik propaganda, the drab little red flags, the posters and banners. They had heard the Communists turn into apostles of commiseration, pitying them for having to live under the rule of American imperialism. Under their arms they carried the voluminous History of the Communist Party of the Soviet Union and a dozen pamphlets by Molotov, Vishinsky, Pieck, and Grotewohl--farewell presents that soon would lie discarded in a mountain of waste paper.[23]

Although it was difficult to talk to the "fearful and distrustful" POWs, Knop surmised that once they had reached their homes and rejoined their families, they would

170

regain their confidence and be willing to talk about their experiences. Almost unanimously, he discovered, the POWs hated Russian communism as a system, were contemptuous of the backwardness of Russian life, and harbored no deep animosity toward the Western occupation officials--especially the "Ami's," as they called the Americans.[24]

The relatively few air force and army intelligence specialists then in the reception centers in Germany generally agreed with Knop's evaluation. They also observed that very often ex-Wehrmacht men enjoyed the best rapport with the POWs because they talked to the returnees in their own jargon about their common experiences fighting the Russians. One German working for the Americans, who later became an outstanding WRINGER interrogator, explained why the POWs rejected communist propaganda and the blandishments of the political agents in the Soviet labor camps: "Na, they had eaten from the pudding."[25]

WRINGER Gets a Name and
Air Force Backing

The young air force intelligence officer who created the WRINGER effort was Major Robert F. Work. In Austria during the Berlin crisis, he met some of the first POWs to be repatriated to that country and recognized their value as informants. A German linguist and graduate of the Army Air Force Intelligence School at Harrisburg, Pennsylvania, Work interrogated captured Luftwaffe personnel in Allied custody during World War II and knew by training and experience that small bits of information about an enemy, extracted by detailed questions from a carefully prepared checklist, could result in an accurate appraisal of his capabilities and intentions. As the officer in charge of a small Air Intelligence Field Office working out of Linz and Vienna, he gleaned disturbing news about Soviet actions in Central Europe from the displaced persons and other refugees from the East who sought sanctuary in Austria. One day in March, 1948, he received information from the headquarters of the American military government in Vienna that a trainload of POWs from Russia was scheduled to reach the border. He took a small team of intelligence personnel to meet the train:

It was a sight that rivalled the worst we had just seen in the concentration camps. Some of the prisoners were dead on arrival; some, I am sure, died beside the tracks when they were rolled out of the freight cars. I remember stooping over one young man, picking him up by the shoulders, which were pure bone, his face taut and gaunt, in the final stages of starvation. "My God!" I said. "How did you come to this condition?" "They worked us to death in rebuilding their war factories," he said. That was the first WRINGER report.[26]

Major Work hastily instigated some screening and debriefing operations among this group of returnees. Shorthanded in German-speaking assistants, uncertain how the POWs would be processed through the receiving centers and sent home, and lacking specific collection requirements or maps for the new targets in the Soviet Union, he and his teammates perforce located the most promising sources almost by instinct and quizzed them in the most general terms, e.g., "Did you see any airfields in Russia?"[27] While Work and his men thought they had produced a few good reports, they were frustrated because they had obviously missed many other potential sources of information about urban areas and military plant installations. Was such information, however, the type air force intelligence really wanted, or would such data duplicate that being collected elsewhere?

Work requested more official guidance and more trained men from the First Air Intelligence Service Organization located at Fürstenfeldbrück Air Base in Bavaria. The commander there, citing his basic mission to keep his linguists and air technical intelligence experts on short call for fast-breaking assignments,[28] and his continuing commitment to furnish translators and intelligence assistants to the Headquarters, USAFE, refused to assign his men to temporary duty in Austria. Besides, he intimated, ex-POWs were not as good an intelligence source as high-level defectors. Major Work realized, however, that there were not many high-level defectors coming out of Russia in those days, and none at all from the Soviet air force.[29]

Disturbed by such experiences but determined to prove the worth of human intelligence collection and develop a program commensurate to the opportunities in Europe,[30] Major Work moved to his next assignment--duty in the Office of the Director of Intelligence, Headquarters, United States Air Force. Because of the Berlin crisis and with a 70-group air force under consideration,[31] the late summer of 1948 was a propitious time to present proposals to the air staff. Work's views also coincided with those of Major General Charles Cabell, who had recently been advanced to Director of Intelligence, Headquarters, United States Air Force.[32] General Cabell brought to his new job not only a thorough familiarity with the strategy and execution of air warfare, derived from his wartime experience in high command and staff (operations and intelligence) positions in both the European and Mediterranean war zones,[33] but also an extraordinarily broad knowledge of the international disputes that were the root cause of the Cold War.

Having seen the Soviet Union defer, rebuff, and ultimately betray American efforts to establish an eastern air force in the Soviet Union to help the Red Army fight German forces on the Russian front during the war, and having witnessed the disastrous results of the later use of Soviet air bases at Poltava to facilitate the shuttle bombing of Germany, Cabell concluded that the Soviets respected military power alone; and he was convinced that Joseph Stalin would terminate Allied military assistance when Russian power was sufficient to defeat Germany.[34] Cabell realized the Soviets wanted German military power destroyed permanently, and he understood their desire to have a protective buffer of friendly states on their borders; but the Soviet forces in Europe had been maintained at a level of strength and readiness far in excess of the capability of meeting those goals, and Soviet conduct in Germany was certainly menacing. Whether the confrontations of the late 1940's would result in war with the Soviet Union, he did not know. Readiness to meet a war threat was essential, however, and the air staff required that forces be ready to implement the various alternatives then being considered in the new Department of Defense. The air strategists in Secretary of Defense James Forrestal's planning sections had necessarily considered employing nuclear weapons in the air war phases of hostilities. General Carl Spaatz, the first Air Force Chief of Staff, explained to the Air Policy

Board in late 1947 how such a war "within the next 4 to 15 years" might be conducted:

> We will first employ our long range strategic bombers in a retaliatory action as expeditiously as possible. Atomic bombs will be used and the system of targets to be attacked will be those which would produce the maximum 'blunting' effect [emphasis mine].[35]

In terms of war with the Soviet Union, though, significant intelligence gaps existed. What were those targets? Where did they lie? What was their relationship to the Red Army forces committed to the field? How well were they defended? The air staff planners were certain that the air force's Strategic Air Command would have to be a viable force; its crews would have to find, identify, and hit the targets. That meant the exhaustive task of target-intelligence collection and operational planning lay ahead.

At the end of 1948, General Cabell authorized a greatly expanded intelligence program in USAFE. He allotted $400,000 to cover the expected cost of the WRINGER activities; he reorganized his directorate to handle the flood of incoming data they expected; and he dispatched Work and Lee Canfield, one of his senior air force intelligence analysts in the headquarters, to Paris and Wiesbaden to urge the theater commanders to provide organizational support. A Far East counterpart to the collection effort was planned for Japan, but the major operations to exploit intelligence sources would be conducted in Germany where the greatest pool of knowledgeable informants about Russia lived.

In the spring of 1949, Work and Canfield surveyed and evaluated POW utilization in Germany and then briefed Colonel William C. Bentley, the Assistant Chief of Staff/Intelligence, Headquarters, USAFE, and members of his staff concerning the air force's new plans and backing for expanded operations. They estimated the numbers and language skills of the required intelligence personnel and offered suggestions for managing the heavy flow of incoming collection requirements and outgoing reports expected to result from the new program. At this briefing, the nickname WRINGER was adopted for the overall effort. As Work recalled the scene:

174

Colonel Bentley . . . had visibly warmed to the idea as I was standing at the briefing charts . . . . I had always described what we were after as 'wringing out' every last bit of usable data from every single person who had been inside of the USSR . . . . I remember the look in Bentley's eyes as I described this wringing process and, at that instant, I knew I had the name for the project . . . and said so.[36]

In June, 1949, U.S. EUCOM established a unit designation and a table of organization for the 7001st Air Intelligence Service Squadron (AISS), whose primary mission was "to collect positive Air Intelligence Information from overt sources."[37] The squadron was allotted 40 officers, 101 airmen, and 103 foreign nationals to do its work. Collecting their language dictionaries, classified documents, background-investigation files, and intelligence source registries, the first assignees began operation in a vacated office building just across the courtyard from 13 Luisenstrasse, Wiesbaden, the interim home for USAFE headquarters personnel. Assigned to the 12th Tactical Air Force with its personnel projected for assignment to field teams throughout the American zone of occupation, the 7001st AISS still carried its original function of "providing foreign-language assistance to the Office of the Deputy Chief of Staff/ Intelligence, Hq USAFE, as required." Air force headquarters initially allocated only $27,000 from its confidential funds to pay for source reimbursement and furnished scant additional guidance about the information desired on 50 Soviet cities, but WRINGER was now official.[38]

The squadron selected small teams of officers and airmen from its Wiesbaden nucleus and located them in the populous, easily reached main cities of central and south Germany. Working out of nondescript indigenous buildings, and in the closest coordination with local German authorities, the teams contacted and invited for interviews the most promising of the "untapped hundreds of thousands of POWs." The squadron established "USAF Historical Research" teams in Ulm (am Donau), Hof, Hersfeld, Frankfurt, Munich, Nuremberg, Stuttgart (Esslingen), Mannheim, Königstein (im Taunus), and Oberürsel (im Taunus) and arranged for adjacent United States Army

military posts to supply and maintain their physical facilities. The teams in the city centers then sent three- or four-man detachments into the German reception centers for POWs and refugees to screen new arrivals for current intelligence information and to card and identify for subsequent work in the city centers any sources with important knowledge bearing on the WRINGER requirements. Air force screening officers were stationed in the main federal camps for returnees and refugees; they were also sent to the numerous small camps maintained by the German states for persons awaiting resettlement whenever the size and character of the camp populations warranted a search. To keep track of this influx of potential informants, the squadron operations personnel adopted an all-purpose production-control form used in the business world, the McBee Keysort Card. In the camps, the screening officers recorded on the McBee cards each ex-prisoner's name, his probable future location in Germany, and such biographical particulars as his general education and military training--a most valuable index to his reliability as an observer. In addition, they assigned a code letter to each source indicating the relative value of his potential intelligence information, and then forwarded a copy of the McBee card to the squadron headquarters for the preparation of a letter inviting the man to come to the nearest center for an interview. The city centers compiled a parallel biographical file on the POW sources already in Germany, and the two lists were ultimately combined into a register of nearly 400,000 names.

Enter the Germans

The need for German-speaking operatives initially was greater than the 7001st AISS could supply from among its air force personnel, so the squadron teams began hiring Germans to fill their authorization of 103 foreign nationals. The first recruits were often the same German officials the air force screening officers had encountered in the camps; occasionally they were demobilized Wehrmacht men already employed at neighboring United States Army sub-posts but looking for better paying and more responsible employment. Especially trustworthy and capable Germans in the military government whose jobs were terminating were sometimes recommended by their superiors for transfer to the squadron.

A good example of this first hiring system was Rolf Bömmelburg of Munich, a former lawyer and cavalry officer from Berlin who had lost an arm in the war on the eastern front. Requisitioned after the German surrender as the translator for a small, roving air force team assigned to a graves-registration and missing persons search unit, he traveled across Germany in a jeep attempting to determine the fate or the burial place of downed Allied fliers. His team questioned both American and German officials in their search, and Rolf acquired a good knowledge of American military organization and procedures as well as a familiarity with the systems in effect in the German camps for handling refugees and POWs.[39]

The increasing numbers of POWs being processed required a move to the facilities of the Hotel Stadt Rosenheim in a Munich suburb; and the many new intelligence collection demands also required more inter- viewers. Advertisements were placed in the local news- papers:

> . . .The U.S. Air Force is seeking skilled German personnel for linguists and translators. . . . . technical and professional backgrounds desireable but not necessary.[40]

Dr. Rudolf Pietzsch was typical of the Germans hired for the WRINGER program. A chemical engineer with long experience in the manufacture of metal alloys by electro- chemical processes, Dr. Pietzsch had avoided military service in the German army because he had been needed to manage a family-owned factory in Munich for the German war effort. To escape the increasing threat of Allied bombing raids over south Germany in 1944, he had moved the plant to Dresden--only to have it suffer almost total destruction in the devastating Allied bombing raids of 13-15 February 1945 on that city. Salvaging enough to build a factory that manufactured insulation panels for the con- struction industry, he was forced into bankruptcy when his partner absconded to Portugal with the company funds. Back home in Munich by early 1950 and in a precarious economic situation, but with a good command of English and engineering experience that he thought would be useful in the rebuilding of Germany, he applied to "some Americans of the Air Force" for one of the advertised jobs, submitting

a personal history and a photograph. He was interviewed and given a written examination which required him to translate into English some passages from a German technical journal. "I must have been what they were looking for," he recently recalled, "for the very next day they called me back and a sergeant took me into a room, introduced me to a prisoner from Russia who had worked on the oil pipeline from Saratov to Kuibyshev, and told me to get everything I could on the pipe line!"[41]

WRINGER Helps the Strategic Air Command Attain War-Readiness Status

More than half of the POWs contacted between the autumn of 1949 and the spring of 1951 accepted the invitations to "talk about the real circumstances surrounding their lives in recent years." Their observations and memory sketches provided the substance for 99,825 separate intelligence reports. In compliance with the primary WRINGER requirement for city plans, over half of the reports consisted of area descriptions of military and industrial sites in the Soviet Union obtained from 70 percent of the sources questioned. Also included as attachments, however, were detailed maps of specific installations, technical drawings of weapons and machinery, copies of official Russian documents, photographs, material samples and machine parts--a total of 140,000 separate items of intelligence data.[42] WRINGER was able to furnish new or corroborative data on such subjects as military uses of television in Russia; developments in the field of rockets and missiles; the mechanics and manufacturing technology for gear-reduction equipment in propeller-driven aircraft; technical secrets about how to make parts for jet engines, particularly the blades for the air compressors; meteorological instruments; the technology of Soviet synthetic fuel plants; water control and storage facilities of key Soviet cities; flight-test data on new Soviet aircraft; the compactibility of the soils and roadbed strength of transportation nets in certain strategic corridors to support heavy vehicles; and information about the sites, support facilities, and foreign scientific personnel connected with the Soviet intercontinental ballistic missile programs. While the reports dealing with the Soviet Union's vital industrial targets were only fractional percentages of the total--metals industries 10 percent, munitions and armaments 8 percent,

aircraft industries 5 percent, power plants 5 percent--the number of transmittals was a remarkable achievement and demonstrated that mass exploitation of human intelligence sources was not only feasible but indispensable.

Most of the Air Intelligence Information Reports prepared during this formative period went into making target materials for the Strategic Air Command and served to alert its planners to the ever-expanding requirements of their bombardment mission. Indirectly, then, the reports played a significant role in justifying the regeneration of SAC's air strike forces. Some of the WRINGER reports revealed enough reliable evidence about the physical vulnerability and the defenses of certain targets that Strategic Air Command planners could organize their total list of important targets into priority groupings for attack and assign appropriate ordnance to each. Invariably, however, as the planners studied their target materials, they found that designating the routes and altitudes of attack raised hundreds of new questions, such as what obstacles lay along the routes. Periodically they initiated new sets of requests for information, which the air force in turn passed on to the field collectors. Ultimately the WRINGER teams claimed that they produced more than half the total number of reports covering Russia and the satellite nations used by the Strategic Air Command.[43]

General Curtis E. LeMay, who took command of the Strategic Air Command in the spring of 1948, has given some insight into the use of WRINGER intelligence. Noting that "we didn't have one crew in the entire command who could do a professional job . . . . no one of the outfits was up to strength--neither in airplanes, nor in people, nor anything else,"[44] he determined "to make certain that what we had was going to be ready to go and could fight":

> We fathered a master war plan. Everyone knew, eventually, what he was going to do. Each crew was assigned an enemy target, and they studied those targets . . . . People working for us and with us invented and constructed training aids whereby a man, if he was assigned a target at Moscow, could bomb Moscow hundreds of times, merely by using his training aid. . . [emphasis mine].[45]

WRINGER reports on urban areas played a major role in the development of the radar target simulators he referred to. The Russian landscape had been sufficiently delineated by POW memory sketches so that three-dimensional models of the key Russian cities could be constructed and photographed on radar-prediction film. Strategic Air Command crews on a simulated bombing run could see the terrain and the configuration of the target itself exactly as they would appear during a mission.[46]

A dramatic example of the way in which WRINGER-extracted intelligence served to update existing target materials concerns the production of a radar-simulation film for the city of Magnitogorsk, the third largest steel producing city in Russia. Earlier target charts showed a large steel factory lying beside a lake west of the city. The lake, which supplied water to both the city and the steel plant, had been formed by an earthen dam across the Ural River. For a bombing attack on the factory, the center of the lake would make a good aiming point because of its high radar-reflective characteristics. Hundreds of POWs had since labored to build a new cofferdam several kilometers downstream, however; when questioned by WRINGER interrogators, they reported that the water basin had quadrupled in size and that its approximate center now was located several miles south of the steel plant. On an actual mission against Magnitogorsk, then, a bomb run using the radar-located center of the lake as a release point--assuming a run from west to east--would have resulted in a relatively harmless impact on the small village lying to the south of the main city.[47]

The Berlin crisis of 1948-1949 was one of several Cold War confrontations hastening the creation of a war-ready Strategic Air Command. Beginning with its direction of the Berlin airlift and spurred by its new requirement to provide tactical air forces for Allied Command Europe, USAFE achieved a revolution in its organization, training, and theater operations.[48] The Third and Twelfth Air Forces were re-established and re-equipped under USAFE command in January, 1951, and the atomic-armed Seventeenth Air Force was created in April, 1953, thus giving the Commander-in-Chief, USAFE, serving as the commander of the 4th Allied Tactical Air Force, a nuclear weapon striking force to spearhead NATO's Allied Force Center in Germany.

180

These three new air forces, as well as the troop carrier, aircraft-control-and-warning, and auxiliary squadrons in the theater, were voracious in their demands for explicit, current air intelligence information about Russia. In addition, USAFE was made responsible for conducting several training and exercise operations in the other thirty-four countries embraced in its area of responsibility, primarily ferrying large numbers of aircraft to countries receiving American military aid. Finally, in response to the projected rearming of Germany envisioned by the incorporation of German forces in the recently established European Defense Community, USAFE began to provide equipment, flying training, and mission-associated air intelligence to the fledgling German air force. Since the above tasks generated a need for expanded strategic intelligence on the entire Soviet bloc, a heavily augmented and more diversified air intelligence collection program for USAFE was mounted, including a great expansion of the WRINGER operations.

Establishment of the 7050th AISW and the WRINGER at Maximum Strength

In February, 1951, Brigadier General Millard Lewis became Deputy Chief of Staff, Intelligence, Headquarters, USAFE, and began strengthening the entire range of air intelligence activity in Europe. He increased the number of personnel in the 7001st AISS to the point that the squadron was elevated to the status of a major-command Air Intelligence Service Wing, the 7050th AISW.[49] By the spring of 1951, it was authorized to recruit the following: 115 officers and warrant officers, 265 airmen, 71 Department of the Air Force civilians, and 589 foreign nationals, of which the great majority would be Germans. General Lewis brought Air Technical Intelligence personnel from the United States, formed them into Air Technical Liaison Officer teams covering a number of scientific subjects, and placed them on direct call to any 7050th AISW interrogators who encountered high-level, scientific sources requiring a specialized debriefing. Finally, with the concurrence of officials in the former British zone of occupation in Germany, where Royal Air Force personnel had already compiled biographic data on approximately 50,000 returnees in that area, he stationed two interrogation flights at Essen and five smaller teams at Dusseldorf, Hanover, Bad Salzuflen, Cologne, and Hamburg.[50]

To provide for the exploitation of the future thousands of returnees they were now soliciting, General Lewis and his air force intelligence staff officers obtained larger urban facilities for use as interrogation centers, including the famous Palace of Justice in Nuremberg. Within the Headquarters, USAFE, a small reports-reproduction branch was enlarged into a veritable printing plant, so that WRINGER transmittals could be duplicated and disseminated to an expanded list of interested agencies: Allied Command Europe, Radio Free Europe, the Voice of America, and friendly governments.

One of the first beneficiaries of the increased collection and publication efforts was the German Federal Republic. Forbidden by the original United States Military Government decrees from possessing any national military forces, it was nevertheless faced with a critical need for a border police force adequate to control the increasing number of political refugees, illegal border crossers, and communist agents slipping across the zonal boundries. When the Federal Border Police was established in 1950, its size (approximately 20,000 officers and men) and deployment were predicated upon data furnished by American intelligence agencies, including many WRINGER reports.[51]

Another important new German agency receiving United States intelligence reports in this period was the Federal Office for the Protection of the Constitution (known as the "German FBI"). Responsible for conducting surveillance on communist agents and spies, it was seriously undermanned initially. Because of this early limitation, agency officials appreciated the explicit WRINGER reports on German collaborators working with the communist agencies in the German Democratic Republic.[52]

Changing Attitudes

The strategic reappraisals that paralleled the developments of the Cold War all stressed the need for a revitalized West Germany and the friendship of the German people. The eleven-month long Soviet blockade of West Berlin marked the beginning of an historic reversal of Western international alliances and a basic change of mutual attitudes on the part of the American and West German

peoples. The embattled mayor of (West) Berlin, Ernst Reuter, noted the shift of sympathies:

> Without any question the people of Berlin have felt during the last year that they are fighting for something in common with the West. You can see for yourself that the relationship between American soldiers and the people around Templehof is very friendly. It is a great difference. Our people no longer have a feeling that the United States is an occupying power. Now the man in the street feels you are here to defend us.[53]

American-sponsored surveys of attitudinal changes among Germans in the early 1950's[54] indicate that their pronounced shift in opinion--away from an attitude of postwar indifference toward their military occupiers, American and Russian alike, and toward militantly pro-American positions--came earlier in Berlin than in the Western occupation zones because of the longer anti-totalitarian tradition of West Berlin residents, their front line situation in the Cold War, and the dramatic nature of the airlift that broke the Soviet blockade. Something akin to that warmer relationship between American soldiers and the German people, compounded of the humanitarian policies of military government and the assurance of military protection guaranteed by the presence of American forces in Germany, was noticeable in public opinion in Western Germany by 1951.

WRINGER deserves a significant amount of credit for the improvement in German-American attitudes. As Herman J. Eckhardt, one German national who received a commendation for his unusually helpful reports, recalls, "We came to rely more on each other to get the mission accomplished, commanded each other's respect, and finally became friends."[55] Out of this esprit de corps and the sense of mutual jeopardy in the face of the growing Soviet threat, a sense of comradeship in arms developed which also characterized the later relations between German and American soldiers deployed along the border of East Germany.

The End of the WRINGER

In the spring of 1953, the exploitation of large numbers of intelligence sources came under critical review. As one visiting analyst stated, "WRINGER reports are subject to the law of diminishing returns; the last 1000 reports are not as valuable as were the first 1000." The relative value of POW-furnished data declined as other instruments of air intelligence collection on the Soviet Union reached a state of reliability, and air force budget allocations for intelligence collection were increasingly devoted to the programs for developing electronic sensors of all types. Inevitably the Germans in the WRINGER program, now fluent in technical and scientific terminology and well informed about Eastern European industry, moved to better paying jobs in the German economy. A number of them were hired by American firms opening up branches in Germany, not only for their experience and language skills but also because they were now familiar with American managerial characteristics.

The WRINGER had a major impact on German-American relations. The German nationals employed and trained by the air force units conducting WRINGER operations were almost equal in number to the German cultural leaders, government officials, university students, and teenagers taken to the United States for indoctrination under the State Department's justly praised German-American Exchange Program.[56] The Germans working incognito in the 7050th AISW, in addition to their contribution to the building of NATO, may have exerted during their WRINGER service and then in civil life an equal influence upon their countrymen, especially in the field of foreign relations for the German Federal Republic. As a general rule, after their WRINGER career they entered business or commercial life, or in a few cases continued their same type of work for the intelligence services of the new Bundeswehr rather than going into politics, so their influence in the formation of German public opinion was indirect. Contemporary public opinion surveys of the changing attitudes of Germans toward communism, the Soviet nemesis, and the United States defense policies in the early 1950's, indicate that it was those very elements in German society that had a personal or closely reasoned basis for their fear and hatred

of the Soviet Union--POWs, refugees, ex-military person-nel--that most strongly supported German rearmament and Germany's membership in NATO in the decisive period between 1950 and 1955. Certainly the Germans who entered into the life of their new nation, and who had had some experience with the WRINGER debriefings, carried into the political arena a revised world view of great significance for the future course of European history: that the United States was both sincere and capable in its promise to defend them, provided they shouldered their share of the common task of protecting their new democratic republic and fulfilling their responsibilities to the Atlantic community to which they now belonged.

[1] George E. Lowe, The Age of Deterrence (Boston, 1964), pp. 1-5, 9-12, 93-120. The doctrinal core of the traditionalist position was that "we must be prepared to meet the enemy at his level of provocation and set up as many 'hurdles' as possible--military, political, economic, moral and psychological--before being driven to use nuclear weapons." Additionally, there must be conventional forces in NATO to provide a deterrent alternative to the clear capacity of the Strategic Air Command to launch the nuclear holocaust. A "utopian" doctrine held that the United States and its free world allies should threaten to use their superior power, in the mode of the atom bomb, "to force our adversaries to relax their global pressure on the Free World."

[2] These were to be augmented by forces from the United States Air Force's Tactical Air Command based in the United States.

[3] The U.S. EUCOM was established in 1949. Formerly its components were grouped under the command of the United States Forces, European Theater. For information on the command structure, see Lord Ismay, NATO, the First Five Years 1949-1954 (Paris, 1954), pp. 34-38, and the NATO Information Service's definitive history, NATO, Facts and Figures (Brussels, 1976), pp. 26-33.

[4] The strategic planning went through three main phases: the Short-Term, Medium-Term, and the Long-Term Defense Plan. The latter two generated the bulk of the WRINGER collection requirements. See Roger Hilsman's astute essay, "NATO: The Developing Strategic Context," in Klaus Knorr, NATO and American Security (Princeton, 1959). General Andre Beaufre highlighted the major strategic considerations of this era in his concise volume, NATO and Europe (New York, 1968), a study based upon his experience as chief of the General Staff of Supreme Headquarters, Allied Powers Europe (SHAPE) during its formative period.

[5] This recapitulation of the Soviet threat as it was perceived in the early 1950's and the comparative data on Alliance strengths is based on Lord Ismay's officially compiled summary, "The Military Situation in May 1950," in his account, NATO, the First Five Years 1949-1954, pp. 29-30.

[6] Ibid., p. 4; Hilsman, "NATO: The Developing Strategic Context," p. 14.

[7] History of the 7050th Air Intelligence Service Wing, January 1952 to February 1952, p. 1, file K-WG-7050-Hi, Albert F. Simpson Historical Research Center, Air University, Maxwell Air Force Base, Alabama (hereafter cited as AFSHRC/ HOR). The center is the repository of all air force unit histories prepared under air force regulations during and after the Second World War.

[8] Over the next year the requirement was raised, first to 200 and later to 403 Soviet cities, by the United States Joint Chiefs of Staff classified directives to the U.S. EUCOM commands.

[9] Seized by the Western Allies from Luftwaffe headquarters in Berlin in the spring of 1945, the film was stored at a Royal Air Force base in England. No use was made of it in the following years by the World-Wide Mapping Project, undertaken by the United States Air Force after the surrender of Japan, probably because the original aerial reconnaissance missions were flown over terrain where ground battles were taking place and showed nothing of interest about Soviet permanent installations or urban areas. This absence of air information about Russia had much to do with the subsequent decision to employ aircraft designated the U-2 for missions over Russia by the Central Intelligence Agency in 1956.

[10] These early air intelligence reports on talks with ex-German POWs were actually prepared by roving agents of the USAFE Office of Special Investigations as adjuncts to their background investigations of German nationals seeking employment with USAFE units.

[11] Concurrent efforts of the United States "Intelligence Community"--mainly the production of the secret, multi-volume National Intelligence Survey by the CIA--to fill gaps in the analysis of the Soviet Union undoubtedly account for the cities placed on the priority targets list. They were the military-industrial complexes on which the greatest number of specific requests for information from the military services and the national intelligence agencies had been focused.

[12] The First Air Intelligence Service Organization was a diversified group of intelligence specialists who were assembled in August, 1946, at Fürstenfeldbrück Air Base in south Germany to provide translation or interpreter services--anywhere in Europe--to high-level American commanders, or to interrogate informants coming into air force purview from behind the "Iron Curtain."

[13] Headquarters, 7707 EUCOM Intelligence Center, Report RT-17-49 (PI-572), 11 January 1949, 321.4, "Prisoners of War in USSR," U.S. State Department records, RG 84, National Archives, Washington, D.C. (hereafter cited as D/S File #).

[14] Adenauer called the Soviet retention of the POWs "a measure of cold atrocity." New York Times, 12 January, 27 October, and 20 November 1950.

[15] See the digest published by the German Federal Republic Press and Information Office, Germany Reports, 4, "Land and People" (Bonn, 1964); New York Times, 5 May 1950.

[16] Helmut M. Fehling, One Great Prison: The Story Behind Russia's Unreleased POW's, with Documents and Official Announcements Concerning German and Japanese War Prisoners in the Soviet Union, trans. by Charles R. Joy (Boston, 1951), pp. 95-101. Various official and unofficial documents for the period 1947-1950 are reprinted in Part II.

[17] New York Times, 20 September 1950.

[18] Quoted in Fehling, One Great Prison, p. 96. This unofficial remark was matched at this time by several statements from TASS, the Soviet news agency.

[19] History of the 7050th Air Intelligence Service Wing, 23 March 1951 to 30 June 1951, pp. 29-31, 12.

[20] New York Times, 15 August 1948.

[21] Headquarters, 7707 EUCOM Intelligence Center, Report RT-362-49 (PI-518), 28 March 1949, 321.4, "Antifa School, PW Camp 2040, Riga-Ogre," D/S File #321.4. This comment was specifically noted by Ambassador Robert Murphy, the United States Political Adviser for Germany, in an airgram to the Secretary of State, 25 February 1949, which forwarded copies of these ominous EUCOM reports to the Department of the Army.

[22] New York Times, 22 September 1950.

[23] Werner Knop, Prowling Russia's Forbidden Zone: A Secret Journey into Soviet Germany (New York, 1949), pp. 146, 153-54. Also see Heinrich von Einsiedel, I Joined the Russians (New Haven, 1953), pp. 84-106.

[24] A favorite--and often sarcastic--nickname for the Americans in Germany, formed from the contraction of "American" and the French word for friend, "Ami."

[25] As told to the author in Munich, 19 July 1979. Still engaged in the work of keeping track of military

developments and orders-of-battle in the Soviet or Warsaw Pact forces, my source requested anonymity.

[26] Colonel Work to the author, 18 May 1978.

[27] Colonel Work to the author, 18 May and 12 October 1978, and telephone conversation, 13 August 1979.

[28] See footnote 12.

[29] Telephone conversation with Colonel Work, 13 August 1979.

[30] The four elements in Work's plan, all executed in the next two years, were: (1) the procurement and training of a sizable corps of men to perform the screening and debriefing of thousands of sources who "didn't know how much they knew"; (2) the assembling and secure transmittal to field intelligence stations of a large compilation of collection schematics; (3) the advance of considerable funds to pay for new costs of accommodating sources in a friendly environment over extended periods of time and for the writing and reproduction of multi-copy, highly technical reports; (4) the procurement of report evaluations from the army of current-intelligence briefers, order-of-battle and physical-vulnerability experts, and map-makers in Washington so that the collectors could focus on the intelligence needs of the operational commands.

[31] Daniel Yergin's recent study, Shattered Peace: The Origins of the Cold War and the National Security State (Boston, 1977), analyzes why the United States in 1948 placed primary reliance on a 70-group air force for its national defense. He also makes clear that the architects of the "National Security State" were divided until 1955 over the role the nuclear-armed air strike forces would play in the implementation of national strategies.

[32] "Charles Pearre Cabell," Generals of the Army and the Air Force and Admirals of the Navy (Washington, 1954), pp. 2-3.

[33] Cullum's Biographical Register, 1940-1950 (Chicago, 1950).

[34] General Cabell's views have been taken from a telephone conversation with Colonel Work, 14 August 1979; from conversations with Colonel James L. Monroe, USAF, Retired, who worked with him after he became Deputy Director of the Central Intelligence Agency, April, 1953-1957; and from various files in the Cabell Papers, AFSHRC/ HOR. For information on the proposed shuttle-bombing of Germany from Russian soil, see Glenn B.

Infield, The Poltava Affair: A Russian Warning (New York, 1973), pp. 217-30.

[35] From an air staff paper entitled "Requirements Based Upon U.S. Air Force Concept for the Employment of Air Power," 28 January 1948, quoted in Yergin, Shattered Peace, p. 478.

[36] Colonel Work to the author, 18 May 1978.

[37] 12th Air Force Regulation #24-26, Headquarters USAFE Organizations, "Mission of the 7001 Air Intelligence Service Squadron," 3 June 1949.

[38] Fletcher Pratt noted the United States' growing awareness of the urgency of collecting intelligence information on the Soviet Union--even by patient research--in his article, "That Real Spy, The Researcher," New York Times, 15 August 1948.

[39] Interview with Rolf Bömmelburg in Munich, Germany, 21 July 1979.

[40] Texts of the letters of invitation varied from team to team. See the various squadron histories attached as appendices to the 7050th AISW histories, file K-WG-7050-Hi, AFSHRC/HOR.

[41] Interview with Dr. Pietzsch in Munich, 23 July 1979.

[42] Data extrapolated from a 7050th AISW "Wing Summary of Reports by Type of Information," December, 1952, History of the 7050th Air Intelligence Service Wing, 1 January 1953 to 29 February 1953, file K-WG-7050-Hi, AFSHRC/HOR.

[43] Ibid., from resume of "Previous History" at the beginning of each 7050th AISW history.

[44] General Curtis E. LeMay with MacKinlay Kantor, Mission with LeMay, My Story (Garden City, New York, 1965), pp. 429-31. See also Air Force Association special edition of Air Force Magazine, The Golden Anniversary, United States Air Force, 1907-1957, pp. 212-20 and 242-49.

[45] LeMay with Kantor, Mission with LeMay, p. 436. See also Office of the Historian, Strategic Air Command, Development of Strategic Air Command, 1946-1976 (Offutt, Nebraska, 1976).

[46] The models were placed in a large tank of water, lighted, and photographed by a camera traveling across the tank on a crane. The layers of water in the tank provided the equivalent refraction of the light waves to the image on the film that the radio waves in an air to ground radar set

in a bomber would make passing through tens of thousands of feet of layers of the atmosphere.

[47] Standard "Wringer Mission" briefing charts, used in the headquarters to illustrate how the WRINGER worked, included representative USAF target charts to show how they were being amplified and kept current by the addition of WRINGER-extracted air intelligence on Soviet cities.

[48] Walton S. Moody, "United States Air Forces in Europe and the Beginning of the Cold War," Aerospace Historian 23 (Summer/June 1976): 75-85.

[49] A 7050th Air Intelligence Wing was first designated and organized, effective 23 March 1951, by USAFE General Order #19, dated 21 March 1951.

[50] History of the 7050th Air Intelligence Service Wing, June-July 1952, pp. 35 ff., file K-WG-7050-Hi, AFSHRC/HOR.

[51] A good view of these border patrol operations is presented in Life magazine's special issue entitled "Germany, A Giant Awakened" 36 (10 May 1954), subsection "On the Edge of the Iron Curtain," pp. 36-39.

[52] Personal knowledge of the author, who was assigned as Headquarters, USAFE Intelligence Liaison Officer to the Office of the Coordinator and Adviser to the High Commissioner, Bonn, Germany, February-August, 1955.

[53] C. L. Sulzberger, A Long Row of Candles: Memoirs and Diaries, 1934-1954 (New York, 1969), p. 460.

[54] Henry J. Kellermann, Cultural Relations as an Instrument of U.S. Foreign Policy, The Educational Exchange Program Between the United States and Germany, 1945-1954 (Washington D.C., 1978), pp. 211-17.

[55] Eckhardt to the author, 28 January 1980.

[56] Kellermann, Cultural Relations as an Instrument of U.S. Foreign Policy [Appendix III], p. 264. Totals of Germans taken to the United States: 298 in 1947-48; 942 in 1949; 2,465 in 1950.

PAUL H. NITZE, NSC 68, AND THE SOVIET UNION

Joseph M. Siracusa

In conjunction with the decision to initiate research on the production of an American hydrogen bomb in late January, 1950, President Harry S. Truman directed the Departments of State and Defense to undertake jointly a reappraisal of United States objectives in peace and war and the effect of these objectives on the nation's strategic plans, particularly "in the light of the probable fission bomb capability and possible thermonuclear bomb capability of the Soviet Union."[1] The burden of this work, which was completed on 5 April 1950 and referred to the National Security Council (where it was called NSC 68) on 12 April, fell to Paul H. Nitze,[2] successor to George F. Kennan as head of the Department of State's Policy Planning Staff.[3]

Having already assisted Secretary of State Dean Acheson on the more immediate problems associated with the development of what was then called the "superbomb,"[4] Nitze perceived his brief as twofold. First, and of critical importance, the Harvard-trained investment banker sought to provide the Truman administration with a rationale for producing and stockpiling "thermonuclear weapons in the event they prove feasible and would add significantly to our net capability"; and second, also of great importance, Nitze sought to provide an effective argument, at least by implication, for lifting the budget ceiling of the national military establishment from approximately $13.5 to $50 billion.[5] According to Nitze, NSC 68 did not so much attempt to "lay out a program in detail as to what kind of military capabilities were needed" as to obtain the President's "agreement to the broad analysis [contained therein] before he could authorize the appropriate people to lay out a specific plan, including the number necessary to support the policy."[6] Put another way, NSC 68 was designed to do "better in getting from general objectives to the details of what the problem was and how to get from where you were to where you wanted to go."[7]

While it is probably questionable to assert that NSC 68 was, to quote Acheson, "one of the great documents in our history,"[8] there can be no question that the document's

192

impact has been profound and far-reaching, both in governmental and academic circles.[9] The purpose of this essay is to describe and examine the ideas and beliefs contained in National Security Council Planning Paper Number 68 from the perspective of the paper's principal author, Paul H. Nitze, in light of recently declassified materials.[10] This essay will also seek to delineate the parameters of the Cold War paradigm[11] that emerged in Washington in the late 1940's and early 1950's in the wake of such events as the Soviet breaking of America's atomic monopoly, communist successes in the Far East, and other related and perceived threats to the national interest.

From the beginning of his review of the nation's political-military strategy, Nitze relied heavily on the observations of State Department colleagues, including Kennan, Robert Tufts, and Herbert Feis, and, outside of the department, on a former business acquaintance, Alexander Sachs of the Wall Street firm of Lehman Brothers, and Edward Teller, a prominent physicist. Nitze believed that the Soviet threat, outlined earlier by Kennan in the NSC 20 Series in general and in its culminating paper NSC 20/4 in particular (approved as policy in November, 1948), was basically consistent with his own analysis and continued to remain valid. What had changed was the presumed immediacy of the threat. "The growing intensity of the conflict which has been imposed upon us," wrote Nitze, "requires the changes of emphasis and additions that are apparent; coupled with the probable fission bomb capability and possible thermonuclear bomb capability of the Soviet Union, the intensifying struggle requires us to face the fact that we can expect no lasting abatement of the crisis unless and until a change occurs in the nature of the Soviet system [emphasis mine]."[12] This was a theme that would appear over and over again. Edward Teller persuaded Nitze of the practicality and probability of developing a fission bomb; hence, Nitze's concern with providing the administration a rationale for including it in the national arsenal.[13] From Robert Tufts, a member of the Policy Planning Staff, Nitze became familiar with and influenced by the work of sometime-novelist Pierrepont B. Noyes, America's Rhineland Commissioner to the Weimar Republic. Noyes's prophetic and neglected novel, The Pallid Giant, published in 1927, focused on the course of mutual annihilation pursued by two ancient and fear-ridden

societies in possession of the ultimate weapon.[14]   Finally, Alexander Sachs convinced Nitze of the reality of the Soviet military threat.

According to Nitze, Sachs (who had introduced Albert Einstein to President Franklin Roosevelt) visited him in early 1950 when he was working on NSC 68; Sachs brought with him a series of charts and graphs and supporting papers.   One set, related Nitze, dealt with the Soviet doctrine now more commonly known as the "correlation of forces,"[15] in which it was "argued that the Soviets felt themselves duty-bound to nail down gains at any time that they felt the correlation of forces had moved substantially in their favour."[16]   The second paper "dealt with the impact on Soviet strategic thinking on the defeat of the Chinese Nationalists . . . and the Soviet testing of a nuclear device," and "concluded with the judgment that these two developments would be assessed by the Soviets as a basic change in the correlation of forces calling on some initiative on their side."   The third paper "dealt with a map of the world showing the various crisis situations and the various places where the Soviets might move," with the firm prediction "that the most likely place was an attack by the North Koreans into South Korea."   Why South Korea? Because, Sachs argued with conviction, "such an attack would be the least risky way for the Soviets to test the validity of their assessment."   The last paper in the series was essentially "a true analysis of past periods when there had been a change in the correlation of forces," with yet another prediction that the North Koreans would probably attack the South by June or July, 1950.[17]

Above all, the Director of the Policy Planning Staff sought to delineate the motives of the Kremlin and in doing so develop a thesis that would carry the burden of the arguments and subsequent recommendations enumerated in NSC 68.   Working from the central premise of the NSC 20 Series, that "Communist ideology and Soviet behaviour clearly demonstrate that the ultimate objective of the leaders of the U.S.S.R. is the domination of the world,"[18] Nitze tried to order the Kremlin's priorities.   "The fundamental design of those who control the Soviet Union and the influential communist movement," observed Nitze, "is to retain and solidify their absolute power, first in the Soviet Union and second in areas now under their control."   To effect this goal "requires the dynamic extension of their

Mr. Paul H. Nitze

authority and the ultimate elimination of any effective opposition to their authority." Nitze elaborated:

> The design . . . calls for the complete subversion or forcible destruction of the machinery of government and structure of society in the countries of the non-Soviet world and their replacement by an apparatus and structure subservient to and controlled from the Kremlin. To that end Soviet efforts are now directed toward the domination of the Eurasian land mass.

It followed that the United States, as the principal center of power in the non-Soviet world and the bulwark of opposition to Soviet expansion, "is the principal enemy whose integrity and vitality must be subverted or destroyed by one means or another if the Kremlin is to achieve its fundamental design."[19] State Department Russian specialist Charles E. Bohlen, who visited Washington from his post in Paris, strongly disputed Nitze's characterization of Soviet fears, contending that these views originated from the continued maintenance of their power at home. Nitze countered that the Soviet Union's doctrinaire leaders were governed by fears of American atomic power and what they as Russians would have done if the U.S.S.R. had had an atomic monopoly, a critical distinction to the Director of the Policy Planning Staff.[20]

In his memoirs, Bohlen reiterated that while there was much he agreed with in NSC 68, "particularly the basic recommendations that American military power be increased so as to be more commensurate with commitments forced on us in the world," it had been a mistake to present Soviet policy "as nothing more than an absolute determination to spread the Communist system throughout the world." To Bohlen, the Soviet Union tended to behave as a national state in pursuit of traditional national interests, the spread of communism being a secondary objective: "The main Bolshevik aim is to protect the Soviet system above all in Russia and secondarily in the satellite countries."[21] Bohlen did not convince Nitze or Acheson, however, with his views.[22]

At the heart of the Cold War, Nitze argued, lay the underlying conflict in the realm of ideas and values.

196

"There is," he wrote, "a basic conflict between the idea of freedom under a government of laws, and the idea of slavery under the grim oligarchy of the Kremlin, which has come to a crisis under the polarization of power [created by the aftermath of World War II] . . . and the exclusive possession of atomic weapons by the two protagonists."[23] In Nitze's clearly defined perception of the world, freedom was seen as subversive to slavery although the reverse was not necessarily true. A free society, where the individual has "the positive responsibility to make constructive use of his freedom in the building of a just society," welcomes diversity. Also, Nitze continued, a free society "derives its strength from its hospitality even to antipathetic ideas." In a real sense, it is "a market for free trade in ideas, secure in its faith that free men will take the best wares, and grow to a fuller and better realization of their powers in exercising their choice."[24] Nitze, believing in the indivisibility of war and peace that had been popular among anti-appeasers in the 1930's, postulated that in current circumstances a defeat of free institutions anywhere constitutes a defeat everywhere, the most recent case being the destruction of Czechoslovakia in February, 1948. Acknowledging that in the material sense Czech capabilities were already at the disposal of the Soviets, Nitze lamented that "when the integrity of Czechoslovak institutions were destroyed, it was in the intangible sense of values that we registered a loss more damaging than the material loss we had already suffered."[25] Such sentiments characterized Cold War thinking in the years ahead.

Perhaps more important than the Soviet threat to American values, according to Nitze, was the growing Soviet threat to the nation's capability to protect its material environment. "Thus," Nitze went on to explain, "we must make ourselves strong, both in the way we affirm our values in the conduct of our national life, and in the development of our military and economic strength."[26] The United States must lead the way "in building a successfully functioning political and economic system in the free world," accepting without hesitation "the responsibility of world leadership." The strategy, which treated the U.S.S.R. as an ideology in the possession of a state, was eminently simple: "It is only by developing the moral and material strength of the free world that the Soviet regime will become convinced of the falsity of its assumptions and that

the pre-conditions for workable agreements can be reached."[27] In other words, "by practically demonstrating the integrity and vitality of our system, the free world widens the area of possible agreement and thus can hope gradually to bring about a Soviet acknowledgement of realities which in sum will eventually constitute a frustration of the Soviet design."[28] Short of this goal, however, Nitze conceded that "it might be possible to create a situation which will induce the Soviet Union to accommodate itself, with or without the conscious abandonment of its design, to coexistence on tolerable terms with the non-Soviet world [emphasis mine]."[29]

The Soviet Union could be checked by employing a policy of containment, the outlines of which had been developed by George Kennan during and immediately after the war. As interpreted by Nitze, containment meant a policy that sought "by all means short of war to (1) block further expansion of Soviet power, (2) expose the falsities of Soviet pretensions, (3) induce a retraction of the Kremlin's control and influence, and (4) in general, to foster the seeds of destruction within the Soviet system that the Kremlin is brought at least to the point of modifying its behaviour to conform to generally accepted international standards."[30] A key feature of containment was the United States dealing with the Soviets from the position of strength. "In the concept of 'containment'," noted Nitze, "the maintenance of a strong military posture is deemed to be essential for two reasons: as an ultimate guarantee of national security and as an indispensable backdrop to the conduct of the policy of containment." To Nitze, there was no substitute for the maintenance of force: "Without superior aggregate military strength, in being and readily mobilizable, a policy of 'containment' - which is in effect a policy of calculated or gradual coercion - is no more than a bluff."[31] Negotiations were not to be ruled out, however, for "a diplomatic freeze . . . tends to defeat the very purposes of 'containment' because it raises tensions at the same time that it makes Soviet retractions and adjustments in the direction of moderated behaviour more difficult"; conversely, it tends "to inhibit our initiative and deprives us of opportunities for maintaining a moral ascendency in our struggle with the Soviet system."[32] Moreover, he thought it desirable not to challenge Soviet prestige directly, for this would keep open "the possibility

for the U.S.S.R. to retreat before pressure with a minimum loss of face and to secure political advantage from the failure of the Kremlin to yield or take advantage of the openings we leave it."   It should be noted parenthetically that this view did not originate with Nitze but with W. Averell Harriman at the end of his ambassadorship in Moscow.[33]

Although Nitze recognized that at least on "the military level the Kremlin had thus far been careful not to commit a technical breach of the peace,"[34] he doubted that the Soviets could be trusted in such important matters as the international control of atomic energy.   He explained, "The absence of good faith on the part of the U.S.S.R. must be assumed until there is concrete evidence that there has been a decisive change in Soviet policies."[35]   Yet Nitze thought it problematical "whether such a change can take place without [first] a change in the nature of the Soviet system itself."

Nitze delved at some length into Soviet intentions and capabilities, tending to equate the one with the other.   He maintained that the means employed by the Stalinist regime, whose twin goals were seen to be Soviet consolidation behind the iron curtain on the one hand and elimination of resistance to its will abroad on the other hand, were "limited only by considerations of expediency."[36]   The Soviets did not view doctrines as a necessarily limiting factor but rather as a kind of rationale dictating the employment of violence, subversion, and deceit.   The Soviet Union "is increasingly militant," he wrote, "because it possesses and is possessed by a world-wide revolutionary movement, because it is the inheritor of Russian imperialism, and because it is a totalitarian dictatorship"; powered by this outlook, "persistence, crisis, conflict and expansion are the essence of the Kremlin's militancy."[37]   In turn, "this dynamism serves to intensify all Soviet capabilities." Paradoxically, though, this same "dynamism can become a weakness if it is frustrated, if in its forward thrust it encounters a superior force which halts the expansion and exerts a superior counterpressure"; for the same set of reasons, "the Kremlin cannot relax the condition of crisis and mobilization, for to do so would be to lose its dynamism, whereas the seeds of decay within the system would begin to flourish and fructify."[38]

In a military sense, assuming a near-maximum production basis, the Soviet Union appeared to Nitze and others to be on the verge of developing a military capacity to support the overall goal of world conquest. Accordingly, Soviet forces in being together with its newly acquired atomic capacity provided Russia "with great coercive power for use in time of peace in furtherance of its objectives and serves as a deterrent to the victims of its aggression from taking any actions in opposition to its tactics which would risk war."[39] Not surprisingly, Nitze painted the grimmest kind of picture in the event of a major war with the Soviet Union and its satellites in 1950. The Joint Chiefs of Staff shared Nitze's pessimism, estimating that Soviet forces would probably "overrun Western Europe, with the possible exception of the Iberian and Scandinavian Peninsulas"; "drive toward the oil bearing areas of the Near and Middle East"; "consolidate Soviet gains in the Far East"; "launch air attacks against the British Isles and air and sea attacks against the lines of communications of the Western powers in the Atlantic and the Pacific"; and, finally, "attack selected targets with atomic weapons, now including the likelihood of such attacks against targets in Alaska, Canada, and the United States."[40] Nitze assumed that Russia would strike first, inflicting mortal blows on the West. "At the time the Soviet Union has a substantial atomic stockpile," he pointed out, "and if it is assumed that it will strike a surprise blow and if it is assumed further that its atomic strikes will be met with no more effective defense opposition than the United States and its allies have programmed, results of those strikes could include: laying waste to the British Isles; destruction of the vital centers and communications of Western Europe; and delivering devastating attacks on certain vital centers in the United States and Canada."[41]

In light of the bleak situation, Nitze believed that there were four possible alternatives for the United States: a continuation of current policies; return to isolation; preventive war; and a more rapid build-up of the political, economic, and military strength of the free world.

Nitze postulated that "on the basis of current programs the United States has a large potential military capability but an actual capability which, though improving, is declining relative to the U.S.S.R, particularly in light of

the probable fission bomb capability and possible thermonuclear bomb capability."[42]   Moreover, continued the head
of Policy Planning, "a review of Soviet policy shows that
the military capabilities, actual and potential of the United
States, together with the apparent determination of the free
world to resist further Soviet expansion, have not induced
the Kremlin to relax its pressure generally or to give up
the initiative of the cold war." In fact, the opposite
seemed to be true because "the Soviet Union has
consistently pursued a bold foreign policy, modified only
when its probing revealed a determination and an ability of
the free world to resist encroachment upon it."
Unfortunately, Nitze believed that "the relative military
capabilities of the free world are declining, with the result
that its determination to resist may also decline and that
the security of the United States and the free world as a
whole will be jeopardized." Consequently, "from the
military point of view, the actual and potential capabilities
of the United States, given a continuation of current and
projected programs, will become less and less effective as a
war deterrent."[43]   Thus, Nitze went on to note, "improvement of the state of readiness will become more and more
important not only to inhibit the launching of war by the
Soviet Union but also to support a national policy designed
to reverse the present ominous trends in international
relations."[44]

Particularly threatening was the Soviet development of
an atomic capability. Nitze held that the Soviet Union's
acquisition of the atomic bomb, together with communist
successes in China, "led to an increasing confidence on its
part and to an increasing nervousness in Western Europe
and the rest of the free world," especially as Washington
could not be certain "how vigorously the Soviet Union will
pursue its initiative, nor can we be sure of the strengths
or weaknesses of the other free countries reacting to it."
Keeping in mind Russia's atomic capability, Nitze also
suggested that the free world was inadequately equipped to
check Soviet or Soviet-inspired conventional forces in a
small war. "The free world," he wrote, "lacks adequate
means to thwart such expansion locally." Accordingly, "the
United States will therefore be confronted more frequently
with the dilemma of reacting totally to a limited extension of
Soviet control or of not reacting at all (except with
ineffectual protests and half measures)." The continuation

of such trends, Nitze concluded somberly, would most likely "lead. . .to a gradual withdrawal under the direct or indirect pressure of the Soviet Union until we discover one day that we have sacrificed positions of vital interests."[45]

Nitze recognized that a return to isolationism was a possible second course of action. "There are those," he wrote, "who advocate a deliberate decision to isolate ourselves."[46] He conceded that isolationism did in fact evidence "some attractiveness as a course of action, for it appears to bring our commitments and capabilities into harmony by reducing the former and by concentrating our present, or perhaps even reduced, military expenditures on the defense of the United States." Nitze argued that such thinking overlooked what he called "the relativity of capabilities."[47] For instance, he observed, "with the United States in an isolated position, we could have to face the probability that the Soviet Union would quickly dominate most of Eurasia, probably without meeting armed resistance"; at that juncture, Russia "would thus acquire a potential far superior to our own and would promptly proceed to develop this potential with the purpose of eliminating our power, which would, even in isolation, remain as an obstacle to the imposition of its kind of order in the world." Put another way, Nitze remarked, "there is no way to make ourselves inoffensive to the Kremlin except by complete submission to its will," a position that ultimately condemned "us to capitulate or to fight alone and on the defensive, with drastically limited offensive and retaliatory capabilities in comparison with the Soviet Union." If the United States followed such a policy, Nitze foresaw the possibility that many Americans would come to favor a preemptive strike against the Soviet Union and its satellites, "in a desperate attempt to alter decisively the balance of power." Yet, according to NSC 68, it was "unlikely that the Soviet Union would wait for such an attack before launching one of its own." In any case, if such a surprise attack were successful, "the United States would face appalling tasks in establishing a tolerable state of order among nations after such a war and after Soviet occupation of all or most of Eurasia."

Nitze proceeded to expand on a preventive war as a third course of action open to America. Noting that "some Americans favor a deliberate decision to go to war against

the Soviet Union in the near future," Nitze believed that it went "without saying that the idea of 'preventive' war - in the sense of a military attack not provoked by a military attack upon us or our allies - is generally unacceptable to Americans."[48] Conceding the plausibility of a first strike, Nitze countered that there were other factors to consider. For example, it was doubtful that a surprise attack could alone "force or induce the Kremlin to capitulate and that the Kremlin would still be able to use the forces under its control to dominate most or all of Eurasia." In the process, Nitze added, "this would probably mean a long and difficult struggle during which the free institutions of Western Europe and many freedom-loving people would be destroyed and the regenerative capacity of Western Europe dealt a crippling blow." Aside from this, Nitze went on to say:

> A surprise attack upon the Soviet Union, despite the provocativeness of recent Soviet behavior, would be repugnant to many Americans. Although the American people would probably rally in support of the war effort, the shock of responsibility for a surprise attack would be morally corrosive. Many would doubt that it was a 'just war' and that all reasonable possibilities for a peaceful settlement had been explored in good faith. Many more, proportionately, would hold such views in other countries, particularly in Western Europe and particularly after Soviet occupation, if only because the Soviet Union would liquidate articulate opponents. It would, therefore, be difficult after such a war to create a satisfactory international order among nations. Victory in such a war would have brought us little if at all closer to victory in the fundamental ideological conflict.

Having made a case against a preemptive strike, Nitze emphasized that the Soviets should be in no doubt that the United States would not hesitate to use any weapons at its disposal in a critical situation.[49]

Nitze concluded that there was only one option left: "A more rapid build-up of political, economic, and military strength and thereby of confidence in the free world than is now contemplated. . . ."[50] Developing this theme, he

elaborated that "the frustration of the Kremlin design requires the free world to develop a successfully function-ing political and economic system and a vigorous political offensive against the Soviet Union"; and "these, in turn, require an adequate military shield under which they can develop." The reasons for such a build-up were obvious: the United States must "have the military power to deter, if possible, Soviet expansion, and to defeat, if necessary, aggressive Soviet or Soviet-directed actions of a limited or total character." From a military point of view, "the two fundamental requirements . . . are support of foreign policy and protection against disaster." To prevent such a catastrophe, Nitze was persuaded that the armed forces in being or readily available must be in a position to perform a number of vital tasks. Among these he included the defense of "the Western Hemisphere and essential allied areas in order that their war-making capabilities can be developed"; the provision and protection of "a mobilization base while the offensive forces required for victory are being built up"; the conducting of "offensive operations to destroy vital elements of the Soviet war-making capability, and to keep the enemy off balance until the full offensive strength of the United States and its allies can be brought to bear"; the maintenance of "lines of communication and base areas"; and providing "such aid to allies as is essential to the execution of their roles."[51] In other words, Nitze was calling for military changes that he calculated would allow the free nations of the West to thwart the aggressive designs of Soviet Russia. Finally, Nitze called for cooperation with allies for "the United States cannot alone provide the resources required for such a build-up of strength."[52] He also recommended that the United States initiate a major psychological offensive "to reduce the power and influence of the Kremlin inside the Soviet Union and other areas under its control," the objective being "the establishment of friendly regimes not under Kremlin domination." Nitze rationalized that "such action is essential to engage the Kremlin's attention, keep it off balance and force an increased expenditure of Soviet resources in counter-action." In short, we would be turning the tables on Russia; "it would be the current Soviet cold war technique used against the Soviet Union."

In NSC 68, Nitze called for a comprehensive and decisive program to win the peace and frustrate the

Kremlin. Military expenditures should be increased substantially. Additional military assistance programs were also needed. In the economic realm, foreign aid should be increased (although a balance of payments problem existed and had yet to be attacked). Furthermore, America needed to intensify intelligence-gathering activities and implement internal security and civilian defense programs. In the end, reasoned Nitze, "the immediate goal of our efforts [is] to build a successfully functioning political and economic system in the free world backed by adequate military strength. . . ."[53] Such a program would halt the drift of Western democracies and prevent the Soviet Union from dominating the world by the mid-1950's. The time of action, though, was at hand. For only "by acting promptly and vigorously in such a way that this date is, so to speak, pushed into the future," could America "permit time for the process of accommodation, withdrawal and frustration to produce the necessary changes in the Soviet system." Though one could dispute all or part of NSC 68, which incidentally became the official policy of the Truman administration on 30 September 1950, none could deny that it marked the fullest expression of the Cold War paradigm that dominated the thinking of American policymakers for the coming generation. Of these statesmen, few would play a greater role than Paul H. Nitze.

Subsequent to his years as head of the Policy Planning Staff, Nitze has served successively as "special adviser" to the so-called Gaither Committee (1957), whose still-classified report recommended a stronger nuclear deterrent and build-up of conventional forces;[54] Assistant Secretary of Defense for International Security Affairs (1961-1963); Secretary of the Navy (1963-1967); Deputy Secretary of Defense (1967-1969); and member of the United States delegation to the Strategic Arms Limitation Talks (1969-1974). In recent years, and particularly in his capacity as a spokesman of the Committee on the Present Danger, Nitze has continued to voice warnings of what he perceives to be the declining military strength of the United States vis-à-vis the Soviet Union. In fact, Nitze's observation of only several years ago in the influential pages of Foreign Affairs suggests that in some ways not much has changed since 1950, and that the Cold War is still very much with us today:

. . .the trends in relative military strength are such that, unless we move promptly to reverse them, the United States is moving toward a posture of minimum deterrence in which we would be conceding to the Soviet Union the potential for a military and political victory if deterrence failed.[55]

The writer would like to thank the Harry S. Truman Library Institute for National and International Affairs and the Australian Research Grants Committee for financial assistance related to the preparation of this paper. An earlier version was read before the annual meeting of the Western Social Science Association in Denver, April, 1978.

[1]NSC 68, A Report to the National Security Council, "United States Objectives and Programs for National Security," 14 April 1950, p. 3, President's Secretary's File, Harry S. Truman Papers, Truman Library, Independence, Missouri (hereafter cited as PSF, Truman Papers).
[2]For an earlier discussion of Nitze's role, see Paul Y. Hammond, "NSC 68: Prologue to Rearmament," in Warner R. Schilling, Paul Y. Hammond, and Glenn H. Snyder, eds., Strategy, Politics, and Defense Budgets (New York, 1962), pp. 267-378.
[3]It should be noted that the National Security Council had decided to begin such a reappraisal on 5 January 1950, the Department of State having set up a group to do its part of the work two weeks later. Thus, the President approved a project already under discussion through NSC channels. Hammond, "NSC 68: Prologue to Rearmament," pp. 294-95.
[4]Dean Acheson, Present at the Creation: My Years in the State Department (New York, 1969), p. 453. Prior to joining Acheson's staff, Nitze had acted in a number of various wartime and postwar capacities, including Special Consultant to the War Department, Director and then Vice-Chairman of the United States Strategic Bombing Survey, and Deputy Director of the Office of International Trade Policy.
[5]NSC 68, p. 39; interview with Paul H. Nitze, 29 April 1977, Center for National Security Research, Arlington, Virginia.
[6]Paul H. Nitze, "The Evolution of National Security Policy and the Vietnam War," in W. Scott Thompson and Donaldson D. Frizzell, eds., Lessons of Vietnam (New York, 1977), p. 3.
[7]Ibid.
[8]Princeton Seminars, 11 October 1953 (evening session), copy 1, folder 1, Dean Acheson Papers, Truman Library, Independence, Missouri.
[9]For example, see Cabell Phillips, The Truman Presidency: The History of a Triumphant Succession (New

York, 1966); Walter La Feber, America, Russia and the Cold War, 1945-75 (3rd ed., New York, 1976); Alexander L. George & Richard Smoke, Deterrence in American Foreign Policy: Theory and Practice (New York, 1974); John C. Donovan, The Cold Warriors: A Policy-Making Elite (Lexington, Mass., 1974); and, most recently, Daniel Yergin, Shattered Peace: The Origins of the Cold War and the National Security State (Boston, 1977).

[10]The author has dealt separately with the origins and impact of NSC 68 in his forthcoming study, The Intellectual Origins of the Cold War.

[11]For a discussion of what is meant by Cold War paradigm, consult the preface in the author's The American Diplomatic Revolution: A Documentary History of the Cold War, 1941-1947 (Sydney and New York, 1976).

[12]NSC 68, p. 10. Interestingly, Nitze departed markedly from Kennan's views on such other matters as the international control of atomic energy. George F. Kennan, Memoirs, 1925-1950 (Boston, 1967), pp. 471-76.

[13]Interview with Paul H. Nitze, 29 April 1977.

[14]Subsequently reissued in 1946 under the title Gentlemen: You Are Mad.

[15]Specifically, by "correlation of forces" Nitze is referring to what he believes the Soviets mean by "the balance of political, economic, ideological, propaganda and organizational forces, as well as the military balance, at any given time." See Paul H. Nitze, "A Plea for Action," New York Times Magazine, 7 May 1978, p. 42 ff.

[16]Nitze, "The Evolution of National Security Policy and the Vietnam War," p. 4.

[17]Interview with Paul H. Nitze, 29 April 1977.

[18]NSC 20/4, A Report to the President by the National Security Council, "U.S. Objectives with Respect to the U.S.S.R. to Counter Soviet Threats to U.S. Security," 23 November 1948, p. 1, PSF, Truman Papers.

[19]NSC 68, p. 6.

[20]Interview with Paul H. Nitze, 29 April 1977.

[21]Charles E. Bohlen, Witness to History, 1929-1969 (New York, 1973), p. 307.

[22]Interview with Paul H. Nitze, 29 April 1977.

[23]NSC 68, p. 7.

[24]Ibid.

[25]Ibid., p. 8.

[26]Ibid., p. 9.

[27]Ibid., p. 10.

[28]Ibid.

[29]Ibid.

[30]NSC 68, p. 21. For a current analysis of what Kennan had presumably hoped to achieve by his version of containment, consult John L. Gaddis, "Containment: A Reassessment," Foreign Affairs 55 (July 1977): 873-87.

[31]NSC 68, pp. 21-22. For insight on this point, see Robert Legvold, "The Nature of Soviet Power," Foreign Affairs 56 (October 1977): 49-71.

[32]NSC 68, p. 22.

[33]Interview with W. Averell Harriman, Georgetown, Washington, D.C., 25 April 1977. Also see chapter 2, "Suspicions about the Future of Soviet Intentions," in Siracusa, The American Diplomatic Revolution, pp. 55-57.

[34]NSC 68, p. 11.

[35]Ibid., p. 42.

[36]Ibid., p. 13.

[37]Ibid., p. 14.

[38]Ibid., p. 16.

[39]Ibid., p. 17.

[40]Ibid., pp. 17-18.

[41]Ibid., p. 20. Kennan's Policy Planning Staff had earlier doubted that the Soviet Union would ever have recourse to atomic weapons, "except by way of retaliation for attacks made on Russia." NSC 20/2, A Report to the National Security Council, "Factors Affecting the Nature of U.S. Defense Arrangements in the Light of Soviet Policies," 25 August 1948, p. 5, National Security Council Files, Modern Military Records Division, National Archives, Washington, D.C. (hereafter cited as National Security Council Files).

[42]NSC 68, p. 48.

[43]Ibid., pp. 48-49.

[44]Ibid., p. 49.

[45]Ibid., pp. 49-50.

[46]Ibid., p. 50.

[47]Ibid., p. 52.

[48]Ibid., pp. 52-53.

[49]For some earlier thoughts on America's atomic use policy, consult NSC 30, A Report to the National Security Council, "United States Policy on Atomic Warfare," 10 September 1948, National Security Council Files.

[50]NSC 68, p. 54.

[51]Ibid., pp. 54-55.

52Ibid., pp. 56.

53Ibid., p. 59.

54See Donovan, The Cold Warriors, pp. 130-49.

55Paul H. Nitze, "Assuring Strategic Stability in an Era of Detente," Foreign Affairs 54 (January 1976): 227.

Publications of Professor Daniel M. Smith

Books:

Robert Lansing and American Neutrality, 1914-1917.
    Berkeley and Los Angeles, 1958.

Major Problems in American Diplomatic History: Documents
    and Readings, ed. Boston, 1964.

The Great Departure: The United States and World War I,
    1914-1920. New York, 1965.

American Intervention, 1917: Sentiment, Self-Interest, or
    Ideals?, ed. Boston, 1966.

Aftermath of War: Bainbridge Colby and Wilsonian
    Diplomacy, 1920-1921. Philadelphia, 1970.

War and Depression: America, 1914-1939. St. Louis, 1972.

The American Diplomatic Experience. Boston, 1972.

Essays in Books:

"Robert Lansing (1915-1920)," in An Uncertain Tradition:
    American Secretaries of State in the Twentieth
    Century, ed. Norman A. Graebner. New York, 1961,
    pp. 101-27.

"Rise to Great World Power, 1865-1918," in The
    Reinterpretation of American History and Culture,
    eds. William H. Cartwright and Richard L. Watson,
    Jr. Washington, D. C., 1973, pp. 443-64.

Articles:

"Robert Lansing and the Formulation of American Neutrality
    Policies, 1914-1915," Mississippi Valley Historical
    Review 43 (June 1956): 59-81.

"Robert Lansing and the Wilson Interregnum," The Historian 21 (February 1959): 135-61.

"James Seagrove and the Mission to Tuckaubatchee, 1793," The Georgia Historical Quarterly 44 (March 1960): 41-55.

"President Wilson and the German 'Overt Act' of 1917--A Reappraisal," University of Colorado Studies, Series in History No. 2, (November 1961): 129-39.

"President Wilson and the State Department, 1913-1921," American Philosophical Society Year Book 1962 (1963), pp. 426-27.

"Bainbridge Colby and the Good Neighbor Policy, 1920-1921," Mississippi Valley Historical Review 50 (June 1963): 56-78.

"National Interest and American Intervention, 1917: An Historiographical Appraisal," Journal of American History 52 (June 1965): 5-24.

"The New Left and the Cold War," Denver Quarterly 4 (Winter 1970): 78-88.

"Authoritarianism and American Policy Makers in Two World Wars," Pacific Historical Review 43 (August 1974): 303-23.

Editors and Contributors

Clifford L. Egan (Ph.D. 1969: "Franco-American Relations, 1803-1814"). Born in Oceanside, New York on 6 July 1940, Egan has been teaching history at the University of Houston since 1967 except for a term spent at the University of Montana in the fall of 1976. He has published articles in the Florida Historical Quarterly, Military Affairs, American Philosophical Society Proceedings, and Early American Literature. His book, Neither Peace Nor War: Franco-American Relations, 1803-1812 will be published by Louisiana State University Press in 1982.

James M. Erdmann (Ph.D. 1970: "USAF Leaflet Operations in the European Theater of Operations during World War II"). Erdmann was born in Minneapolis Minnesota on 16 November 1918 and has been teaching modern European, German and military history courses at the University of Denver since 1966. Before joining the Denver faculty, he served in the United States Air Force as an air intelligence officer. His dissertation was published as Leaflet Operations in the Second World War. Erdmann is currently teaching at the Air University, Maxwell Air Force Base, Alabama.

Michael Holcomb (Ph.D. 1973: "Anglo-American Policy and the Manchurian Crises: The Simon-Stimson Controversy"). Born in Breckenridge, Texas on 5 February 1943, Holcomb is employed at Rutgers University in a non-academic position.

Billie Barnes Jensen (Ph.D. 1962: "House, Wilson, and American Neutrality, 1914-1917"). Professor Jensen was born in Boulder, Colorado on 18 August 1933 and has taught at San Jose State University since 1962. She has published articles in Arizona and the West, Labor History, Pacific Northwest Quarterly, Church History, and American Studies. She has also co-edited a two-volume collection of American humor.

Stephen John Kneeshaw (Ph.D. 1971: "The Kellogg-Briand Pact: The American Reaction"). Kneeshaw was born in Tacoma, Washington on 14 October 1946 and has been teaching history at The School of the Ozarks in Point Lookout, Missouri, since 1974. He has co-authored or written articles for the Colorado Magazine, Mid-America, and Idaho Yesterdays. In addition, Professor Kneeshaw co-founded and edits Teaching History: A Journal of Methods.

Alexander W. Knott (Ph.D. 1968: "The Pan American Policy of Woodrow Wilson, 1913-1921"). Born in Chicago on 14 October 1938, Knott has been teaching courses in American history and diplomacy at the University of Northern Colorado since 1968. He has co-authored an article in The Pennsylvania Magazine of History and Biography.

Judith Papachristou (Ph.D. 1968: "American-Soviet Relations and United States Policy in the Pacific"). Judith Papachristou was born on 17 July 1930. She teaches in the graduate program in women's history at Sarah Lawrence College in Bronxville, New York. Prior to joining Sarah Lawrence, she taught at Hunter College and York College, divisions of the City University of New York. Professor Papachristou has published articles in American Studies and The Colorado Quarterly and a book, Women Together: A History in Documents of the Women's Movement in the United States.

Benjamin Rhodes (Ph.D. 1965: "The United States and the War Debt Question, 1917-1934"). A native of St. Louis, Missouri, Rhodes was born on 7 November 1936. He has taught at Northern Michigan University and, since 1965, at the University of Wisconsin-Whitewater. He has published articles in the Journal of American History, Mid-America, Prologue: The Journal of The National Archives, and Diplomatic History.

Joseph M. Siracusa (Ph.D. 1971: "New Left Diplomatic Historians: A Critical Analysis of Recent Trends in American Diplomatic Historiography, 1961-1970"). Born on 6 July 1944 in Chicago, Siracusa is Senior Lecturer in American diplomatic history at the University of Queensland in Australia where he has taught since 1973. He has pub-

lished articles in the Review of Politics, World Review, Australian Journal of Politics and History. In addition, he has written or edited New Left Diplomatic Histories and Historians: The American Revisionists; The American Diplomatic Revolutions: A Documentary History of the Cold War, 1941-1947; The Testing of America, 1914-1945; and Australian-American Relations Since 1945: A Documentary History.

Brooks Van Everen (Ph.D. 1970: "Franklin D. Roosevelt and the German Problem, 1914-1945"). Professor Van Everen has been affiliated with Metropolitan State College in Denver since 1970.

House, Edward M., 1, 37, 38, 39, 40
    accomplishments of, 32-34
    disarmament ideas, 6, 9, 10, 12, 16, 22, 23, 29, 32
    encourages Wilson as peace-maker, 1
    failures of, 28-32
    first meets Wilson, 3
    "freedom of the seas" idea, 16, 18, 19, 20, 24, 29, 38
    influence with Wilson, 4-6
    intervention plan, 22-27. See also House-Grey Memorandum missions, 1, 2
    1914, 6; importance of, 12-13; in England, 10-12; in Germany, 8-9; in Paris, 10; origin of, 6-8; preparations for, 8
    1915, in England, 16-18, 20-21; in Germany, 19-20; in Paris, 18-19, 20; plans for, 14-15; reactions of Britain and Germany, 15; results of, 21
    1916, House's views of, 28; in England 23-25, 27-28; in France, 26; in Germany, 25; itinerary, 23; purpose of, 21-22
    personality, 3
    relationship with Bryan, 30-32
    relationship with Gerard, 31
    relationship with Page, 31-32
    relationship with Wilson, 2-3
    role in Wilson's nomination, 4
    "second convention" idea, 16-17, 18, 19, 32
    "waste places of the earth" idea, 6, 7, 10, 12, 16
House-Grey Memorandum, 22, 30
Hoyt, Elizabeth Sherman, 64
Hull, Cordell, 62, 71, 78, 80, 81, 99, 114, 115, 119, 121, 122, 123, 140, 141, 145

Immigration Act, 1924, 43, 53, 56

Imperial Conference. See Japan
Institute of Pacific Relations, 96
Iriye, Akira, 56
"iron curtain," 187
Ishii Kikujiro, 53
Izvestia, 119

Jagow, Gottlieb von, 8, 19, 25
Japan Imperial Conference, 124 Privy Council, 48, 49, 52, 59
Japan Society, 59
Johnson, Hiram, 74
Johnson Act, 74, 114, 117

Katsuji Debuchi, 59
Kelley, Robert, 114
Kellogg, Frank B., 43, 44, 45, 46, 48, 50, 54, 57, 59
Kellogg-Briand Pact, 42, 43, 44, 47, 52, 53, 54, 55, 56, 57, 59, 96, 107
    aggressive designs of the United States, 45
    American recognition of Russia, 49, 50
    Article I, 47, 48, 49, 52, 53
    Article III, 49
    immigration issue, 44, 45, 46, 51, 53, 54
    imperial prerogatives, 48, 52
    impractical nature of, 45, 46, 55
    Japanese recognition of Nationalist Government, 49, 50-51, 53
    Manchuria, 44, 46, 51, 53, 54, 55
    multilaterialization of, 44
    reservations, 51, 53
    "special circumstances," 45
    United States membership in the League of Nations, 46
Kennan, George F., 192, 193, 198, 208, 209
Kennedy, John, 90

219

Martin, Edward S., 7

Mills, Ogden, 75

Minseito party, 48, 58

Moffat, Jay Pierrepont, 73, 118, 142

Moley, Raymond, 71, 72

Molotov, Vyacheslav M., 119, 142, 167, 170

Monroe, James L., 189

Monroe Doctrine, 36, 51
    Roosevelt Corollary to, 64, 65

Moore, John Bassett, 49

Moore, R. Walton, 73

Morgenthau, Henry, 123
    attitude toward Germany, 147-48
    influence with Roosevelt, 150
    relationship with Roosevelt, 146

Morgenthau Plan, 141, 143, 147
    provisions of, 149
    Roosevelt rejects, 149-50
    Roosevelt's initial acceptance of, 138, 146

Moses, George, 67

Mukden incident, 42

Murphy, Robert, 188

Mussolini, Benito, 29, 67

National Intelligence Survey, 187

National Recovery Administration, 70

National Security Council, 192, 207

National Security Council (NSC) 20, 193, 194

National Security Council (NSC) 68, 192, 193, 194, 202, 204, 205

"National Security State," 189

Nazi-Soviet nonaggression pact, 121, 122, 123, 128

Nelson, Keith, 30

Neville, Edwin L., 48

New Freedom diplomacy, 12

New York Herald Tribune, 101

New York Times, 44, 45, 48, 52, 116

Nichi Nichi, 46

Nine Power Treaty, 54, 92, 94, 95, 96, 97

Nitze, Paul H., 193, 194, 207, 208
    alternatives to Soviet expansion, 200-204
    build-up of free world strength, 200, 203-204
    capabilities of the free world, 200-202
    continuation of current policies, 200-202
    nature of the Soviet threat, 193-94
    perception of his brief, 192
    policy of containment, 198
    preventive war, 200, 202-203
    reappraisal of United States objectives, 192
    return to isolation, 200, 202
    Soviet capabilities, 199-200, 201
    Soviet intentions, 194-96
    Soviet threat to American values, 196-97
    Soviet threat to American system, 197-98
    views in NSC 68, 204-205

nonrecognition, 92-93, 94, 95, 97, 104-105

Norris, George, 142

North Atlantic Treaty, 162

North Atlantic Treaty Organization, 159, 160, 162, 163, 164, 165, 184, 185, 186
    Allied Force Center of, 180

Noyes, Pierrepont B., 193

Office of International Trade Policy, 207

Olds, Robert, 48

223